TALES FROM THE BACK ROOM

Memories of a Political Insider

MICHAEL DECTER

GREAT PLAINS
PUBLICATIONS

Great Plains Publications
345-955 Portage Avenue
Winnipeg, MB R3G 0P9
www.greatplains.mb.ca

Great Plains Publications gratefully acknowledges the financial support provided for its publishing program by the Government of Canada through the Canada Book Fund; the Canada Council for the Arts; the Province of Manitoba through the Book Publishing Tax Credit and the Book Publisher Marketing Assistance Program; and the Manitoba Arts Council.

Design & Typography by Relish Design Studio Ltd.
Printed in Canada by Friesens

LIBRARY AND ARCHIVES CANADA CATALOGUING IN PUBLICATION

Decter, Michael
Tales from the back room : memories of a political insider /
Michael Decter.

ISBN 978-1-926531-06-9

1. Decter, Michael. 2. Manitoba--Officials and employees--Biography.
3. Ontario--Officials and employees--Biography. 4. Manitoba--Politics
and government--1977-1988. 5. Ontario--Politics and government--
1990-1995. I. Title.

FC631.D42A3 2010   971.27'03092   C2010-903291-8

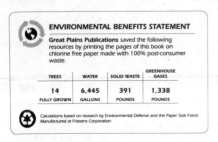

ENVIRONMENTAL BENEFITS STATEMENT

Great Plains Publications saved the following resources by printing the pages of this book on chlorine free paper made with 100% post-consumer waste.

TREES	WATER	SOLID WASTE	GREENHOUSE GASES
14	6,445	391	1,338
FULLY GROWN	GALLONS	POUNDS	POUNDS

Calculations based on research by Environmental Defense and the Paper Task Force.
Manufactured at Friesens Corporation

Mixed Sources
Cert no. SW-COC-001271
© 1996 FSC
FSC

*For my late mother, Una Barry McGilligan Decter,
who loved politics and telling political stories and passed
on her love of all things political to me.*

*For all the fine people who have braved the slings
and arrows of the media and the public to seek political
office and in so doing allowed our democracy to survive
and flourish as well as to entertain us.*

*And finally for the fine Sherpas of Confederation
who bear our leaders towards their summits.*

TABLE OF CONTENTS

INTRODUCTION

WHO SHOULD WRITE autobiography? Normally, one thinks of the famous: prime ministers, generals, movie stars. I am none of those things. Outside of health and political circles, mine is hardly a household name.

However, my years in government in this country have afforded me the extraordinary privilege of meeting and working with many fine public servants and dedicated politicians as well as a smattering of world leaders. Among our Canadian prime ministers, I have had the opportunity to dine with Pierre Elliot Trudeau, Joe Clark, Jean Chrétien, John Turner and Paul Martin. I have also met with Prime Ministers Mulroney and Turner. I have had only two encounters with Prime Minister Harper—once in an elevator and once on national television. Beyond Canadian prime ministers, in my government and post-government days, I have met President Bill Clinton, His Holiness Pope John Paul II and Her Royal Majesty Queen Elizabeth II as well as Princess Anne.

Among our recent governors general, I have enjoyed the hospitality of Rideau Hall during Edward Schreyer's term as our head of state. Much later and to my delight, I was presented the Order of Canada by Governor General Adrienne Clarkson. I met our elegant Governor General Jeanne Sauvé when she visited Manitoba. My very young and very nervous son, Riel, presented her with a bouquet of flowers on that occasion.

Twice in my life, electoral politics beckoned me in a very direct way. On both occasions I was asked to seek political office as a Member of the Parliament of Canada. On both occasions, despite the enormous and seductive pull of political life, I declined to enter the fray. These occasions were two decades apart. It was my second refusal that convinced me that a life in electoral politics was not to be. This struck me as odd because a part of me always believed that someday I would cast my hat in the political ring. It may well be that too long as an observer makes for a reluctant participant.

Political fortune first knocked on my door in 1983 in the form of the constituency executive for Winnipeg North Centre. Stanley Knowles, the legendary house leader of the federal New Democratic Party, had decided to retire from politics following a stroke. The riding executive wondered if I would consider standing as a candidate at the next general election. At the time, I bore the onerous duties of cabinet secretary in the government of Manitoba. Premier Howard Pawley had taken a risk in appointing someone as young as me to such a critical position. I had no intention of deserting him.

There was another equally important reason. I also had the responsibilities of a young family. When our children were young, I promised my wife Lucille that I would not seek political office until they were both in university. We had watched the hardships of too many young families with someone in politics. The hours of politicians were as relentless as the rewards were bittersweet. I kept my promise.

In 2004, Prime Minister Paul Martin called to ask me to seek office as a Liberal candidate and to consider becoming health minister in his government. We met in a hotel room in Toronto for a long discussion. It was only our second conversation. Earlier, while he was still finance minister, Martin had arranged a lunch and interrogated me about health care. I remember it as an unusual experience. Often when someone in political life asks you your opinion after a very short period of time they will tell you their opinion, often at great length. Paul Martin did exactly the opposite. For over two hours at lunch he sought my views, in meticulous detail. I was both intrigued and flattered. Martin proved to be that rare creature, a politician who really could listen.

This time, our discussion was once again engaging and flattering. Martin brushed aside my hesitations about stepping into the political arena. He told me that I would have a far greater impact as health minister than as chair of the Health Council of Canada, the position I held at the time. He was probably right. I asked him to wait until the last possible minute to formally ask me. The call came several months later. The prime minister was on a plane bound for Washington to meet President George W. Bush. His approach was direct.

"Michael. I am asking you to run."

My reply came in the form of a question, "How long do I have to think about it?"

The prime minister chuckled. "When Raymond Garneau asked me to run for the very first time, that was what I asked: 'How long do I have to think about it?' He told me that if you think about entering politics you would never do it."

The longtime Quebec politician who had served ably as finance minister proved to be wise on the decision to enter politics. I thought about it and the doubts overwhelmed me. I didn't do it.

These were both golden opportunities for anyone with political ambition. The first offer was of one of the safest and most historic NDP seats in Canada following in the footsteps of the giants of the movement. Cooperative Commonwealth Federation founder J.S. Woodsworth held the seat for seventeen years and Stanley Knowles, who followed him, held it for twenty-five more years.

The second invitation came from an incumbent prime minister who had been Canada's best finance minister. Yet I declined both offers. Why?

By the time Paul Martin asked, one of my children was in university and the other had already graduated. Still I declined. The partisan feelings that I had when I was younger had long since departed. I am no longer one hundred percent for any political party, left or right or wrong. Over the years in public service I came to admire individual politicians from various parties. I became more concerned with pragmatism and compromise than the pure octane of ideology. The more I witnessed the behaviour of "true believers" of any ideology, the less convinced I became of the virtue of rigid views. Much progress in our nation has been achieved through hard work and compromise based on pragmatism. Still, I readily concede that politics would be a dull place if every decision was made by consensus.

Politics may have passed me by but its stories have not. Stories are as important to politics as facts are to science. In the end, politics must be entertaining just as life must be entertaining or who could bear either? It must also be purposeful, earnest, and by its nature, contentious, but without the entertainment value, why bother?

What follows is an effort to distill some entertainment value from five decades around politics in my younger years and in and out of government in my middle life. As my late Irish mother Una Barry McGilligan Decter would be careful to note, stories are improved by their telling and re-telling. Many of my stories have grown better in their telling over the years. Does this undermine their historical accuracy? Perhaps. Others, who lived these events, may well remember them differently. That is as it should be. At their core these tales are as I remember them. No claim is advanced for their complete accuracy. Memory plays tricks. Historians beware. Lovers of politics draw near. Enjoy them for what they are, simple stories of politics and political life in all its curious glory.

I know that the telling of political stories is infectious and contagious. Nothing would please me more if reading these accounts convinces others to write their own tales from the back room.

CHAPTER ONE

GROWING UP POLITICAL

WHEN I REACHED THE GRAND AGE of nine years, the New Democratic Party was formed by the alliance of the Cooperative Commonwealth Federation (CCF) and the Canadian Labour Congress. Because my mother was very active in left-wing politics in Winnipeg, I was soon put to work delivering election pamphlets door-to-door for the NDP. Due to the success of my surgeon father, Percy, we lived in the well-to-do area of south Winnipeg which was rather infertile ground for the NDP. This slogging from doorstep to doorstep began my early childhood education in politics. I reached the first rung of the political ladder—deliverer of pamphlets.

My mother, Una Barry McGilligan Decter, was Irish. Her family thrived in the rough and tumble of Irish politics. My grandfather, Eugene McGilligan, served time in the Irish jails in the 1930s for his activities in the Irish Republican Army (IRA). At that time it was a legitimate political organization and only a precursor to the terrorist nightmare it later became. There was also an Irish uncle, known as Uncle Toady around our household. I never met him. It was only years later, upon the occasion of his death, that a long obituary in the *Irish Times* taught me that Uncle Toady had, in reality, been Patrick McGilligan, a pillar of post-war Irish governments. As a cabinet minister, he brought Ireland modernization in the form of both Keynesian economics in finance and the massive Shannon hydroelectric development scheme. In Ireland, some histories referred to the Statute of Westminster as McGilligan's Charter because of Patrick McGilligan's role in drafting it. In addition to serving as attorney general of the Irish Republic, Patrick McGilligan also served as dean of the Law School of University College. Recently I have learned that there are thirty-seven boxes of Patrick McGilligan's papers archived in Dublin. Someday I hope to go and read his papers and understand more about my Irish political heritage.

My mother arrived in Canada pregnant with me. She had met my father, Percy, in London, England, after the war, when he travelled there for post-graduate medical studies in the early 1950s. They married and sailed for his home and native land, Canada. Una and my father bounced over 2,400 kilometres of gravel road that would later be called the Trans-Canada Highway, all the way from Montreal to Prince Arthur and Fort William and then on through the United States to Winnipeg because the Trans-Canada was not yet completed between the Lakehead (later renamed Thunder Bay) and Winnipeg. My Jewish grandparents had met them in Montreal. They refused to speak to my mother because she was Catholic. Safe in the womb, I arrived in Winnipeg, shaken not stirred.

Percy grew up in the North End of Winnipeg amidst the many people driven from Europe by war and prejudice. My grandparents were Russian Jews who had fled the pogroms of the Ukraine to find safety in the new land of Canada. My grandfather, Harry Decter, drove a streetcar for the Winnipeg Gas & Electric Company. He belonged to the One Big Union (OBU) that organized the 1919 General Strike in Winnipeg. His three sons all became doctors; two of them, Alan and Percy, became surgeons. Percy's success brought our family to the more comfortable surroundings of River Heights in south Winnipeg. This is a piece of well-to-do political geography that had never elected a New Democrat to either the Manitoba legislature or the parliament of Canada until many years after my birth.

In the early days of my involvement in electoral politics, my mother had the dominant influence. My father took me fishing and told me stories of his work as an orthopedic surgeon. My mother took me to political rallies and protest marches and taught me how to be against the established order of things. She also sent me out to deliver pamphlets for every New Democrat who sought political office in south Winnipeg.

VOICE OF WOMEN

WE SIX DECTER CHILDREN, of whom I was the first-born, grew up in a rambling, green shingle and limestone, barn-like house on Ash Street in Winnipeg's leafy River Heights neighbourhood. Our mother became very active in the peace movement. Una emerged as a driving force locally and nationally in an organization called Voice of Women (VOW). The VOW represented a fascinating mix of 1950s and 1960s peace activism, incipient feminism and a smattering of world federalist views. The VOW had links to women's peace groups around the world. This lead to the Voice of Women and everyone associated with it being monitored by the RCMP as possibly dangerous subversives.

In North America in the 1950s and 1960s amidst the Cold War and the arms race, peace was a subversive concept. Strange to consider now but then the United States viewed peace as a pro-Soviet notion. The prevalent Cold War mentality directed hostility towards all those "radicals" who thought that perhaps people living on the other side of the Iron Curtain were just as frightened of nuclear war as we were. I wonder now, with the meltdown of the Soviet Union and the democratic revolution in eastern Europe, how I will ever explain the Cold War or communism to my children, now in their twenties. Sean "P. Diddy" Combs is a more prominent figure in their lives than Lenin, Stalin or Karl Marx. They do exhibit an interest in former President John Kennedy, but via Oliver Stone's paranoid, conspiracy-filled view of the assassination. My efforts to put forward another, more moderate view are met with taunts of "I suppose you believe the Warren Commission—yeah right, pops!"

Voice of Women intruded upon our childhood lives in intriguing and sometimes disturbing ways. For example, the annual Remembrance Day Silent Peace Vigil proved memorable. Every Remembrance Day, when others would commemorate the war dead and the sacrifices made to protect freedom, my mother and her determined band of Voice of Women activists would journey to the cenotaph in downtown Winnipeg and stage a silent vigil in support of peace. This display of anti-war sentiment generally did not sit well with war veterans. Because of the internationalist alignment of Voice of Women, it grated particularly on those who had escaped oppression in eastern Europe and viewed internationalism as clearly pro-Soviet.

We older children were often dragged along to these Remembrance Day peace vigils to sit silently, often in the fiercely cold November rain, at the base of the cenotaph. My mother viewed this as "character-building" although at the time this opinion was not shared by the participating children. We saw it as punishment for the crime of having an activist mother.

One of the most vivid memories I have of these protests was of the kindliness of the police towards us. They believed the protesting women to be at worst harmless, misguided fools standing out in the cold and rain. Harmless we most certainly were, for as the name "Silent Peace Vigil" implied, the rules of protest required us to maintain quiet and not to respond to provocation of any sort. That said, provocation in the form of several large ex-east European men spitting on you is a little hard to ignore, especially when you are nine years old.

One bitterly cold November 11, a particularly obnoxious fellow, who must have weighed upwards of 300 pounds—from my vantage point he loomed as a giant—screamed verbal abuse at us and began spitting upon the demonstrators. Clearly, I lacked the full self-control of the seasoned protestors as well as their devotion to the peaceful civil disobedience doctrines of Martin Luther King and Mahatma Gandhi. I lunged at the evil giant and kicked him as hard as I could on his shin. It was completely ineffective. I did him no damage. However, my assault, pitiful as it had been, provoked him to a furious but ill-conceived effort to swat me. The friendly policeman, weighing in at about 250 pounds, grabbed him, threw him roughly to the ground and hauled him away. Later, I was mildly admonished for injecting a note of combative violence into the proceedings. But, it has always been my conviction that the group took secret and appropriately silent delight from my action.

My mother's involvements with the Voice of Women also led to a visit by the mayor of Moscow, one of the many guests over the years to stay at our home. She was given my bedroom for her stay, forcing me to bunk in with my younger brothers for a night of pushing and shoving and little sleep. The mayor of Moscow presented a powerful figure who reminded me of my own grandmother, Baba Edith. With her roots in Ukraine, my Baba might well have shared a physical heritage with the mayor's ancestors.

I grew up with the distorted view that everyone had notables like the mayor of Moscow, Rabbi Fineman of Toronto and later, Senator Thérèse Casgrain drop in for dinner and a party. Una made our home an eclectic, political salon that she hosted with great grace and style.

Years later, when I had learned more of the history of the rambling barn of a house on Ash Street in which we lived, it seemed fitting that the mayor of Moscow should have stayed there during the Cold War. Early owners of the house included the Moodys, who were the family of Maryon Pearson. She became the wife of distinguished prime minister, peace activist and Nobel Laureate Lester B. Pearson. When my father bought the house it was the home of a widow of one of the colourful Gee brothers. The Gees were the leading concert promoters and impresarios of Winnipeg for a quarter of a century. They booked acts from all over the world. When they brought the famous black American singer, actor and social activist and alleged communist Paul Robeson to Winnipeg in the 1930s, the hotels would not have him. His race, not his political beliefs, was the issue. Consequently, Paul Robeson stayed in the same modest bedroom that I later surrendered to the mayor of Moscow. In 1975, after a narrow defeat in the leadership convention of the NDP, Rosemary Brown occupied the same room. I have always wondered if a strange karma was attached to the house and to the room that three quite different soulmates would sleep in some decades apart. Did this karma affect me?

The Voice of Women provided a bond for my parents in what sadly became a marriage strained and finally rent asunder by an unending contest of wills—the passionate Irish political woman and her relentless Jewish surgeon husband. They may have had different beliefs, but both Una and Percy loved to entertain. The Voice of Women furnished a steady stream of lively, unusual visitors to Winnipeg and our home as well as good reasons for entertaining.

The ritual of the party preparation included my father sweeping around the grand curved driveway with his Jaguar sedan loaded with wine and spirits for the bar and wonderful food. Among his favourites were mountains of shrimp which we children would be pressed into service to peel. The house buzzed with the anticipation of the party. There were dishes to polish, ice to chip, the bar to array. And tantalizing smells wafted from the two large ovens in the kitchen. To this day the sight of a peeled shrimp takes me back forty-five years and 1,500 kilometres to the three-storey house with its noisy chaotic life force and my mother's political salon.

Voice of Women was a combination of women's auxiliary to the peace movement and an emerging feminism organization. This led to diverse projects. Among the most memorable were Betty Nickerson's art kits. The assembling of art kits became the decade-long fundraising approach for the vow. The art kits themselves were a folio with crayons and co-loured construction paper. The idea was to sell the art kits to the parents for use by their artistically inclined children. Unfortunately, the Decter children, carried away in their zeal at aiding the cause of world peace, manufactured several hundred more kits than the market would absorb. They were stored in the cedar closet on the third floor for many years afterwards. Occasionally the kits were raided by the children for needed school supplies. They were too nice to throw out. I wonder if they are still safe in the cedar closet protected forever from the ravages of time and more importantly, from the ravages of the moths.

Another vow project started by one of the British Columbia members was to knit socks for the North Vietnamese. With the assistance of the vow, she would dispatch these large, hand-knit socks by the box-load to North Vietnam. I was a callow enough youth to point out that the North Vietnamese featured on the nightly news seemed, in a phrase, "sock-less." This was taken as yet another sign that youth did not understand the serious problems of the world. I always felt, in my own defence, that py-jamas would have been a more welcome garment, albeit harder to knit.

The news of the world caused great debate and argument at our din-ner table. I learned from my parents that the many harsh realities of the world were never to be accepted. Challenging the conventional wisdom and the accepted order were the cornerstones of my early childhood edu-cation. My father regarded virtually all those in authority as a "bunch of bastards." Though more refined in her language, my mother fully shared his sentiment.

Against the volcanic outpouring of anger at the unjust state of the world, a sense of humour seemed a necessary element of activism. I gained it early and have clung to it ever since. Politics without a sense of humour is an unbearably grim business.

JEFFERSONIAN VIOLENCE

IT WAS AT THE HEIGHT of the Cold War in the mid-1960s when one incident catapulted Voice of Women and my mother onto the front page
of national newspapers and into a confrontation with the government
of Canada. It began innocently enough when the Voice of Women invited a professor from the University of Minnesota to give a speech in
Winnipeg. Professor Mulford Q. Sibley was a well-known advocate of
"Jeffersonian Violence." The term "Jeffersonian Violence" derived from
Thomas Jefferson and his fundamental belief in the ballot box and electoral process as an instrument of change. In short, Sibley was an advocate of nothing more revolutionary than getting the vote out on behalf
of whatever cause one supported. For the Canadian immigration department the word "Jeffersonian" did not in any way explain or excuse
the word "violence." To these literal-minded authorities, the professor
was a menace to Canada's national security. He was turned back at the
Winnipeg Airport and not allowed to enter Canada.

It must have been rapidly evident to the thinking people in Ottawa,
likely found in the Department of External Affairs rather than the
Department of Immigration, as soon as they examined the Sibley dos-
sier, that a ghastly mistake had been made. Moreover it was a mistake
not easily retreated from. The communist revolutionary menace they had
repelled at the border turned out to be a mild-mannered academic, well
regarded by his colleagues. Certainly no one in his own country regarded
him as a threat to the national security of that dramatically more paranoid nation, the United States of America.

My mother's Irish temper, combined with her flare for publicity, catapulted the incident forward onto the front pages. Una demanded, and
got a meeting with the minister of immigration. He flew to Winnipeg.
As reported by Una, the meeting consisted of the minister in full retreat.
He sought to distance himself from the folly of his officials' actions. He
agreed most readily that Professor Sibley would be welcome to come to
Canada at any time.

The ultimate event was a smashing success—240 in the audience, ver-
sus the twenty-five that might have been expected without the extra publicity sparked by the original Immigration Department decision. The
speech was not revolutionary. In fact, one honest but tactless guest at my
mother's post-speech party noted that the speech itself had been a colos-
sal bore, draining to listen to. Jeffersonian violence may have inflamed

the officials of the Immigration Department but it did not inspire the audience.

Una responded forcefully in her full Irish brogue. "That was not the important point. The important point is that the nonsense of the Cold War was confronted in Winnipeg and exposed for the utter folly that it is."

In that sentiment, she had the full support of the crowd, by now recovering their energy through a combination of shrimps and martinis.

MONKEYS, ORGAN GRINDERS AND WINNIPEG SOUTH

IN THE FIRST DOZEN election campaigns in which I worked, the New Democratic Party candidates were soundly defeated. Often, there were few or no votes for the NDP in many of the polls that comprised the riding. This did not deter us. By age eleven, I had command of a motley crew consisting of my younger brothers and sisters and the children of Lionel and Anne Orlikow. Our mission—to deliver NDP leaflets to every door in Winnipeg South. Every election, whether federal, provincial or municipal, we would make our appointed rounds. Even the local dogs came to know us. And we, warily, came to know them.

One of my early memories is of the rather ill-fated provincial election campaign of 1966 in which Lionel Orlikow, then a well-regarded high school teacher, became the candidate. Lionel was the step-brother of David Orlikow, a long-time elected school trustee, city councillor and Member of Parliament for Winnipeg North. He was persuaded by my mother and others to cast his political fortunes before the electorate of River Heights as the NDP candidate. This solidly Tory stronghold cried out for a sacrificial NDP lamb. Lionel was chosen. I suspect he drew the short straw at the nominating meeting.

Lionel was a wonderful human being, a marvellous teacher and brilliant educator. He was, however, not an ideal politician. He wore his heart on his sleeve and despite years of facing classrooms of high school students, was painfully shy. In fact, I have rarely met a brand new "wannabe" politician eager to knock on a strange voter's door. Lionel, however, proved to have a case of extreme reluctance to go door-to-door. On his first canvass with my mother, his unease became apparent. At the very first house, my mother rang the doorbell. When the voter appeared she said, "I would like you to meet Lionel Orlikow, our candidate for River Heights." Turning to Lionel, she discovered him fully two houses away, hiding behind a hedge. This caused a great crisis of confidence in the campaign. An emergency meeting of the campaign committee was convened and extensive canvass training sessions organized for Lionel. I was cast as "Mrs. Jones," the door answerer and undecided voter, eager to be swayed by clarity on the issues. A number of rehearsals were held.

After a period of intensive coaching, the trainers pronounced Lionel fit for active canvassing duty. We sallied forth. He had worked up a hearty greeting style in a booming voice. In keeping with the instructions of his tutors, Lionel pounded on the first door. A woman appeared. Glancing at his voter's list, Lionel grasped her hand and declared, "I am Lionel Orlikow, the NDP candidate in River Heights. I am pleased to meet you. Would your good husband be at home also?"

Mrs. Jones promptly dissolved into tears. Her good husband had died between the time of the preparation of the voter's list and candidate Orlikow's hearty but untimely call. This incident finished Lionel on the door-to-door canvass.

Undeterred by this setback, the campaign committee decided to shift the field of action. The proper place for Lionel's candidacy to gain the necessary momentum was not on the doorstep but in the supermarkets. My mother and Sidney Green, later a prominent Manitoba NDP cabinet minister, also decided that simply imposing Lionel and the leaflets on unsuspecting shoppers would be underwhelming. They figured that Lionel needed a little hoopla to accompany his tour. The campaign committee decided on an organ grinder and monkey to draw the crowd. By now, these slave monkeys have likely been freed by the animal rights movements. In 1966, they hustled for peanuts.

A suitable monkey and organ grinder were found. Arrangements were made by telephone. On the appointed day, two of us were dispatched to pick up the monkey and his organ grinder master from a tiny apartment just off north Main Street. On our arrival, the organ grinder confessed that his monkey had not been well lately. Despite this warning, monkey, organ grinder and organ were transported to join candidate Lionel in the parking lot of a local food market. An early supermarket, the designated Safeway possessed a spacious parking lot. Here the organ grinder team was to charm the voters into supporting Lionel. We left them there amidst the unsuspecting electorate shopping on Corydon Avenue and went off to continue the leaflet campaign. We promised to return in two hours to collect the triumphant campaigners.

When we returned two hours later, there, seated on the curb, each with his head in his hands were the monkey, the organ grinder and Lionel. The three resembled nothing so much as the "hear-no-evil, see-no-evil, speak-no-evil" monkey trio of caricature fame. It turned out the monkey had been violently ill. Due to the smell of vomit, few of the shoppers had wanted to linger in the general vicinity. Fewer still had been interested in Lionel's election leaflet. It had been a total fiasco. We all vowed that a monkey would never again be a part of our campaign. Ill or well! It was not a difficult promise to keep.

The election was a predictable debacle. On election day, Lionel ran a distant third, garnering fewer than 1,000 votes as the Progressive Conservative candidate Sidney Spivak swept into office. The Liberal finished second.

Lionel's career moved him from the classroom to the Department of Education. As assistant deputy minister and later deputy minister, Lionel Orlikow provided the leadership for many innovative educational initiatives. He did not return to political life for twenty years. In the 1980s, Lionel was easily elected to the Winnipeg School Board. He served with energy and intellect and was re-elected. When he retired from the board, one of his sons successfully contested the seat. The son, likely one of my Ash Street irregular leaflet distributors, was asked by a reporter whether his father had played any part in his decision to seek political office. He replied that Lionel had informed him that the Orlikows had served their community for forty years in electoral office and that it was now his turn.

There has been no evidence of monkeys or organ grinders in the recent electoral efforts of any member of the Orlikow family.

POLITICAL RALLIES

MY MOTHER WAS not only active in the Voice of Women but later in the NDP and even in its radical left wing, the Waffle. My parents believed that a broad exposure to politics was the best approach for the education of children about politics. We were hauled along at every opportunity to hear politicians and others speak, either because my parents supported them or because they opposed them. What really counted was that they could speak well. An articulate and forceful presentation of a point of view was to be valued. This logic of broad exposure also extended to religion. My mother was a lapsed Catholic, actually "lapsed" would understate her dislike for the Catholic Church. The height of my mother's ambition, at one stage in her life, was to lock the Bishop of Dublin and the Bishop of Galway in a room and play them Tom Lehrer's song "Vatican Rag" until they lost their faith or went mad. She never expressed a clear view of which outcome was to be preferred.

My father was a less than conscientious Jew. We were exposed on a haphazard basis to several religions but never formally enrolled in any particular religion. Often the older women hired to look after us when my parents travelled took us to their churches, generally fundamentalist ones. As schoolchildren, we were instructed, when asked our religion, to write the letters N.F.R. We were ready to explain, if asked, that N.F.R. stood for "No Formal Religion" but no one ever asked. I can presume that we were regarded as belonging to some odd cult.

When I was thirteen years old, John Diefenbaker spoke at the Winnipeg Auditorium during the 1965 federal election campaign. He was a marvellous orator, in the same league as Tommy Douglas, whom we heard speak with passion more often during the 1960s. The old auditorium had banging steam radiators, creaking floors and a steep balcony terrifying to young children. The room was warm before it was full and doubly so when the lights were on. It soon became unbearably hot. This humid, steamy atmosphere gave Diefenbaker occasion to use one of his finest lines.

One of the scandals of the era was Lucien Rivard's escape from one of Canada's most secure penitentiaries by using a water hose to climb over the prison wall. The scandal had two prominent issues—one a fact and the other an allegation. The fact was that Rivard had been sent out to flood the skating rink on a very warm evening. The allegation was that the Liberals had somehow aided Rivard's escape.

Mopping the sweat from his brow and gazing out at each one of us in the hot and wilting crowd, Diefenbaker declared with astonished indignation, shaking his jowls, "it was on a night like this that they sent Lucien Rivard out to flood the skating rink." That was all he needed to say. The crowd went wild.

Major political rallies were the exception in Winnipeg. Far more frequent were small nominating meetings, sometimes very, very small nominating meetings. My younger brothers and sisters and I were often dragooned into service to pack a meeting. There were six of us. With Lionel and Anne Orlikow's seven children we could make a reasonable show of filled chairs just between the two families. Sometimes, in a contested nomination, the support of a few large families could secure a nomination for a candidate. I learned how real politics rested largely on attendance rather than beliefs.

As a consequence I was always impressed by Robert Fulford's comment that the Liberal Party of Canada, like United Church, required not so much faith as regular attendance. It seemed to me that all our modern political parties require not so much faith as regular attendance.

DEMOCRACY IN MOTION

A NORMAL NEW DEMOCRATIC PARTY nomination featured two or more candidates competing for the support of the local party faithful. New memberships would be sold over weeks or months with the various campaigns culminating in the nomination meeting. The nomination meeting was usually held in a church or union hall rented for the occasion. Candidates would work hard to sell memberships in advance of the nomination meeting. It was highly unusual for an elected incumbent to be challenged successfully at a nomination meeting. The most determined nomination battles followed a retirement in a safe riding.

The extent to which entrenched incumbents would go to avoid a nomination fight was brought home most colourfully by one New Democrat who had held a provincial seat in the North End of Winnipeg for many years. Upon hearing the news that a challenge was being mounted to his re-nomination, the incumbent turned up at the provincial office with signed nomination papers. Party officials were puzzled. His opponent was outraged.

When had the actual nomination been held, they all wanted to know. Where had it been held? Who had been invited to attend?

The incumbent's explanation was that a nomination meeting had indeed been held. Under grilling, he conceded that the meeting had not actually involved notice to the membership or the renting of a hall. On being repeatedly asked who had actually nominated him and where, he confessed that, "well a bunch of guys had gotten together," and a "bunch of guys" had nominated him. As it turned out, the particular nomination in question had been held in the backseat of a car filled with five people, including the candidate. To be fair, they had been driving around the right riding. Even the most skillful of organizers will admit that it is tough to overturn a nomination by packing a meeting when that meeting is travelling at sixty kilometres per hour in a Chevrolet. To my knowledge this was the one and only "bunchnik" nomination on wheels.

The local left-wing of the party accused the establishment of supporting incumbents for nomination as long as they were breathing or, failing that, if their body was still warm. This claim crystallized the moniker the "bunchniks." It stuck.

THE EARLY CANDIDATE GETS THE NOMINATION

ONE OF THE MOST UNUSUAL nomination battles to take place in Winnipeg was the titanic struggle over the Liberal nomination in the St. Boniface federal seat in 1968. Veteran's Affairs Minister Leo Teillet held the riding for the Liberals. Joe Guay was the mayor of St. Boniface. He held one enormous advantage over the incumbent. Unlike Minister Teillet, Joe Guay had supported Pierre Elliott Trudeau in his successful bid for the leadership of the Liberal Party. Teillet had not. Trudeau's team set out to dump Teillet at his own nomination meeting. It took me many years and a decent bottle of scotch to learn the full story.

The defeat of Leo Teillet marked the first time in Commonwealth political history that an incumbent cabinet minister lost his own renomination. It was quite a dark moment in the history of a party steeped in continuity and stability. The defeat of Teillet was engineered with a very simple yet powerful manoeuvre. Joe Guay's supporters bussed in all of their Liberal members an hour before the scheduled time of the nomination meeting. They literally packed the arena. When the Teillet supporters arrived there was no room in the hall. Many of the Teillet supporters were turned away. By the simple strategy of showing up early, the Guay forces triumphed. In life it is said that the early bird gets the worm. In politics sometimes the early candidate gets the nomination.

SUING THE WINNIPEG SCHOOL BOARD

ANOTHER CLOSE ENCOUNTER with electoral politics came with my mother's election to the Winnipeg School Board in the late 1960s. As an activist high school student, I had a keen interest in the issues of education policy but was quite unprepared for the politics. My mother equally was not versed in how politics was practised on the Winnipeg School Board. In particular, Una was not prepared for a local gentleman, reputed to be a bootlegger, who had gained a seat on the board through diligent efforts to supply the afterhours needs of all available political parties. Among this bootlegger's classic moments on the board was his verbal assault on a teachers' delegation for the use of the word "niggardly" in their brief. He took it to be a racist term. He also questioned sabbatical leave for senior teachers in the division with the remark, "I thought we gave all the teachers Saturday off."

There were many evenings of delight occasioned by my radical mother's generally unsuccessful attempts to have an impact on the board's decisions. A bastion of conservatism, the Winnipeg School Board repelled the reform-minded invader at every turn. Still, she would return home after each meeting and regale us with grand stories of the board's follies. The board reflected the character of Winnipeg itself. The Communist Party held a board seat from the North End. A few Liberals held seats from the centre of the city. The Communist trustees were joined by New Democrats from the North End and the centre of Winnipeg. The Conservatives held the south Winnipeg seats and commanded a majority on the board.

At one juncture, due to a narrow split on the board—an eight-seven division amongst the fifteen trustees—and the hospitalization of one of the elderly conservative members, it appeared as though the election of the new chair of the board might go to a progressive. My mother was delighted. She explained how it would all unfold. For the first time in living memory, the long-entrenched conservative school trustees were about to face a major setback. We listened enthralled by her passion for the anticipated victory over the forces of darkness.

On the night of the fateful meeting, Una swept off in her favourite Irish tweed suit—the elegant burgundy one—filled with the righteousness of her cause and the warm glow of the great and moral victory to be achieved. Certain in her heart that she would return to announce the election of a chair that could show progressive leadership.

Una had not reckoned with the formidable instinct for self-preservation of the conservative majority. In defiance of anything representing democratic tradition, which requires the presence of an elected member to cast a vote, they had their hospitalized member vote by mail. Given that no one had yet been nominated for the post of chair, the mail-in ballot required an act of incredible imagination.

Una arrived home after midnight in a towering Irish rage.

"We were hijacked. It was a travesty of democracy!" she declared.

Her immediate reaction, once her anger subsided a little, was to call her best political friend and ally, Sidney Green. At the time, Green served as a member of the Manitoba legislature representing the NDP in the North End riding of Inkster. Una became Sidney Green's campaign manager and one of his chief backers when he ran for leadership of the provincial NDP on two separate occasions. Although we all worked tirelessly for Green, none did so with more determination than Una. He lost both times.

Green is a complex, remarkable, brilliant man who fought his way up from poverty through to a gold medal at the University of Manitoba Law School where he became a tremendous orator. His political career passed through the NDP where after failing to become party leader twice he served with distinction as a minister in several portfolios during the Schreyer administration in the 1970s. Eventually he left the NDP and formed his own political party, the Progressives, that enjoyed little electoral success.

From a role at the centre of reform in Manitoba politics he returned to a life as a lawyer. Sidney Green has always made a powerful impression, for good or ill, on everyone he ever encountered. In his non-political life, Green represented his legal clients with formidable intellect and powerful oratory.

Sidney arrived within twenty minutes of the phone call, no doubt alarmed by Una's anger. They engaged in a loud discussion for nearly an hour. Then Green declared, "We will sue the Winnipeg School Board." He said it with such dramatic flair that he ended consideration of any other alternatives. After all, he was the lawyer. If he said sue—then it must be a good idea. And sue is exactly what they did.

The debate that long night then turned to who exactly would sue the Winnipeg School Board. Sidney decided that it would be improper for my mother to sue. As a member of the board she would be suing herself. I volunteered but was not of legal age. My father went to bed due to his morning surgery schedule; he too was out of the running. So a citizen had to be found who would consent to sue the board to reverse the outrage against democracy that had been perpetrated that very evening. My mother and Sidney were of one mind. This could not wait nor could they rest until the enraged citizen was found. To my astonishment, Sidney Green picked up the telephone and began dialling. Noting that it was now 3:00 a.m., I was certain an enraged citizen could be found at the other end of the telephone. Though it seemed unlikely that a citizen's first waking thought would be to launch a lawsuit against the Winnipeg School Board. Sidney called the head of the Steelworker's Union, a tough, effective leader by the name of Len Stevens. Awakened from the depths of sleep and discovering that it was his good friend Sidney on the phone, Stevens readily consented to sue whomever Sid wanted if only he could hear about it in the morning. By noon the next day, Hugh Leonard Stevens, a.k.a. Len Stevens, whose full name I would never have known if not for the suit, was, in fact, suing the Winnipeg School Board.

The legal action was successful. Eventually the election was overturned and a new one ordered. However, victory was fleeting. The previously hospitalized Conservative trustee rallied and appeared to vote in person. Nevertheless justice and democracy had triumphed—another small moral victory had been won. Until Ed Schreyer won the provincial election in 1969 and became Manitoba's first NDP premier, we had to be satisfied with a large number of moral victories.

POWDER PUFF DERBY

MY MOTHER'S DECISION to contest the newly-formed constituency of Fort Rouge in the 1969 election on behalf of the NDP was not her own choice. In the re-organization of ridings, it appeared that either Osborne or Crescentwood would be better ridings for a New Democratic candidate. However, my mother, then a vice-president of the party was called upon to contest the nomination in Fort Rouge because the alternative candidate was not someone the party hierarchy felt would well represent the party. The irony of this particular decision was that the NDP swept narrowly to power under Premier Ed Schreyer in the 1969 election. The candidates in Crescentwood and Osborne were both elected. My New Democratic mother was not elected in Fort Rouge even though at the time she was seen as the strongest of the NDP candidates across the three ridings.

Women candidates were not by any means mainstream in 1969. In fact, there had been only a few women members of the Manitoba legislature. Thelma Forbes had been the only woman member to serve in a cabinet. But in response to Una's nomination, both the Conservative and Liberal parties nominated women—Inez Truman for the Tories and Jane Heffelfinger for the Grits. Sadly, the race was dubbed the "Powder Puff Derby" in the daily press, underscoring the lack of respect for women in politics at that time. Each of the three candidates was talented, serious and capable.

Although the NDP swept the province, Fort Rouge stuck by its conservative inclinations. At least it could be said that Una's nomination and the ensuing "Powder Puff Derby" ensured the election of a woman to the legislature.

BUSTING THE SLATE

IN MY YOUTH, I attended the annual conventions of the Manitoba New Democratic Party. My mother's active involvement in the party ensured my interest and my own curiosity led to my involvement. In 1969, the NDP moved from opposition to government. The key elements of a party convention were the delegates. Most delegates were elected by their regular party constituency organizations. However, the various labour unions as founders of the party were also entitled to elect delegates.

Voting at the conventions was structured in a fashion that allowed certain groups, primarily the larger unions led by the United Steelworkers, to have disproportionate control. The union delegates, sensibly from a political power point of view, tended to caucus and vote together on issues. They would put forth a slate of nominees previously agreed to in their own caucus. From my youthful point of view this was democratic as long as it only involved the labour members of the party executive. What struck my young democratic soul as unjust was the idea that one group—labour—albeit a group I had respected, would pick the entire executive of the party. And by voting in a block, the unions would ensure their slate's election.

I puzzled over how one might change the system and hit upon the idea of a sneaky solution. The day of the voting, representatives of the United Steelworkers would hand out their slate on green or yellow or some predetermined colour of paper. The arriving delegates would get this one sheet and it would allow them to conveniently fill out their ballot not only for party leader, president and vice president and treasurer but for members of the provincial council at large. It occurred to me that since the slate was an unofficial document, I thought if I obtained a copy it might be possible to substitute multiple copies, creating confusion and busting the slate.

This is exactly what I proceeded to do one convention morning with the aid of a couple of friends who shall remain anonymous. I should note, since she was later blamed for the resulting chaos, my mother not only had nothing to do with this but no knowledge of it. This was an act of youthful defiance of the convention hierarchy by yours truly.

It worked splendidly. I found the slates printed on pale yellow paper so I set about obtaining the same colour paper. Sensibly, I left intact all of the key positions, that is, Ed Schreyer, party leader and the party president. I also left the actual union representatives but changed everybody else on the slate. The scene was one of confusion since everything seemed in the right place. I did not hand out the altered slate but left that to the representatives from the United Steelworkers union and their allies who handed delegates multiple different slates. The resulting chaos cheered my young rebellious heart and completely antagonized those in authority.

In the end, people were forced to actually vote for candidates they knew and respected. They all ignored the slate since the slate had proven to be unreliable. Only a few positions changed. At the time, I viewed it as a triumph of democracy. Several years later, working for national leader Ed Broadbent, I would be very much more conservative, preserving the established order instead of rocking the boat.

LADY BOUNTIFUL OF THE WELFARE APPEAL BOARD

UNA ALWAYS INTENDED TO WRITE about her eight years as chairperson of the Welfare Appeal and Advisory Board. Her words would have been filled with wonderful humour. My mother told the best stories of anyone I have ever met. Tragically a stroke ended her life before she could undertake the task of summing up her epic struggle on behalf of the rights of the poor. Her stories of the Welfare Appeal Board years were bittersweet. She put endless energy into bettering the lives of the poor.

At her memorial service, my brother Derry read from W.B. Yeats poem "Her Praise":

Though she had young men's praise and old men's blame,
Among the poor both old and young gave her praise.

When the NDP formed the government with Ed Schreyer as premier in 1969, my mother had been an unsuccessful candidate. As one of the talented, she presented an obvious choice for appointed office. Her friend and supporter Sidney Green had been named Minister of Social Services. He recommended that the cabinet appoint Una as chair of the Welfare Advisory and Appeal Board.

Although this post lacked the grandeur of being a cabinet minister, it was ironically the most wonderful appointment both for my mother and for the Schreyer government. Her fundamental belief in justice and her deep commitment to the poor lead her to champion many vital reforms. She totally revamped the board, altering its composition as well as its function. She transformed a moribund board which had kept the right of recipients to appeal welfare decisions a secret. Una believed that the poor had a right to know that they could appeal ... and they did. Many unfair practices and abuses were identified through the appeal process and corrected.

One of the actions Una undertook as chair of the board was to convene an appeal panel in response to an appeal by a Treaty Indian living on a First Nations reserve in northern Manitoba. Her ally, Sidney Green, by then minister of another department, was outraged. Sid was a lawyer with strong and rigid views. He believed Aboriginals were a federal responsibility and Una's board had no jurisdiction. My mother's legal opinion, which she sought carefully, was that the provincial social assistance act referred to all residents of Manitoba. Treaty Indians were indeed residents of Manitoba so her board heard the appeal. It determined that the welfare rates paid by federal Indian Affairs were below the level of subsistence. As a consequence, an embarrassed Department of Indian Affairs raised its welfare rates to the benefit of both the Indians and the provincial economy. They took this remedial action despite their continuing assertion that the provincially appointed board had no legal authority in federal jurisdiction. Premier Schreyer was delighted as he yearned for greater federal recognition of the plight of the northern Aboriginal people and a greater sharing of the financial burden. On the other hand, a rigid legalist in such matters, Green was angered at my mother's defiance of his direction. It was all the more galling since Una had supported Green historically against Schreyer for the leadership. In my experience, no candidate for party leadership ever forgets friends or foes later on.

One evening shortly after the decision, I opened the large oak front door of our home to find a highly agitated Honourable Sidney Green pacing back and forth on the porch.

"I need to speak with your mother!" Sid announced.

Naturally I invited him in. As a regular guest in the Decter house I was astonished when he refused to enter. He indicated an urgent need to speak with Una.

"Could she come out?"

Puzzled by this odd behaviour, I sought her out and told her that Sidney Green, cabinet minister, awaited her on our front porch. She went out. Sidney informed her in a very formal manner that he disagreed with her decision to hear the Indian appeal and that he had recommended her dismissal as chair of the Welfare Appeal Board to cabinet that very morning.

Una replied "So, Sid, did they fire me?"

"No." Green, chagrined, admitted that the cabinet had not fired her despite his insistence. Further he indicated that his colleagues, not historically fans of my mother, were delighted at the federal government being shamed into paying up.

"So, you will come in and have a drink." Una said and swept Sidney into our home and back into the fold. Such were Una's Irish ways.

A more disturbing tale of the adventures of the Welfare Appeal Board came during a rural hearing in western Manitoba. The board, when my mother was first appointed as its chair, had little representation from the poor and little insight into poverty. Una lobbied for change and succeeded. The Manitoba Indian Brotherhood, Manitoba Métis Federation and anti-poverty groups were invited to suggest nominees. The fifteen-member board came to more clearly represent Manitoba's diverse population. The board's mandate required it to hear appeals against municipal welfare as well as provincial welfare. Many of the municipal officials were openly hostile towards Aboriginals and the poor whom they considered wholly undeserving. In some cases, they endeavoured to drive the poor away from their communities by denying them adequate welfare. They also set grindingly low rates for welfare payments and imposed harsh conditions.

One town on Manitoba's western boundary had a particularly nasty track record on welfare. For its appeal function, the board would designate the chair or vice-chair and two of its fifteen members as a three-member panel. This particular appeal, held in the town's cavernous curling rink in the dead heat of summer, was presided over by one such panel.

The mayor of this town, a short, cigar-smoking man, exploded with rage at the mere sight of the panel. Biting through his cigar he shouted at them "Call this a government board—two women and a goddamned Indian!" As my mother calmed the mayor into a smouldering silence she had the satisfaction of knowing that this one government board had indeed changed.

Una's efforts to reform Manitoba's welfare system, one case and one decision at a time, were not universally applauded. The *Winnipeg Free Press* ran an editorial denouncing her; they compared her to "Lady Bountiful" of Dublin fame. The editors depicted her as dispensing the taxpayers' hard-earned money to the undeserving poor. They were further incensed that Una lived in a large house in a wealthy neighbourhood.

Municipal officials would regularly pass resolutions at their annual conventions demanding that her efforts cease and that she be removed from office. Premier Schreyer was unmoved. His own egalitarian soul must have appreciated the efforts of his Lady Bountiful. The premier kept Una in her job for the full eight years of his time in office. Every year as a result he endured the organized wrath of the municipalities. Schreyer carried this burden stoically. Each year at the annual NDP convention, the premier would quote U.S. President Franklin Delano Roosevelt: "The test of our progress is not whether we add more abundance of those who have much; it is whether we provide enough to those who have little." Those words captured not only the political philosophy of FDR but also my mother and Ed Schreyer.

At an early age, I learned that the two daily newspapers, the *Winnipeg Free Press* and the *Winnipeg Tribune*, were a source of both keen interest and extreme displeasure for my parents. Frequently one or both of them would be so offended by an editorial or column that I would be instructed to "Cancel the Damn Paper!" As the dutiful oldest son, I would call the offending paper and cancel our subscription effective immediately. The next day I would hear my parents complaining about the non-appearance of the *Free Press* or the *Tribune*. My efforts to explain their previous day's demand for immediate cancellation were met with complete loss of memory. "You did what?"

Gradually, I evolved a very successful coping strategy. I would phone the offending paper and instruct them in a loud voice to cancel their damned paper. At once, then I would hang up without leaving our name or address. My parents' indignation would be transmitted, much to their satisfaction, and I would be spared explaining the absence of the paper the next day.

STUDENT POLITICS

FOR ME, GROWING UP in a political household meant finding opportunities to put my fledgling political skills to the test. That led to an active involvement in student politics. I ran for student council president at River

Heights Junior High School. I lost, finishing second to a very popular athlete, Eric Winograd. I served Al Gore-like as his vice-president. Three years later, I ran for president of Kelvin High School's student council with Tim Stuart, a very popular athlete, as my vice-presidential running mate. We won. Political lesson learned—if you want to be president of your school, team up with a popular jock! Politics 101.

Our student campaigns, while spirited, lacked imagination and creativity. Others did better on this score. At nearby Gordon Bell High School, Arthur Green, son of Sidney Green, found himself in a tough battle for the student body presidency. His opponent's major campaign pledge was that if he were elected he would lobby the administration to paint basketball court lines on the schoolyard. The school had an entirely paved schoolyard. While informal basketball occurred frequently, the absence of lines made it difficult to organize formal games or to referee disputes. Arthur Green went his opponent one better and in so doing swept the election. On the morning of the election, Arthur rose very early and with a can of paint and sturdy brush, painted the basketball lines on the paved schoolyard. As the student body arrived at school, Arthur, paint can in evidence, shook each of their hands, saying, "My opponent only promised a basketball court with proper lines; I delivered." He won the election handily!

Student politics also provided an opportunity to learn about the harsh realities of the press. During my high school days, in the late 1960s, Brian Gory, an enterprising journalist, published a newspaper directed at high school students. In my final year of high school while I was serving as student council president, *Youth Beat* reprinted an article from *The Atlantic Monthly* which contained some extremely forceful language (the word 'motherfucker' to be precise). This antagonized the very proper and determined principal of Kelvin High School, Mr. M.R. Thompson. I never learned what his actual names were. He was the kind of man that demanded to be called Mister.

Although I viewed him as an unreasonable tyrant in those days, from my current vantage point, Mr. Thompson was an extremely capable administrator, if a tad humourless. He decreed that the offending rag would no longer be distributed on school property. The student body, which I headed, reacted negatively. Our response was sparked more out of dislike for Principal Thompson than due to a determined understanding of the principle of freedom of speech. The student council got sufficiently fired up to proclaim that we would distribute the newspaper on school premises in spite of the principal's decree.

The incident escalated. Gory fanned the flames by running a full front-page story declaring that freedom of the press was under threat. The article made personal the battle between me and Mr. Thompson. In reality it was not. The student council was unanimous in defying the principal's edict. I, as elected leader, was under obligation to pursue the course of action it had selected. It was also true that Thompson and I were not the best of friends and that he had all of the appropriate authority on his side. An objective observer might have been hard-pressed to believe that freedom of the press was really at stake. Mr. Thompson did not threaten the publication of *Youth Beat*, only its distribution within Kelvin High School. Nevertheless Gory's inflammatory article provoked him to go one step too far. He threatened to call the police and have members of the student council arrested if they tried to distribute the newspaper within the four walls of his sacred school. This proved too much. Among the student council members were the daughter of the Conservative premier of Manitoba and the son of his somewhat progressive but still Conservative minister of education. Principal Thompson had overplayed his hand. Parental opinion swung heavily to our side. A compromise was hastily reached. We were allowed to distribute the newspaper to students on their way out of the school not on their way in, as had previously been the case. It seemed a complete victory from our point of view but one which saved the administration some face.

What I learned—a valuable lesson—was that the press is chiefly interested in selling newspapers. If a good confrontation helps sell papers, as it usually does, then that is what will be portrayed, regardless of the subtle nuances in the minds of the protagonists. Gory cemented my fate with Principal Thompson by running a banner headline "Principal Backs Down," along with a very large photo of each of us above the fold. After that, my relations with the principal were never better than chilly. We rarely met, opting instead to send memos. It was excellent preparation for my subsequent years in government.

During this era, the nine high schools within Winnipeg School Division No. 1 banded together to form the Inter-High School Council. I became its president and my good friend Brian O'Leary, president of the student council at Gordon Bell High School, became its vice-president. At one point in our last year of high school we mounted a protest and marched en masse to the Winnipeg School Board offices. I do not remember our particular cause. The march did lead to a brief bit of fame and to an invitation to go on the dominant hotline call-in show on CJOB radio which was hosted by John Harvard, who later became a Liberal MP and eventually lieutenant governor of Manitoba. In those days, he was a hard, bullying radio voice. A shock jock before Howard Stern was even born. O'Leary and I were complete neophytes, radio virgins, lambs to the broadcast slaughter!

We arrived at the CJOB Portage Avenue studio and were greeted by a jovial Harvard. He regaled us with stories from his own high school days and put us in a completely relaxed and trusting mood. That polite Dr. Jekyll-like, John Harvard vanished the minute the "On Air" light glowed red. Suddenly, we were confronted by a grim, angry host who had fully transformed into Mr. Hyde. His first words were, "Tell me Michael and Brian, isn't it true that the Inter-High Council is simply a communist front?"

We were both speechless. Nothing could be further from the truth, at least as far as we knew. My mind reviewed the entire ranks of not only the Inter-High Council but my own council at Kelvin High. I had a difficult time identifying anyone who was New Democratic, let alone a communist. In those days, John Harvard seemed to view the NDP and communism as synonymous. In any event, we endured several minutes of accusation and denial, whereupon Harvard cut to an advertisement, the On Air light darkened, and in a stunning reversal he resumed his friendly Dr. Jekyll persona. Suddenly he was friendly again, worried about our welfare, concerned about how things were going. This process continued throughout the interview. We grew less bewildered and angrier. We also realized it was largely show business. Unfortunately, we were the show.

It was my only experience with what McCarthyism must have been like and even so, it was extremely mild experience, an annoyance, rather the ruination of a life. The interview taught me a number of lessons about the media which have proved valuable over the years. Avoidance, unless you have a cause that is on the side of the angels, is an essential lesson. Be prepared to be challenged, even baited if that is a way of eliciting a strong reaction. Keep your cool and your sense of humour. As comic theatre it is much more compelling than the truth.

Nearly thirty years later I sat in the same CJOB radio station preparing to be interviewed about my newly-published investment strategy book. The host, Charles Adler, asked if I had ever visited the station before. I told him my John Harvard story. I asked him to be gentle in his interview. Fortunately, he was.

Since that first interview, I have never again mistaken friendly banter in the green room or on the set before the microphone is live for genuine intent. This caution has proven invaluable over the years.

CHAPTER TWO

HARVARD DAYS

IN 1969, WHEN POLITICS CHANGED the face of Manitoba, I set off for an adventure far from home. I was accepted at Harvard University in the United States. My departure for what Bob Dylan described as the "green pastures of Harvard University" was not without humour. My high school adversary, Principal Thompson, grasped my hand at graduation and wished me well at university. Apparently my acceptance at a prestigious university reversed all the trouble I had generated during my student days. He seemed genuinely pleased. Some modest confusion had set in between Cambridge, the university in England and Cambridge, Massachusetts, location of Harvard. Believing his biggest troublemaker was leaving the country, the principal let his optimism overcome him. Convinced I was also leaving the continent, never to darken his office door again, he shook my hand and intoned, "All the best with your studies in England." I nodded and thanked him. It seemed best not to point out the difference between Cambridge, England and Cambridge, Massachusetts. It seemed an appropriate end to our odd relationship. I had, in truth, learned much from Mr. Thompson. It just took me a long time to understand just how much.

My parents, nervous about the American Empire, drove me to Cambridge, Massachusetts. "Friendly Manitoba" declared our license plates. After we crossed the American border south of Montreal I spotted my first New Hampshire plates. "Live Free or Die" proclaimed the more aggressive motto of the Green Mountain state. I realized that American values, as reflected by at least their license plates, were more lofty and declarative than our own. Years later, I would learn that Canada's constitutional principles of peace, order and good government were mild compared to the bolder American "life, liberty and the pursuit of happiness."

GREEN POLITICAL PASTURES

CAMBRIDGE, MASSACHUSETTS is really part of the larger city of Boston; it has only the Charles River to protect it from that city's encroachments. I felt, at first, awkward about any involvement in American politics. I was a Canadian. I was also a social democrat. In my Canadian mind, Americans equated U.S. Republicans with Canadian Conservatives and the Democrats with the Liberals. I had formed the impression that the American left—if it existed at all—had no role in electoral politics. As was often the case, I had underestimated the remarkable diversity of the American political landscape. Regionally, the Republican and Democratic parties were vastly different. There were many Democrats who were far to the left of the mainstream of the Canadian NDP. Gradually, I became fascinated by the Democratic Party and its electoral machine in the state of Massachusetts. This powerful electoral machinery was really the Kennedy apparatus. The Kennedy political organization, built to elect presidents, took the election of a mere senator, namely Ted Kennedy, as an easy, but nevertheless, serious undertaking.

Loosely attached to Harvard was a marvellous place called the Harvard Institute of Politics. Located in a small house on Auburn Street, the institute was where various politicos out of favour and needing time for a rest would hang out. A wide array of seminars was offered, non-credit, but it was probably more fascinating for students of real politics than much of what went on inside the Harvard Kennedy School of Government. I always found it interesting that the Americans called it "government" whereas in Canada, we stuck to the term "political science." "Government" seemed more confident to me and less of a fraud that "political science." This was yet another example of social science masquerading as a real science.

I attended a number of interesting seminars at the Institute of Politics, meeting people whom I would recognize years later as they ran for president (Joe Biden), or were elected to the Senate or House (Barney Frank), or otherwise achieved their destiny in American politics. The most entertaining and informative seminar was run by a man named Ed King who had an innocuous job as Harbor Commissioner or some such thing. In reality, however, his real life was spent working for the Kennedy machine as the election day organizer.

In Canada, the election day organizer was someone who might work for three or four weeks on a campaign to get everyone ready to pull the vote on voting day. For Ed King, this was his life's work. He would begin a day after one election preparing for the next one four years hence. On election day, he would typically have 10,000 people arrayed across the state of Massachusetts to ensure that the Kennedy in question or whoever else the Kennedys liked was elected to office.

Among the gems gleaned from attendance at these seminars was that on election day, King would hire all the pinball machine repairmen in Massachusetts and put them in vans with two-way radios. It was not uncommon for Republicans to smash the voting machines commonly used in U.S. elections in Democratic-minded districts and vice versa. Pinball machine repairmen were capable of fixing the voting machines. King would rush them in to ensure that the vote could go on. He would only do this however, if the damage had occurred in a heavily Democratic precinct.

King entertained us with other stories. His visit with Senator Ted Kennedy to the Soviet Union was a particular favourite. The visit took place long before glasnost. When the group reached Moscow, King had arranged secretly with the bus driver to take the tour bus, filled with American reporters, to the site of a modest building in central Moscow. King then grabbed the bus microphone.

"The tallest building in Moscow!" he proclaimed to his surprised audience. They gazed out uncomprehendingly at a non-descript five-storey structure.

"Spook central." King continued, "Five floors up but forty stories down. I give you the KGB headquarters building."

The Russian guides were not amused.

It was through the Institute of Politics that I ended up assigned as an intern on the primary campaign of Robert Drinan for the U.S. Congress. Reverend Drinan was a distinguished Bostonian and dean of the Boston College Law School, a Jesuit priest, and someone who called for the impeachment of Nixon before Watergate. He was seeking the Democratic nomination in the primary against Philip J. Philbin, who was a hawk, a longtime Congressman, and number two after Representative Mendel Rivers on the powerful Armed Services Committee. For this reason, the congressional district was filled with defence contractors' plants, including such notables as Raytheon. For the first time in my life, I found myself on the other side of the unions, who were heavily for Philbin in the primary. Nevertheless, the student zeal from Harvard, coupled with large donations from people such as Harvard Professor John Kenneth Galbraith, allowed the super-Dove, Drinan, to win the primary.

Philbin then decided to play mischief by running as an independent in the general election, thus splitting the Democratic vote and offering the possibility of a Republican beating Drinan. We simply redoubled our efforts and pushed on. Father Drinan succeeded in securing the congressional seat as the legitimately nominated Democrat.

Walt Isaacson, who went on to write for *Time* magazine (who became, in fact, its national editor as well as the author of a brilliant book on the Cold War years), was my fellow intern on the campaign. He told a wonderful story of being out with Drinan, who was not the most sensitive of individuals, campaigning at some small Massachusetts centre. As they went up the steps of the town hall, they encountered an elderly black gentleman who was sweeping the steps. Drinan shook the man's hand and said to him, "You know, when I was a boy, I had a job sweeping steps." Isaacson nearly grabbed Drinan by his clerical collar and dragged him up the rest of the steps and away from the upset voter. Such was the one-on-one political skill of our candidate in his early campaign days. Nevertheless, he prevailed, both in the primary and in the general election. Congressman Drinan served with distinction in Congress until the Pope decided that active politics was verboten for Catholic priests. Drinan was forced to resign.

RENÉ LÉVESQUE AT THE HARVARD BUSINESS SCHOOL

RENÉ LÉVESQUE, THE FIERY ORATOR and champion of Quebec nationalism, left the Liberal Party in the late 1960s to be a founder of the separatist Parti Québécois. Lévesque had been the champion of the Quiet Revolution and it was Lévesque who pointed out the history of domination and oppression of French-speaking Quebecers by the Anglophone minority. But the Quiet Revolution had not gone far enough for Lévesque.

Before stepping into the political arena, Lévesque had been a journalist. An interesting reality to me is that Quebec views journalists on a much higher social and intellectual plane than do the people in the rest of Canada. Journalists in the rest of Canada rarely go into politics as leaders although sometimes politicians become hotline radio show hosts!

René Lévesque's television experience was invaluable to him in the making of his political career. It was Lévesque who inspired the Jean Lesage Liberal government to nationalize Shawinigan Power and the other privately owned utilities to create Hydro-Quebec. It was Lévesque, along with Eric Kierans, who reorganized health and social services in Quebec, and it was eventually Lévesque who broke ranks and became the leader of the nationalist and separatist Parti Québécois.

I heard Lévesque speak only once before he came to Harvard. That speech took place in a hot, overcrowded, smoky auditorium at the University of Manitoba in the mid-1960s. I had been invited by my parents to hear Lévesque, whom they both greatly admired. Lévesque was electric, his speaking style powerful and his message emotional.

Lévesque's speech shook the rafters. Words and passion poured out of this tiny, Charlie Chaplin of a man as he recounted the history of a province kept as a colony and a downtrodden people. Quebecers were a people suppressed so that their labour could be exploited by the English minority, by the English bankers. A people kept docile and subservient by their own church. A society cast as hewers of wood and drawers of water toiling in a society where the English minority owned all the businesses. Labouring at the bad jobs in a society where English speaking Quebecers had all the good jobs. His people were cheated and made poor. I can still hear the powerful blow of Lévesque's fist hitting the top of the lectern. His voice, larger than the man himself, was booming across the sweaty auditorium. "No more cheap labour Quebec!" he thundered. "No more cheap labour Quebec!" The crowd took up his cry. "No more cheap labour Quebec!" we shouted his own words back at him until our throats grew hoarse. Later this would be crystallized into the Lesage slogan, "Maître chez nous"—masters in our own house—and later still, on the license plates of Quebec, "Je me souviens"—I remember. What was always to be remembered was the oppression, even when two decades of legislation had firmly established the rights of the majority against the rights of the minority in Quebec.

This image of the feisty René Lévesque was burned into my memory. The champion of the workers and the champion of Quebec, René Lévesque stood as the fiery orator and reformer. In the early 1970s, about the last person on earth I expected to see as a guest of the Harvard Business School was René Lévesque. But there it was on the poster. The leader of the newly-formed Parti Québécois, the self-same Lévesque, a guest speaker at the most prestigious training school for American capitalist managers—the oppressors, the ugliest of the ugly Americans, or so I thought in my radical school days. I could not resist seeing my hero amidst these foreign surroundings.

On the way to the speech, I was asked for direction by a young woman who turned out to be a journalist visiting from Edmonton. She was a very entertaining and talented young woman. She and I decided that it would be entirely appropriate for us Canadians to crash the speech at the Harvard Business School. We did just that, sitting near the back in our jeans and long, messy hair in stark contrast to the well-dressed, short-haired, and all-male members of the Harvard Business School class of the day. While we had been walking through Harvard Square down to the Charles River and across the bridge from Harvard to the Business School on the other side of the River, I had been regaling my journalist friend with stories of the power of this diminutive orator and my memories of his earlier radical speech.

Alas, Lévesque had a new tune. In a modest and moderate speech, he argued that Americans should share common cause with the Parti Québécois and that they should welcome getting rid of the English Canadians who extracted their profit in the middle. His message, far from "No More Cheap Labour Quebec," seemed to be "Quebec and American capitalists, arm in arm." I was appalled. In those days, not only was my Canadian nationalism at a boiling point (driven by the total ignorance of our country by Americans about whom we were expected to know so much), but I was also more determinedly socialist than I have been since. The spectacle of this hero of Canadian and Quebec socialism pandering to an American business audience was too much.

My journalist colleague and I crashed the rather small reception for Lévesque afterwards and I proceeded, in my best indignant, long-haired, angry-man style, to express my disappointment to hear him so willing to invite American capitalism into Quebec when he had just finished fighting English Canadian capitalism. Lévesque was a little taken aback, clearly feeling some sensitivity on this point but he vigorously defended the views he had expressed in his speech. We were joined in our discussion by an overly large, well-dressed, member of the invited entourage. He was a caricature of the cigar-smoking, capitalist plutocrat. On hearing my remarks, particularly the use of the words socialism and capitalism, he leapt to Lévesque's defence. What the hell was I doing to this guest of the Harvard Business School? Obviously, Lévesque was someone who believed in the American Dream and American capitalism, how could I offend such a man? I inquired as to the line of business this gentleman was in and received the reply, "pharmaceuticals."

This was too much for Lévesque. Numbered among his many villains in the world, the international drug industry ranked among the worst. What I could not accomplish by my earnest argument was readily accomplished by the misguided flattery of this captain of the industry. Whatever he hoped to accomplish at the Harvard Business School, Lévesque could not abide being seen as on the same side as this pharmaceutical company blowhard. He launched a long tirade against the global pharmaceutical industry, puffing on his cigarette all the while and jabbing at this pudgy representative of the American business class. This was more like the old Lévesque. Whatever accommodation he had planned between an independent Quebec and American Capitalism, the drug industry was not likely to be an early beneficiary.

We toasted each other before parting—Lévesque, the woman journalist and I. We were three Canadians in the heart of the American Empire, three Canadians with quite different destinies but with a strange sense of camaraderie nevertheless. After all, we were not Americans and never could be.

WATERGATE

THE EARLY 1970s proved to be a roller coaster ride in the carnival of American politics. As the war on Vietnam dragged on and Nixon expanded it to Cambodia, protests continued to grow in university campuses across the nation. The 1972 presidential election that initially offered such hope in the candidacy of the decent Eugene McCarthy turned into a complete rout for Richard Milhous Nixon.

His landslide victory carried every state except Massachusetts and the District of Columbia. We drew what solace we could from the brilliant irreverent gonzo journalism of Hunter S. Thompson writing in *Rolling Stone* magazine. Despite Hunter's words after the election, a deep mood of gloom settled over the Harvard campus at the prospect of another four years of Tricky Dick Nixon in the White House. Bumper stickers emerged post-election day. They read DON'T BLAME ME—I'M FROM MASSACHUSETTS!

As Harvard and MIT professors proudly displayed their bumper stickers on their Volvos and Land Rovers, a disturbance began to emerge in the Nixonian era. Watergate! At the beginning it was a whisper and no one dared to dream that this act of simple burglary would bring down the very foundations of the Nixon presidency. The invulnerable and unbeatable Nixon had come back from his loss to JFK in 1960. He had never given up his long, lonely and ultimately successful quest to be president.

An aspect of the unfolding Watergate era proved to be the rise of "Doonesbury." Gary Trudeau began drawing the political cartoon strip for the *Yale Daily News*, the campus student paper, in 1971. The brilliance of his wit and political insight rapidly moved his daily strip into a broad range of newspapers. One of the papers carrying "Doonesbury" was *The Boston Globe*. Many of us became avid daily readers of the *Globe* beginning with the "Doonesbury" strip. We followed the adventures of BD and Duke and we viewed the unfolding story of Watergate through Gary Trudeau's eyes and through his characters.

In the early Watergate days, it was not clear that Nixon would ever be connected to the burglary or that he would be held accountable. The Watergate saga unfolded slowly—aided by the journalistic determination of *The Washington Post* reporters Woodward and Bernstein. "Deep Throat," their confidential source, also played a major role in moving the Watergate investigation forward.

One of the big breaks came with the accusations levelled by Martha Mitchell, whose husband, John Mitchell, served as Nixon's attorney general as well as chair of the Committee to Re-elect the President or "CREEP" as it became known. This was revealed to be the organization through which the funds were funnelled to pay the Watergate burglars. There were setbacks and moments when the investigation stalled.

At a pivotal moment, "Doonesbury" appeared with a very simple strip that declared in the first panel JOHN MITCHELL IS GUILTY—the second panel the same declaration was repeated in larger type and in the third panel in even larger type. *The Boston Globe* did not run "Doonesbury" that day. Instead, it ran a very stern editorial declaring that if its editorial board came to the view that the attorney general of the United States of America was guilty of a crime it would not communicate that opinion in a cartoon strip. The non-publication of "Doonesbury" proved a very public and much debated event. Many pundits applauded the *Globe*'s decision. How dare a cartoonist, a college cartoonist to boot, pronounce upon the innocence or guilt of the attorney general? What gall! What rudeness!

"Doonesbury" did not run again in *The Boston Globe* for several weeks. We were saddened but found "Doonesbury" elsewhere—including the *Yale Daily News*.

Then one fine morning our world changed for the better. Attorney general John Mitchell was indicted. When *The Boston Globe* landed on our dormitory doorstep it carried "Doonesbury" on its front page. That famous cartoon declared John Mitchell to be GUILTY, GUILTY, GUILTY. The *Globe* editors also published an editorial acknowledging that Gary Trudeau's "Doonesbury" had been right and that their august newspaper's editorial board had been wrong. It was a moment of delicious triumph for all "Doonesbury" fans.

As the Watergate saga gained momentum, John Mitchell resigned as attorney general. Then Vice-President Spiro T. Agnew resigned and eventually went to jail. He was replaced by Gerald Ford who ultimately became president. Elliot Richardson, a former Republican governor of Massachusetts, was named attorney general. Remembering that Massachusetts had not voted for Nixon but had voted for Richardson, it is worth noting that they were at opposite ends of the ethical scale. Richardson moved to appoint Harvard law professor, Archibald Cox, as special prosecutor for the Watergate scandal. Cox was a man of outstanding integrity and substance. The White House was not amused by the choice.

In what came to be dubbed the Saturday Night Massacre, President Nixon ordered his attorney general to fire Cox. A man of conscience, Richardson refused. He tendered his own resignation, which Nixon accepted. Deputy Attorney General William Ruckelshaus became acting attorney general upon Richardson's resignation. He also refused to fire Cox and he also resigned. It took Nixon three tries to find his man but he found him in Robert Bork, then solicitor general and only too willing to fire Cox. Bork did Nixon's bidding at the dark time of Watergate. But his role in the Saturday Night Massacre did not go unpunished. When nominated to the Supreme Court by President Ronald Reagan, his nomination failed in the Senate. Many senators had long memories regarding Bork's role in the Saturday Night Massacre.

That night, the night of the Saturday Night Massacre, many of us were up late spurred on by our anger at the firing of good men by evildoers. Someone had a friend who had a friend who had a print shop. We all pitched in to help channel our anger into creativity. By Sunday dawn spreading across the bumpers of thousands of cars in Cambridge and into Boston were bumper stickers that read bluntly "IMPEACH THE COX SACKER."

The firing of Archibald Cox did not save Nixon. Quite the contrary, the grisly spectacle of a president firing men of integrity to prevent an investigation and in all likelihood his own impeachment galvanized the nation against Nixon.

CHAPTER THREE

CONFESSIONS OF AN OUTSIDE ORGANIZER

MY STUDENT YEARS and early career days were interspersed with political campaign involvements. During the four years I studied at Harvard I returned to Manitoba for my summers. One summer I helped Brian O'Leary with an organization named the Coalition for Better Schools. We endeavoured to elect more progressive school trustees in Winnipeg. Three other summers I worked in the cabinet office of the Manitoba Government.

Eventually I graduated from the south Winnipeg school of political hard knocks and moral victories and the more philosophical school of government and politics at Harvard University. I expect that many years of political campaigns were more valuable to organizing than my undergraduate degree in economics. After this long apprenticeship, it was my happy fate to be one of what the NDP called, "outside organizers." That is, organizers sent into various key ridings across the country to assist the local organization in mobilizing the campaign and in eventually getting the vote to the poll on election day. The godmother to all NDP organizers, Jo-Anne McNevin, had become a friend of mine in the early 1970s. I met her on Willy Parasiuk's 1973 campaign in the Riel riding in south Winnipeg.

Between 1974 and 1979, I worked as an outside organizer on four separate election campaigns. Two were at the provincial level, in Saskatchewan and Nova Scotia, and there were two at the federal level, Oshawa for Ed Broadbent in 1974 and Winnipeg North Centre for Stanley Knowles in 1979. These four campaigns across four of Canada's provinces proved both educational and fascinating. The role of an outside organizer is to be both a manager of a campaign but more than that, bringing to bear the knowledge of previous campaigns, generally in an area where the party has perhaps not always enjoyed success.

In this regard, I was fortunate to be assigned a preponderance of winning campaigns; in three of the four, the New Democratic Party proved victorious. Both the re-election of Stanley Knowles and Ed Broadbent were not particularly difficult challenges. Nor in the end was the re-election of Norman Vickar in Melfort, Saskatchewan in 1978. However, Pictou Centre in New Glasgow, Nova Scotia, was a defeat, hard fought with many lessons learned.

Jo-Anne McNevin graded all organizers as A's, B's, or C's. Out of consideration of our friendship, I was never allowed to know my rank. My suspicion always was that I wasn't quite an "A" organizer. My lack of devotion to the disciplined canvass approach and my overemphasis on policy were my greatest weaknesses. However, "outside organizing" was a fascinating way to roam about the country and to experience the democratic process close-up and personal in an array of places. Out where the rubber meets the road, politics is not theoretical and democracy is not an ideal. Doors are knocked, signs are stuck in windows and in lawns, voters are identified and persuaded. In short, campaigns are organized. On these mundane tasks our democracy is constructed and sustained. Every canvasser for every party who talks to a neighbour or friend about who should govern a village, town, city, province or the nation is a foot soldier of our democracy.

RIEL, MANITOBA 1973

I WAS NOT an outside organizer on this campaign but a canvasser and foot soldier. Willy Parasiuk decided to enter politics in 1973 by running in the provincial general election in the riding of Riel. Willy had become a mentor and my boss in the Manitoba government where he headed the Planning Secretariat to the Cabinet. We had also rapidly become great friends. Held for many years by the Conservative MLA Don Craik, the Riel riding was comprised of a good slice of St.Vital, an older suburb on Winnipeg's southeast side. As well, the new and expanding area of Southdale was included in the riding.

Jo-Anne McNevin came in from British Columbia to run the campaign. She brought with her Judi Korbin, also from Vancouver, to serve as one of the canvass organizers. Irene Rossman and Doreen Dodick were recruited from the riding to serve as the other two canvass co-ordinators.

Canvass organizing, for those unfamiliar with the classic NDP approach to elections, is the activity that begins with the recruitment of a group of workers. The canvassers themselves are trained in NDP methodology and they then set out with their canvass kits. Their mission is to reach every voter in their particular poll in the riding. Polls generally consist of anywhere from 180 to nearly 300 voters, although there are only about eighty to 150 doors, depending on whether one is dealing with residences housing families or apartments with singles.

The object of the canvass technique is not fundamentally to persuade voters (since the general view is that this is unlikely) but rather to show an interest in the voter, to communicate with them, and most of all, to identify supporters. Canvassers have canvass cards open which they mark voters as hostile (this does not mean that they necessarily are hostile personally, but rather that they are clearly supporting one of the other parties), positive (which means that they are definitely NDP supporters), or undecided. Each canvass turns around a particular leaflet. The canvasser is to present the leaflet and elicit comment, if possible, from the voter. The leaflet is the proverbial foot in the door to get the voter talking, sharing their views of the election and if possible, to identify where their thinking is taking them. In a properly executed NDP campaign, there would likely be three canvasses, although McNevin, one the harder-nosed practitioners of the art, had been known to drive campaigns through four and even five canvasses if she thought it would identify late-breaking voters.

Door-to-door canvassing is not for the faint of heart. The Riel campaign provided plenty of examples of the difficulties involved in campaigning on this basis. My own best story of the campaign was when I was canvassing a poll, which, while it had some new construction, had a lot of forty and fifty-year-old smaller homes. When they were first built, they were in a rural area, and over time the city had engulfed them. These small wood frame structures housed the ever-challenging electorate of Riel.

At one such house, having evaded the compulsory large dog and having discovered that no one was home, I reached the garage. Two legs were sticking out from under a car, obviously belonging to someone of a mechanically-inclined nature. Boldly I knocked on the car door and introduced myself. I was greeted with a muffled grunt from under the car. Based on the muffled grunt, I could not decide whether this person was hostile, positive or undecided. I rapped again on the door and got a somewhat louder but still indecipherable grunt. At my third rap, the legs shot out from under the car and the mechanic appeared, lying on some sort of dolly. He jumped up, completely covered in grease and, waving a socket wrench, said some extraordinarily foul things about what he intended to do at me. At this point, my response was, "I suppose you don't want a leaflet either." This was too much. With a howl of rage, the car mechanic set out after me. Fortunately, I had youth on my side and I was able to escape from his property without him throwing the socket wrench at my rapidly retreating back. A block later, as I regained my breath, I put him down as hostile. In brackets I wrote, "In every sense of the word."

My friend David Martin had a somewhat different canvassing experience. He was going door-to-door in one of the most affluent polls in the riding. These people were extremely supportive of the Conservative candidate and were somewhat opposed towards the NDP and its various efforts to redistribute income and tax burden to the poor from the better off. At one household, David, who has gone on to be a successful Toronto lawyer, was confronted by a voter. This individual took the leaflet, looked at it and said, "Willie Par-a-suk, another dumb hunky plumber running for the NDP, eh?" This was too much for David who pointed out that our friend and candidate Wilson Parasiuk had not only been a distinguished Rhodes Scholar from Manitoba at Oxford University, but was a holder of two master's degrees. He further rubbed salt into the wound by asking the belligerent voter what educational qualifications he had. The voter in question had a Bachelor of Commerce degree from the University of Manitoba. It was on this basis that David launched his rather ill-fated attempt to gain this voter's support by reviewing the academic achievements of Wilson Parasiuk. The voter's retort to this impressive resume was to look at David and grunt "Overeducated, eh?" and slam the door in his face. Another hostile.

Some measure of satisfaction was in store for David and me. The campaign was joined by an old hockey playing buddy of Willy's, a large fellow by the name of Jim Quail who had departed from the Winnipeg police force. Legend had it that he had locked his gun in the trunk of a car and had taken on a large number (estimates range from six to a dozen) of motorcycle gang members of some particularly virulent variety with his bare knuckles. The result of the brawl was that the gang members ended up in the hospital and Quail ended up as a very able representative of Canon copiers. He went on to great business success but he remained someone with an extremely short fuse. Willy Parasiuk's father told me that whenever he went to hockey games and arrived late there was always a pile of players on the ice after some brawl. As the bodies were pried loose from one another, Jim Quail was always at the bottom of the heap, usually with a firm grip on an opposing player's throat.

Much to my astonishment, Quail insisted on becoming a canvasser and Jo-Anne relented. She took the precaution of sending him out with Syd Hepworth, a very calm man who worked as a probation officer and was therefore used to defusing difficult situations. However, even Syd was unprepared for Quail's reaction the first time that someone on a doorstep took a personal run at the candidate. Quail simply reached over, picked the fellow up, and slammed him against the brick exterior of the house. It took all of Hepworth's training to talk Quail into relinquishing his grip on the man's collar and to soothe the fellow. No charges were filed.

Willy Parasiuk did not win Riel in 1973. Despite a relentless campaign and the valiant efforts of all of us, the Conservative tendency of the place was too much and Don Craik was elected. Or perhaps we didn't knock on enough doors. Perhaps Willy was overeducated. My dark and secret view was that we didn't let Jim Quail reason with enough voters.

I'd gone to Vancouver following the unsuccessful Riel campaign in the Manitoba election to attend the federal convention of the New Democratic Party. After that convention, Riel campaign organizer Jo-Anne McNevin and her husband John invited me to visit their home on the spectacular Sunshine Coast north of Vancouver. It transpired that among the other invitees were the Premier of Manitoba, Ed Schreyer and his wife Lily, my friend Willy Parasiuk and Ed Broadbent, then a member of the federal caucus but not yet its leader.

I took the ferry up from Vancouver to the picturesque Hopkins Landing at the foot of the Sunshine Coast. I was deputized to bring Ed Broadbent with me and I don't remember the exact circumstances of who had the rental car, but we travelled up together and I began to appreciate this rather remarkable scholar of John Stuart Mill, son of auto workers, as both an intellectual and an activist.

Several of us, Jo-Anne McNevin, Bill Knight, and Mary-Ellen McQuay, had chatted about supporting Ed Broadbent for the leadership of the party when it became vacant. Little did we dream how soon that circumstance would be upon us. In the 1972 to 1974 period, the NDP ably led by David Lewis held the balance of power in the House of Commons. Lewis demanded and got numerous concessions from the Trudeau Liberals anxious to cling to power. By the spring of 1974, Trudeau had decided that he had a reasonable prospect of regaining its majority and called an election for June of 1974. After my summer meeting with Broadbent, I'd returned to complete my studies at Harvard.

We determined to run a superb campaign in Oshawa at the next federal election to get Ed Broadbent the secure majority and safe seat he would need to lead without fear of losing his own seat. We could have found no better champion for this effort than Jo-Anne McNevin. Nicknamed "General Jo-Anne" for her tendency to take control, she is, in my experience, the best political organizer I've ever met. There will be those who tell you they've seen someone better, and they'll mutter about a campaign here and there, but there is actually no one in Canada who has run as many campaigns with as consistent success as Jo-Anne McNevin. In saying this, I take nothing away from the rather stellar performances over the years of Joyce Nash, Penny Dickens, Rod Dickenson and others. But for my dollar when it comes to a tough campaign, General Jo-Anne trumps them all.

OSHAWA, ONTARIO 1974

THE OSHAWA CAMPAIGN of 1974 began for me in a shower at Cambridge, Massachusetts. I was scrubbing down when Ed Broadbent called to ask me to join his 1974 constituency campaign. Broadbent was worried for two reasons. First, he had never won the riding by very many votes;

in fact, in 1968, his first outing, he got by the veteran Conservative cabinet minister Michael Starr by only fifteen votes. Four years later in 1972, he again beat Starr, this time by 824 votes. Secondly, there were rumours that the Conservatives would run Harvey Kirk, a popular national news broadcaster for the CTV network. Kirk had a much higher national profile than had Broadbent and therefore might be expected to do well.

The third reason for Broadbent's call was the relentless organizing by Jo-Anne McNevin. In her desire to see Broadbent as the next leader of her party, Jo-Anne was determined to get him a significant majority in Oshawa so he need not be one of those leaders perpetually worried about the safety of his own seat. To this end, Jo-Anne was assembling a heavy-duty team to manage a large Broadbent win. Unbeknownst to Jo-Anne, events were unfolding that would accelerate the change of leadership to the party. During the 1974 campaign, David Lewis would lose his seat in Toronto, precipitating a much earlier leadership race than had been contemplated by those of us supporting Broadbent.

As I stood dripping wet in my Cambridge apartment, I realized that saying "yes" to Ed Broadbent meant commuting from Oshawa back to Cambridge to write my final exams. As I prepared to finish my days as a student and enter the working world, the invitation to Oshawa proved irresistible. In May and June, I commuted back and forth as necessary for exams and skipped my Harvard graduation ceremony because we were entering an all-important second canvass.

In 1972, Jo-Anne had gone in late to the Oshawa Broadbent campaign after the first organizer had collapsed from the nervous stress of trying to keep the campaign going amidst the factitiousness of Oshawa. The dominant force in those years in NDP politics in Oshawa was Local 222 of the United Auto Workers. The difficulty with this local is that it had incited two quite strong factions who fought each other at every opportunity. Often the leadership of these factions was more concerned with their own issues than with election campaigns. In 1972, it had disintegrated to the point of near fist-fights on the campaign between the members of the two factions. Sadly, Ed Broadbent's brother Dave was a member of one of the factions and therefore Ed was always at risk of being inadvertently drawn in on one side or the other. Successful re-elections required that both factions put aside their differences, however briefly, and work together.

I was not present for Jo-Anne's first sermon from the mount to the assembled autoworkers. I do know that two years later when I got to Oshawa, very tough auto workers who could have snapped me across their muscular forearms like a toothpick were still speaking in somewhat hushed tones about the speech. Apparently arriving to find the campaign disintegrating and Broadbent at risk, McNevin had climbed up on the table in the abandoned Safeway that was being used as campaign headquarters and silenced the assembled group of rowdy and quarrelling workers. She delivered in what was described to me in terms that would make a sailor blush, a sermon on why people would either hang together or hang separately. She declared she had no intention of presiding over the defeat of one of Canada's most important politicians. After this she got the campaign moving and pulled out what had looked like a certain defeat considering that there had been a heavy swing towards the Conservatives in 1972, and managed to get Ed Broadbent re-elected with an 824 vote majority.

In 1974, Jo-Anne did not need to make tough speeches. She had the respect of the people she worked with in Oshawa. The team that shaped up around Jo-Anne included Mary Ellen McQuay, who would later go on to be federal secretary of the party, its most senior position. A delightful former teacher, Mary Ellen had drifted into political organizing and shown a remarkable grasp of it. Jo-Anne, Mary Ellen and I would sit nearly every evening after the 10:30 p.m. closing of the campaign office and sip scotch and dissect the day's events. These are some of my fondest memories of politics. Later, we were joined by Sharon McCrae who took on the responsibility for organizing the election day get-out-the-vote drive. Sharon also joined our nightly discussions. I realized that there was much more political wisdom imparted in those late nights than in the political study seminars at Harvard. These were real people. Particularly Jo-Anne, who had been in the front lines and who knew how the electorate thought, and how political parties and politicians worked. I learned more about real politics in Oshawa than I had at Harvard.

Jo-Anne was taking no chances this time. She was planning four or five canvasses of the constituency. It was a feat that required both determined organization and a willingness to drive volunteers well beyond anything that could be conceived as a reasonable contribution to the campaign. For my sins, I was set to work on an assortment of things including policy and the sign crew. An odd mix you might think, but I quite enjoyed the sign crew. The morning ritual was to take the autoworker panel van and to get off to a good start by taking a 40 ounce bottle of scotch whiskey and mixing it half scotch and half coffee. This Oshawa eye-opener was undoubtedly helpful to me in formulating policy as well as helping with the signs.

In the end, Harvey Kirk declined to run and the Conservatives nominated a much weaker candidate, a man named Martin Weatherall. Weatherall owned and operated a chain of "music and instrument" rental stores in Oshawa. Working-class Oshawa folks wanted their children to be musical geniuses, to do things they couldn't dream of doing, and this business essentially catered to that expectation. Better still from the point of view of the Broadbent campaign, Weatherall was not a very good politician.

The Liberal candidate nominated was a more successful politician. Margaret Shaw had served many years on the Oshawa city council. Her style was one of old-fashioned red baiting. She accused Broadbent of having flown immediately to Bulgaria to receive his orders from the Kremlin after getting re-elected in 1972. This was a humorous assertion given that the Kremlin is actually in Moscow and not Bulgaria. It was particularly bizarre because Broadbent had made no such trip. But this did not stop Shaw from letting loose on every occasion. One imagined she could have said roughly the same thing about Pierre Trudeau had she followed his travel itinerary a bit closer. After all, it was the Liberal Trudeau, not the socialist Broadbent, who had gone to China, Cuba and Russia.

Broadbent took an amused, uncomprehending view of the nuts and bolts of his campaign. He poked fun at us when he could. Organizers have their own code. Scrutineers are the people you recruit for election day. In each poll, and there might be 250 polls in a typical riding, you need an inside scrutineer and an outside scrutineer. The inside scrutineer sits and actually supervises the count to make sure ballots are cast properly. In a well-organized NDP campaign, the inside scrutineer has a second duty: to keep track of who has voted and pass numbered sheets to the outside scrutineer. The outside scrutineer's job is to ensure that each and every identified NDP voter in the poll votes. To focus their work, they come by hourly to pick up the list of who has voted from the inside scrutineer. This can be particularly compelling when confronted by a voter at the door who said, "Oh, I already voted." The outside scrutineer is able to say, "Well, for some strange reason they don't have your name crossed off at the polling station. Why don't we go down to the polling station and see if we can correct the error?"

Reluctant voters are the cause of many lost elections. Consider for a moment that Oshawa had 250 polls; in his first election, Broadbent won by just fifteen votes. That is only one vote in each of fifteen polls. Even the 824-vote victory amounted to just three votes per poll. Many elections are won or lost, in fact, whole governments change hands, because someone does a slightly better job at getting the vote out than someone else. Leave one or two votes per poll at home and you may hand the seat and the government to your rival.

One evening near election day, Jo-Anne McNevin declined an invitation from the candidate to come by for drink or dinner because she was busy mopping up scroots. Mopping up scroots, of course, meant no more than filling in the remaining scrutineer spots for election day. But to Broadbent, the phrase mopping up scroots had a kind of magic to it. For many years he dined out on this "I don't know what Jo-Anne's doing. She's mopping up scroots!" This played into his general view that the druids were a viable religion and that organizers were all secretly druids. He would frequently end meetings of the campaign committee by announcing, "Jo-Anne has to go now. She has to mop up scroots!"

One of the delights of being on the sign crew was the ingenuity shown by my fellow sign crew members who were all employees of a bumper plant, represented by Local 222. These were very rough, tough guys. On the morning of the election, they discovered that the Conservative team of Martin Weatherall had placed literally hundreds of election signs in the boulevard that ran up to the General Motors plant. These signs were illegal but pulling them up would have required the better part of the day without the resourcefulness of the sign crew. The van we used for signs was a heavy three-ton truck with a big metal bumper. These guys were used to creative thinking on the assembly line. When I arrived for 7:00 a.m. coffee and scotch, they were already welding a metal rod to the front bumper of the panel van. I puzzled at this. It looked highly dangerous. The metal rod stuck a meter or more out from the edge of the truck rendering it nearly impossible to drive in traffic. However, I had not shared their insight in how to dispose of hundreds of signs quickly. They drove at a good clip along the boulevard as close as they could get to the curb, the metal bar acting as a virtual scythe. Signs were mowed down by some giant three-ton lawn mower. Two passes and the Weatherall signs were all reduced to splinters and rubble.

One of the characters on the campaign team was a giant of a man, dubbed in the working class world of Oshawa, Tiny. He must have weighed 350 pounds and didn't have an ounce of fat on him. His most impressive feat of strength came one day at the committee rooms when scorching heat required us to install an air conditioner. We got quite a sizeable unit and measured that it would fit over the door. We didn't calculate how hard it would be to position it there. Tiny solved this problem by picking up the air conditioner (a feat I thought would've required two if not three strong men), walking up a ladder and installing it over the door. If Canada ever wants to win any Olympic medals in weightlifting they should find out whether Tiny had grandchildren and enlist them in the team.

In addition to being the office strongman, Tiny was a superb canvasser. Tiny and his wife completed five canvasses of their designated poll and made superb detailed markers on each and every voter. Tiny was not someone to be resisted when he came calling. I think people were only too happy to tell him exactly how they were going to vote. Through some accident of domestic housekeeping, the canvass kit with Tiny's precious markings, essential to the election day machine, were disposed of in the trash. I believe Tiny personally tore apart the rather large and smelly Oshawa garbage dump. I don't recall whether he relocated his canvass markings but for the sake of his memory, let's pretend he did.

One of the other characters I got to know well during my stay in Oshawa was Nester Pidwerbecki. He was a solid contributor to the campaign and a genuinely nice human being. Towards the end of the campaign we were having a drink one night at the local pub, and Nester, who seemed eminently qualified, mentioned to me that he might take a run at city council. Then he sadly lowered his eyes and said "Of course I'd probably have to change my name." I got suddenly seized with fear for Nester. It seemed that he had decided to abandon his Ukrainian heritage for the sake of political opportunism. Once he knew he had me, he looked up and said "Yes, I'm thinking of changing my name to Peter."

"Peter...?" I was taken aback, startled. Then we both began laughing.

"Yes. Peter Pidwerbecki!"

Chalk up another defeat for the college boy against the rough humour of the auto city. Nester roared with laughter.

Nester later ran for Oshawa city council. He was elected and served the people of Oshawa ably for many years. He never changed his name to Peter.

We became so completely consumed with the campaign in Oshawa that we largely lost track of how poorly the 1974 national campaign was going for the NDP. On election night, Ed Broadbent swept to victory with a majority, which rocketed past his previous majorities to a genuine landslide of more than 10,000 votes. From then on it was a night of defeat with the NDP dropping from thirty-two seats to a mere sixteen. The Liberals under Trudeau regained their majority.

Worse still, NDP leader David Lewis lost his seat in Toronto and it was clear even on election night that the informal leadership campaign to succeed Lewis was soon to be a much more formal affair.

Later that summer, Ed Broadbent was elected by the NDP caucus to be the interim leader of the party. He invited me to move to Ottawa and become his first executive assistant. I worked in Ottawa for Ed Broadbent for only six months in 1974 and 1975 before returning to Manitoba and rejoining the government. My reason for leaving was Broadbent's decision, later reversed, to exit the leadership race. He later won. But my career would steadily draw me towards government rather than opposition.

PICTOU CENTRE, NOVA SCOTIA, 1978

I SHOULD CONFESS at this point that I'm not a very good flyer. I don't get airsick. I simply get fearful especially if it's turbulent or dark. Family and friends know me as a poor flyer. In those days to steel my nerves, I would have a couple of glasses of scotch on a typical flight. This posed little risk to me and often allowed me to park my fears.

Upon my arrival at the Halifax airport that August of 1978, I was greeted by the official Pictou Centre greeting committee: three wild women— a mother, her daughter and her granddaughter. I think their ages were probably fifty, thirty-three, and sixteen. Ages did not seem to be a good question to ask so I got in the back seat of a very battered and rusty Oldsmobile and we set off at about a hundred miles an hour to New Glasgow, Nova Scotia. If the battered automobile at the rapid speed were not enough to cause me some concern, the passing of the vodka bottle around the car should have been my final clue that I was in for a very different Maritime political experience. After refusing the vodka a few times, I realized that it was definitely in my interest to partake. First, the more I could drink of the vodka, the less the driver could consume, enhancing our chances of reaching New Glasgow alive. This seemed at that point both a highly desirable and a highly unlikely outcome. Second, the more of the vodka I could drink the less pain I would feel when the battered Oldsmobile inevitably careened either off the road or into an oncoming vehicle. So, as the vodka bottle came around I drank at least my share if not more.

The consumption of vodka during the harrowing, one-and-a-half hour trip from the Halifax airport to New Glasgow seemed to have worked. By the time we arrived, I was feeling no pain and miracle of miracles, we were still alive. However, I had not counted on the news given to me as we entered the city limits of New Glasgow that rather than heading for wherever I was billeted we were going straight into a campaign committee meeting. This was a sobering thought. Here I was, collapsed in the back seat of this car, exhausted from my cross-country flight, reeking of vodka. No doubt I would be paraded before the local committee and, with my luck; I would stumble and fall and be dismissed as some drunk who had been foisted off on them in the guise of an outside organizer.

I can't imagine what the campaign committee thought as I stumbled out of the Oldsmobile. They were very good not to say anything, particularly the candidate, the intense, earnest and extraordinarily hardworking Austin Sutton.

Despite my initial appearance, relationships with the campaign committee went well. Up to 1978, the New Democratic Party had enjoyed significant success on Cape Breton Island but little electoral success in the rest of Nova Scotia. In fact, the NDP had never finished better than third in any Nova Scotia provincial constituency. Government alternated between the Conservatives and the Liberals.

The constituency of Pictou Centre turned out to include four towns: New Glasgow, Stellarton, Westville, and Trenton. This was a sprawling constituency which drifted off into rural areas between the towns. Our candidate was an electrician on leave from the local Scott pulp and paper plant, a former stock car driver, and probably the most diligent candidate I have ever seen. He would rise every morning at 6:00 and canvass from breakfast until dark. Largely because of his extraordinary energy, we were able, for the first time in the history of the New Democratic Party in Nova Scotia, to finish second in a mainland seat.

Staffing the campaign for election day in Pictou Centre provided a difficult challenge. We simply did not have enough supporters willing to work. I managed through a friendly high school teacher to recruit and train an entire grade ten class to serve as scrutineers in each of the polling stations to ensure an honest vote and count. I guess my instructions were too forceful. At noon on election day, two students arrived from their polling station with a question. I don't remember their precise concern because my entire attention was focused on what they had brought with them from the polling station—the ballot box. The students had disagreed with a decision at the polling station and convinced those in authority that until they had consulted me the voting should cease. I remember how my mind turned to the disastrous headline that could ensue and how fast I could run in those days. We returned the ballot box in record time. No more was heard of the incident. In future campaigns I stressed that removing the ballot box from the polling station was never a very good idea.

MELFORT, SASKATCHEWAN, 1978

I HAD JUST finished the Nova Scotia election in early September, 1978, when my phone rang one morning and I was asked if I would go to Saskatchewan. Premier Allan Blakeney of the NDP had just called a provincial election. I went home briefly and then jumped on a plane to Regina. Upon my arrival in Regina, I was greeted by my old friend, Bill Knight, who was then provincial secretary of the Saskatchewan NDP. Knight was a former MP who was elected at a young age to represent the difficult Assiniboia seat in southern Saskatchewan, which he did only briefly in the minority parliament of 1972 to 1974. Assiniboia has a habit of changing its MPs as often as some people change their socks. Despite his formidable political talent, Knight only held on for one election and lost his seat in 1974 when the NDP representation dropped by half. Knight had a deep appreciation of Prairie politics, a lifelong commitment to the NDP and a good sense of humour.

Bill met me at the airport and explained to me the importance of the Melfort riding. The government was in a tight fight for re-election and the candidate in Melfort, Norman Vickar, had been the business development minister. He had a solid grasp of small business issues and was an extremely likeable candidate. Essentially, he had been the mayor of Melfort for a long time. As Bill put it, the premier needed this minister, and he also needed this seat.

Bill took me out to the car he had rented for me—what I thought was a grotesquely large automobile by NDP standards. It was a mid-sized Buick of some sort, and in 1978, a mid-sized Buick was still a large car. After my six weeks of poverty-stricken campaigning in Pictou County, Nova Scotia, I was skeptical about the prospect of arriving at my assigned seat in what might be viewed by the locals as a luxury car. I raised this difficulty with Bill who brushed aside my objections, saying that they had gotten a real deal on a whole fleet of these things and I should just get in my car and set off to Melfort where the campaign needed me.

I was particularly pleased to be assigned to Melfort since I had a relative in nearby Kinistino, Saskatchewan. I felt certain that Ernie Field would be able to give me some good local knowledge.

I took off in the Buick, driving north from Regina and arrived in Melfort just in time for the campaign meeting. Melfort is a community of about 6,000, northeast of Saskatoon. I parked at the campaign office noting that what I'd presumed to be an overly large car was in fact the smallest car in the parking lot. Many of the backers of the NDP in Saskatchewan were prosperous farmers or small business operators. The parking lot was filled with Lincoln Continentals, Cadillacs and cars I generally associated with our better-heeled opposition in other parts of the country. This was my first hint that the NDP in Saskatchewan represented not necessarily the poor of the earth but rather a constituency that included plenty of well-off people.

As it turned out, it was the large, successful farmers and businessmen who were supporting Norm Vickar and the NDP. The poorer farmers of the Melfort area all seemed to be Conservatives. This topsy-turvy alignment of economic power and voting preference was common to many parts of rural Saskatchewan. The CCF/NDP had become so much the government party in many regions by 1978 that it was the establishment within local communities that supported the NDP, rather than the downtrodden. The NDP had traded a good deal of its populism for this government party status but I think that is an historical eventuality which happens to nearly all parties in time. It was not fatal in 1978 for the Blakeney government but it would be in 1982 when a Conservative populist named Grant Devine was able to decimate the NDP in a provincial election.

Early in the campaign, I found an occasion to drive over and visit my relative Ernie Field, in the nearby town of Kinistino. Ernie was a fascinating character. He was the father of my aunt Dena. He was by then well into his seventies and still running a clothing and general store as he had for a large part of twentieth century. Ernie was a refugee from Europe who had wandered, as an orphaned child, around war-devastated eastern Europe. He had come to Canada and eventually established himself in Kinistino, where he raised Dena, who would later marry my uncle, Alan

Decter. Ernie had been a continuing feature of our growing up. He would descend on Winnipeg from time to time, a small town Prairie socialist, a CCFer from the word go, and he would engage my mother in long discussions about the state of the CCF/NDP. I do not believe that he ever fully accepted the merger which led to the NDP. He was CCF, pure and simple, and was deeply suspicious that the NDP was becoming too conservative, even though his own values as a small businessman would tend in the same direction in some areas of policy. Ernie was a merchant in the classic, old-world sense. When times were bad, he took grain in trade for furniture and loaned money to local people to keep the economy going. As a Jew, he was close to the Vickars, who were also Jewish, and they were all part of the same small congregation around the synagogue in Melfort. He was, at our first meeting, suspiciously silent about Norman Vickar.

"Norman Vickar is a good friend," he said. That was all. Nothing about his politics, nothing about the rumours I kept hearing that maybe Norman was a Liberal at heart. I thought that perhaps this was just grumbling from the old guard CCFers.

Ernie did treat me to a wonderful Chinese dinner at the major restaurant in Kinistino, the strangely named Sven Café which was run by a Chinese man who served Chinese and American food. Where the Scandinavian name the "Sven Café" came from, I never learned. I saw Ernie a few times during the campaign as we laboured on what turned into a significant landslide victory for Vickar and the Blakeney government.

It was only the day after the election that I learned Ernie's true feelings. I arrived at his furniture store savagely hung over from the election night victory celebration. Ernie took me immediately to the Sven Café for lunch. Ernie's only words to me as we walked were, "So, Michael, my young socialist friend, you come to Saskatchewan, and what do you do? You elect a liberal."

I protested, "Ernie, but he's your friend."

Ernie said, "Norman Vickar is my friend and very fine man. But he's a liberal. Why couldn't you come here and elect a socialist?"

I drove back to Regina in my overly large leased Buick feeling as though I had betrayed Ernie's cause. He didn't seem to hold it against me. It was just one of those things, the fact that his young relative from Winnipeg, who ought to know better, would come out to Saskatchewan and help elect a liberal. I consoled myself with the thought that Norman Vickar was an able minister and the kind of small 'l' liberal that Allan

Blakeney needed in his cabinet if he hoped to hang on to power and govern the province, but I never forgot Ernie saying, "So, you elected a liberal."

On one occasion several years later when Ernie visited Winnipeg, he came to our home. My wife Lucille and I had purchased a large three-storey wood-frame home on a narrow lot in the green and leafy Wolseley section of Winnipeg. We had done considerable work fixing it up. It was cheek by jowl to the next house and other than a spacious interior, had little to commend it—certainly not the tiny yard.

Ernie's daughter Dena and her husband Alan had bought a house only a block from us on the Assiniboine River. Theirs was a smaller but gorgeous, two-storey home with a beautiful vista to the south overlooking the river. Ernie toured our house, then demanded of me, as we were on the third floor and alone, what we had paid. When I told him we had paid $44,000, he slapped his hands together and said, "That Alan, he spends money like water. He paid $70,000 for his house not a block from here, and it's less than half the size of yours."

"But," I protested to Ernie, "his house is on the river."

"The river," said Ernie, "That river is frozen half the year!" as though his son-in-law was an even bigger fool for not recognizing the inherent treachery of residing by a river. Neither Alan nor I were ever able to convince Ernie that Alan hadn't been swindled by buying his house for near double what we had paid. Such was Ernie's view of the world from Kinistino. He was a good soul and I miss him. Ernie had his own obstinate and unshakeable views on frozen rivers and the value of a dollar.

Other memories of the Melfort campaign of 1978 include Florence Vickar, the gentle, kind and extremely energetic wife of the candidate. On election day, we assigned Florence the task of pulling out the vote at the local senior citizens' residence. She was to work there all day, making sure that all of our supporters in the nursing home had voted. Since Norm was popular with the seniors, that seemed a straightforward task. What I had not counted on was Florence returning to our campaign office at about three o'clock in the afternoon. As my job as campaign organizer was to keep things moving, I thought with a sinking heart, how do I get our candidate's wife back to her appointed rounds? After a cup of coffee, I broached the subject with her and said, "Florence, shouldn't you be getting back to the senior citizens' centre?"

"No" she said, causing my heart to sink further.

"Why?" I inquired.

She said, "Oh, they've all voted."

"What do you mean, they've all voted?"

"I had every single resident of the senior citizens' centre to vote before one o'clock because I needed to get back here to help with other things."

In my experience, this was an unprecedented feat. It is nearly impossible to get all of the people in any poll to vote and particularly, to get them all to vote before the polls close, let alone before one in the afternoon. There seems to be some syndrome that afflicts voters—they want to be lined up when the polls close. Well, the formidable Florence Vickar proved to me that with enough determination and charm, you really could get everyone to vote early. As my Irish mother would say, "Vote early, vote often." In Florence's case, fortunately for our campaign, it was just "vote early."

I marvelled and put her to work elsewhere. And sure enough when the votes from the nursing home came in, Norman Vickar carried the election by a large margin.

WINNIPEG NORTH CENTRE, 1979

IN 1979, STANLEY KNOWLES epitomized the history of the CCF and the NDP as well as what was best in Canadian politics. He had represented Winnipeg North Centre since the 1930s except for a brief interruption during the Diefenbaker sweep when he had spent several years at the Canadian Labour Congress arranging the amalgamation of the CCF and the CLC to become the New Democratic Party. Knowles was a legend in the House of Commons for his command of parliamentary rules. I had come to know Knowles as more than a legend but also as a formidable tactician during my time as Ed Broadbent's executive assistant in 1974 and 1975. Working on his campaign, I was not only figuratively stepping into a piece of Canadian history but also, given the quaint cottage building on Notre Dame that acted as his constituency office and campaign headquarters, I experienced the reality of stepping back into history. It is the only campaign headquarters in which I have ever been where election night is celebrated by putting on another pot of tea and where alcoholic beverages are strictly forbidden. It was also proof to me that every bit of the Knowles' reputation had been earned.

Early on in the campaign, one of the older workers, an individual who had served as an alderman in Winnipeg and for whom I did not have a high regard, was contending with a call from someone who was clearly a supporter of capital punishment. The former alderman was, to my mind, doing something indescribably immoral by hedging what position Mr. Knowles actually had on capital punishment. In the middle of the conversation, Mr. Knowles strode across the committee room, took the phone firmly in hand, and introduced himself. "This is Stanley Knowles," he said, "and I've always opposed capital punishment. If you believe that is the only true issue in this election, then you must, of course, vote against me. If, on the other hand, you believe that improved pensions (and here he went on to list a number of important issues), if you believe them to be important, then you might consider voting for me. Thank you and good evening."

Now, you might say that Stanley Knowles was at no risk in this election and with his years of service he could afford the luxury of principle. In my own view, it was exactly the other way around. It had been his lifetime of principle that had secured him his place in Canadian politics and it was the strength of his integrity that had earned him the support of even those who opposed some of his most fundamental positions.

One of my tasks on the Knowles campaign was to ensure that the requisite signs went out. Among the most effective sign canvassers was the Reverend Donald Malinowski, a member of the provincial assembly from the Point Douglas area. I had mistakenly presumed the Reverend Malinowski to be a Catholic priest. As it turned out, he was a member of a relatively obscure sect with its headquarters somewhere in Pennsylvania, but I was to learn that later and more painfully during the visit of His Holiness, the Pope, to Manitoba. What I did learn on the campaign was the black secret of Malinowski's success with the sign crew.

A good friend went out with Malinowski one day to deliver a sign, a particularly large, four-by-eight foot plywood one, to an elderly woman who lived in a very strategically placed corner lot on a main thoroughfare. This was what we called an "A" location and we were eager to have a large sign there. The woman, whose command of English was not good, had obviously misunderstood. She had been expecting a small window or door sign; she was quite adamantly opposed to having this massive plywood billboard in her front yard.

My friend was astonished when the Reverend Malinowski, after giving a forceful pitch for the importance of this sign location, ended his pitch by saying to the terrified woman, "When you die, there is two choices. You can go up," and he pointed up, "or you can go down," and he pointed down. He left the impression that the direction of this woman's soul in the afterworld was inextricably and irrevocably linked to the sign. We got the location but my friend refused to do any more sign work on the campaign with the Malinowski. I never told Knowles this story; I was sure that he would go out personally and take the sign back down. After all, it was a very good sign location!

I went out to the CNR shops with Knowles one morning. It was winter— about forty degrees below zero (either Fahrenheit or Celsius, because they converge at forty below). The only other campaigners waiting for the early morning shift change were two Marxist-Leninist candidates. As it had been for about a decade, their slogan that morning was "Make the Rich Pay." Knowles had a thin coat on and I was not wearing enough clothing for the bone-chilling cold. Standing caused us to become colder and colder.

"We have to get moving, Michael or we will freeze," declared a very frozen Knowles.

"Move how?" I asked.

Without a further word, an elderly Stanley Knowles started jumping up and down yelling, "Make the Rich Pay." The Marxist-Leninists were stunned at our identity theft. I soon joined Stanley and began jumping up and down chanting, "Make the Rich Pay." Causing the Marxist-Leninists anguish was a bonus. The real value came from the warmth of blood moving once again to my frozen toes and fingers and face.

CHAPTER FOUR

PARLIAMENT HILL

AS A VERY young man, working shoulder to shoulder with the living legends of the CCF/NDP had a profound impact on me. As a young advocate and policy devotee, I saw up close how two men had re-shaped our nation. Tommy Douglas and Stanley Knowles had each in their own way changed the direction of Canada and the circumstances of millions of Canadians. They had achieved it in vastly different ways. Tommy Douglas held power as premier of Saskatchewan from 1944 to 1961. He created Medicare. Knowles had only his voice in Parliament and his incredible mastery of the rules of Parliament. Nevertheless he made a huge impact on the pensions of all Canadians.

I still have my faded House of Commons photo identification from 1974. It shows a skinny young man with long brown hair. The card and my position granted me the run of Parliament Hill including the Parliamentary Library, the Parliamentary Dining Room and the gallery. I viewed it as a free pass or golden ticket to a real political education.

From September of 1974 until about February 1975, I worked as executive assistant to Ed Broadbent on Parliament Hill. At the time, Broadbent was parliamentary leader, elected by the caucus to replace David Lewis who had been defeated in his Toronto seat in the 1974 general election. The leadership race was on to determine who would permanently replace Lewis as party leader. As caucus chair, Broadbent was a solid consensus choice of the caucus to hold the reins as interim leader until the leadership convention could be held.

The sixteen remaining members of the NDP caucus in those days were a demoralized lot. The party had lost significant ground from the heady days of 1972 to 1974 when it held the balance of power, keeping the Liberals in a minority government status while exacting important concessions. In contrast, the 1974 election gave the Liberals a majority; they were no longer in need of the NDP support. From the kings of Parliament Hill, the NDP were back in the netherworld of third-party status. Compared to the days when journalists hung on David Lewis's every word, the 1974-era press was keenly uninterested in whatever the NDP had to say.

With its ranks decimated, it quickly became apparent that it was the old stalwarts of the NDP who would provide the firepower. The former premier of Saskatchewan and first leader of the NDP, Tommy Douglas, was the energy critic. Stanley Knowles was house leader, the dean of the House of Commons, and a master of its rules. Stanley had played a major role in the negotiations that led to the bringing together of the Canadian Labour Congress and the trade unions and the CCF to form the New Democratic Party.

Compared to Tommy and Stanley's seventy or eighty years of collective political experience, Broadbent was a relative neophyte, having served only six years as an MP. However, Broadbent was the most likely heir apparent. Ed Schreyer, with one term as premier under his belt, was not in a position to leave Manitoba and seek the national leadership despite pressure for him to do so.

In the fall of 1974, Broadbent and I were both relative rookies. He was the rookie interim parliamentary leader, the person chosen by the caucus to serve as leader until the convention in the spring of 1975. I was the rookie executive assistant who, along with Sharon McCrae, was sent by Jo-Anne McNevin and others in the Oshawa campaign gang to look after Broadbent while they put together a leadership campaign.

This was a delightful period in my life. Broadbent and I would roar off across Ontario in his Pontiac. He would give speeches at nomination meetings. Other weekends we would fly across the country to various NDP provincial section conventions. Broadbent was wonderful company although he still tended to assume in those days that his audiences had the same depth and breadth of political philosophy that he did.

I remember one night in a smoke-filled union hall in Peterborough, Ontario. If I am right, it was the nomination of Gill Sandeman as the NDP candidate. Broadbent abandoned his carefully crafted text and launched a bit of a diatribe which prominently featured the thoughts of John Stuart Mill. Sitting, as was my habit, at the back of the room, I caught a sharp elbow in the ribs from a large auto worker in the next chair. "This guy, Mill," he said to me, "Is he one of ours? A candidate or something?" I thought it best to leave it at the suggestion that Mill was indeed one of ours. Broadbent gradually sorted the wheat of his new political message from the chaff of his university days lectures. He became a powerful advocate for "ordinary Canadians" although Broadbent himself was anything but ordinary.

Ed Broadbent had one particularly good story that fit perfectly with our rolling tour. He began it by stating that it was a story about the august governor of the Bank of Canada. This drew puzzled laughter from an NDP crowd.

"Well, the governor of the Bank of Canada decides that his message just isn't being understood by Canadians." There was laughter. Broadbent continued. "So, the governor's staff arranges a speaking tour beginning in Newfoundland and continuing all the way across the country. As befits the governor of the Bank of Canada, he takes his chauffeur along with him."

Broadbent paused. Some in the crowed chuckled at the prospect of the Bank of Canada governor flying his chauffeur across the country.

He continued. "The governor travels in business class on each flight while his chauffeur sits back in economy class. At each city, the chauffeur goes to pick up the rental car and the governor sits in the back. They do not talk to each other.

"After a dozen cities across Canada, they are on the final flight from Vancouver to Victoria. On this small plane, there is no business class section and so the governor and the chauffeur sit together. Out of politeness, the governor asks his driver, 'You have travelled with me across the country. You have heard me give this speech a dozen times. I was wondering what you thought of it?'

"The chauffeur is wary. 'You actually want my opinion?' he asks. 'Even if it is not positive?'

"'Of course I do,' replies the governor, supremely confident of his speech and the delivery of same. 'I want your real opinion. The unvarnished truth of it,' retorts the governor.

"'Well, Governor, I have heard you give that speech twelve times. To be honest it is not a very good speech. I actually believe I could deliver it better, myself.'

"The governor of the Bank of Canada is outraged but he tries not to show his anger to the chauffeur. Instead he decides to call his bluff. 'No one in Victoria has ever met me. We are about the same size. So if you really think you can deliver the speech better than I can we will put you to the test. When we land, we will change clothing and I will rent the car and drive you to the meeting. You can deliver my speech and we will see how you fare.'

"To the governor's surprise, instead of backing down the chauffeur accepts his challenge.

"At the Victoria airport, they exchange clothes and the governor, now dressed as the chauffeur, drives the rented Lincoln. The chauffeur, now dressed as the governor, reviews his speech until they arrive at the University of Victoria. Much to the surprise of the governor of the Bank of Canada, the chauffeur delivers the speech to the gathering of economic faculty and students flawlessly and in ten minutes less than the allotted time.

"'Will the governor take a few questions?'" inquires the chairperson of the Economics Department.

"'Yes,' replies the chauffeur. 'I would be pleased to take a few questions.'

"The governor of the Bank of Canada allows himself a smile. Reading a prepared speech was an act of mimicry. Let him answer a real question. He will come off the fool!

"The first question comes from a newly-minted PhD in economics, 'Could the governor comment on the impact of the Breton Woods Agreement on post-war exchange rates in Japan and the rest of Asia?'

"The governor thinks now that is a tough question—my chauffeur is done like dinner!

"But the chauffeur stands tall. He says, 'Young man. I have travelled this entire country. I have given this speech before thousands of learned individuals. I have to say that is the dumbest question I have ever been asked.' He pauses. 'In fact it is such a stupid question that I will ask my chauffeur at the back of the room to answer it.' "

As we journeyed about Canada, the governor of the Bank of Canada story always won over audiences. Broadbent got better and better at telling it. And I sat at the back of the room imaging that I was the chauffeur.

I worked diligently on Broadbent's leadership campaign until his decision to withdraw from the quest. I doubted he would stay out of the race permanently but his decision caused me to return to the Manitoba government.

When I left my post as Broadbent's executive assistant, he presented me with a book by Albert Camus, *Resistance, Rebellion, and Death*, that he had inscribed. It still occupies a place of pride in my library. I admire the career of Ed Broadbent, who has stuck to his principles and his passion for equality through decades, even when the popular mood turned against such convictions. He was a wonderful mentor for a young man seeking to turn passion to action.

THE ART OF QUESTION PERIOD

EARLY ON IN my time in Ottawa, I learned that question period was much less spontaneous that it appears on television. There was prior agreement on who would ask the questions. Your order and how many questions you could pose were determined first by how many seats you held. As the third party in the House of Commons, the NDP were entitled to three guaranteed questions each question period by way of agreement among the parties' house leaders. It was up to them to submit a list to the speaker on who the three questioners would be and in what order. Although there was still time for spontaneous questions towards the end of question period, the press would largely focus its attention on the first few questions.

The NDP caucus executive met every morning punctually at 9:00 a.m. to allocate the questions and decide what they would be about. The caucus executive consisted of five members of the sixteen member caucus— Ed Broadbent, Stanley Knowles as house leader, Stuart Leggatt as caucus chair, Lorne Nystrom as whip, and Tommy Douglas. Stu Leggatt rarely attended, Nystrom only occasionally.

A number of things became quickly apparent to me at those morning meetings. First, Broadbent was rarely punctual, something that provoked the silent fury of Knowles. Secondly, at exactly 9:08, the door would open just enough to admit a thin wrist and a hand holding a cup of tea for Stanley Knowles. He would pick up the teacup with a rapid movement without losing his place in a sentence and without spilling a drop of tea. I used to have the urge to run around through Broadbent's other office just to catch a glimpse of the tea deliverer but I never did.

In addition to the unseen choreography of question period, there was a genuine art to the putting of a question. Novice questioners were easily dismissed by a well-briefed or clever minister. (In my experience there are more well-briefed ministers than clever ones.) Questions which are too specific can be skated off into the departmental morass; questions which are too general are dealt with in generalities. Ministers are briefed to dredge up an indiscretion of the MP asking the question to blunt the attack. The effective question must turn upon something very specific and topical and yet raise the spectre of government pursuing a general policy to the detriment of the public.

My only small hand at anything approaching ingenuity in all of the hundreds of questions we drafted occurred late in one question period. I remember leafing through the *Maclean's* magazine which had just arrived, and reading in astonishment an interview by Marci MacDonald who had travelled to Europe with then Defence Minister James Richardson. The story had the usual code words that suggested that perhaps a few drinks had been served. Marci had sweet-talked the usual reticent scion of the wealthy Richardson dynasty into a discussion of his views on Canada's Aboriginal people. The views were not favourable. In fact, the Honourable James Richardson went on to suggest that without the European immigration to Canada, the local Aboriginal population would still be dragging their belongings around behind a horse or oxen on two sticks. Political dynamite!

Sensing the opportunity that was presented, Jean Guy Carrier, Broadbent's press secretary, and I rushed down to the members' lobby seeking Wally Firth, an Aboriginal member who represented the Northwest Territories in the House of Commons. Firth was the only Aboriginal member of the NDP caucus and perhaps the only Aboriginal member of the house. He used to torment visitors by asking them if they knew about the University of his home town of Tuktoyaktuk. Most visitors, myself included, upon a first visit to his office were reluctant to admit a lack of knowledge of the aforementioned Tuktoyaktuk University. Wally would beam and say that it was better known by its abbreviated name, Tuk U.

We succeeded in summoning Wally. He was a quick study. He roared back into the house, gained the speaker's attention and demanded an explanation and apology from a red-faced Honourable James Richardson. Defence Minister Richardson became known partly because of the article and significantly because of Wally's determined questioning of the minister he called "Jimmy Two-Sticks."

There are two lessons to be learned from this. First, never drink on an airplane if you are a cabinet minister, particularly with a member of the press. Actually, drinking with the press is at best a risky business even if you are on terra firma. There is no "off the record" that can be relied upon.

Second, the art of question period and success in it are sometimes determined by fleetness of foot, or fleetness of moccasin. Timing is everything in question period. A day later and the question about the *Maclean's* article would have gone to Robert Stanfield as leader of the opposition. By the next day, Richardson would have had a carefully prepared and rehearsed response and his staff would have worked on the press gallery to put a favourable "spin" on events: their hapless minister had merely dropped his guard on a transatlantic flight. The spontaneity was such that, while Wally got all the credit, we were able to retreat to the gallery, secure in the knowledge that on that day, we had come close to understanding the art of the question period.

Another delight of question period was the ongoing antagonism between George Hees of the Progressive Conservatives, a longtime member for Prince Edwards Hastings, and Prime Minister Pierre Elliot Trudeau. The two disliked each other intensely and Hees went to considerable lengths to think up artful ways of skewering Trudeau in question period.

The release of transcripts in which President Nixon was recorded as referring to Prime Minister Trudeau as "an asshole," caused a furor in Ottawa. When Trudeau was asked about Nixon's comments he replied coolly that Nixon wouldn't know "his razzmatazz from a hole in the ground."

Hees lost no time in preparing his question. His question was along the lines of a play on words and language: a trou, which in French is a hole, and d'eau; hence, water hole. Hees demanded of the prime minister what the difference was between a "Trudeau and a razzmatazz." Hees's definition of a razzmatazz, staying within the bounds of parliamentary language, was "what Nixon referred to Trudeau as." The answer, delivered by a beaming Hees, was that there was no difference between Trudeau, or Trou d'eau (en francais) water hole, and the word razzmatazz. He stood there beaming, reciting, "A Trou d'eau a water hole, a hole in the ground, a Trudeau, a razzmatazz, what Nixon referred to Trudeau as." Quite juvenile upon reflection, but it brought down the house.

STANLEY AND TOMMY

STANLEY KNOWLES AND TOMMY DOUGLAS took great delight in my youthful naïveté when I first arrived in Ottawa. I knew they had both graduated from Brandon College in my home province of Manitoba the same year, 1930, as members of the same class. Both were church ministers. One morning, typical of their style, Stanley said to me, with genuine sadness in his voice, "You know Michael, when Tommy and I were in university together, he took all the medals." Knowles paused to let this sink in. Tommy Douglas looked suitably like the cat with the Cheshire grin.

I was completely taken aback. My immediate impression was that after forty-five years, Stanley Knowles was still suffering because he had been bested by Tommy Douglas. I wondered sadly if he had resented all those earlier years when Tommy was party leader and he merely house leader.

This must have been a well-rehearsed gag. Just as I was feeling my newfound pity for poor old Stanley, Tommy Douglas gave me a big grin and said, "Of course, I had to put all the medals back after I took them." Both Tommy and Stanley slapped their knees and laughed uproariously at the discomfort they caused me. This was one of many good-humoured jokes I had to endure as new kid on the block. I smiled weakly after being taken in by their oft-told tale, another neophyte taken in by two old pros.

Stanley Knowles had a tremendous sense of humour. At one point in the fall of 1974, we arranged for the entire caucus to go up to Wakefield. We also imported a number of policy advisors, including Abe Rothstein from the University of Toronto and Jack Weldon from McGill University, to try and refocus the dejected caucus members on the new policy context—how to find meaning in third party opposition and how to be effective? One of the bits of analysis we had prepared was data on who had actually voted for the NDP broken down by age. We had noted in our research that there was a preponderance of the elderly who formed a great, grey core of the party's support.

Uncharacteristically, Stanley Knowles was late for this meeting. In his absence, the colourful Max Saltsman, a renegade MP from Waterloo, was holding forth on the merits of Stanley as an appeal to elderly voters. "Why," he declared, "every election Stanley comes to Waterloo and we put him in the front seat of the car and drive him around and I'm re-elected."

Just as Max was delving into the difficult future that lay ahead for the NDP in general and his own re-election in particular, Stanley appeared and stood just in the doorway. Only Max could not see him. The rest of us listened in horror as Max went on and on about the great disaster that would befall the party with the loss of Stanley, the great symbol and magnet for the elderly vote. Finally Max caught the message in some frantic eye and looked around to see Stanley watching him with a patient smile.

Stanley simply looked Max right in the eye and said, "Don't worry, Max, after I die, I have arranged to have myself stuffed. You can still put me in the front seat of the car and drive me around Waterloo. I can still get you re-elected."

Ironically and sadly, Max succumbed within the decade to cancer— long before Stanley passed. After a debilitating stroke in 1981 and his retirement from politics, Stanley Knowles sat at the clerk's table on the floor of the House of Commons. He remained a fixture of the institution of Parliament, the place he loved more than any other. It was a privilege granted him by the great grace of Pierre Elliot Trudeau on the advice of the magnificent Jerry Yanover, long-time advisor to Liberal house leaders, who cared deeply about both Stanley and the institution of Parliament.

THE ART OF RECOGNITION

IN THE FALL OF 1974, a provincial by-election was called to fill a vacant seat in Carleton East, an Ottawa riding. At that time I was sharing a rented house near Parliament Hill with one of my co-workers, the lovely and talented Sharon McCrae. We had extra room, so organizer Rod Dickenson arrived to stay with us. Rod delighted us by performing scenes from Shakespeare on the dining room table when he was not running the campaign. The distance between acting and running a campaign, while never very large, became unimaginably small when Rod Dickenson was the organizer. He was extremely skilled at both tasks.

The nomination meeting was set and we all made our way to help Rod pack the hall. The candidate to be nominated was Evelyn Gigantes, a journalist who later served in Bob Rae's Ontario Cabinet. The guest speaker was Stephen Lewis, then leader of the Ontario NDP.

I had not been in Ottawa very long. I felt lonely not knowing very many people in the city. This situation seemed unlikely to improve as I spent most weekends touring the country with Ed Broadbent. I was rapidly getting to know people across Canada but few in the city I now called home.

Stephen Lewis was introduced. I was sitting with Rod and Sharon in the very front row as we had arrived quite early. Then a remarkable and completely unexpected thing happened.

"Before I begin my speech," began Stephen Lewis. "I want to say how delighted I am to see Michael Decter sitting in the front row." He may have been delighted but I was truly astonished to be singled out and recognized.

"Seeing Michael makes me remember all of the wonderful campaigns I have been involved in Manitoba. Campaigns for Ed Schreyer, for Stanley Knowles and for David Orlikow."

After his speech, many people in the room came over to welcome me to Ottawa. His simple act of kindness taught me a hugely important political lesson. When you have the pulpit you can use it to recognize those in your audience and win their support for life. It is one of the many wise and generous things that I have learned from Stephen Lewis over the years.

RUSSIANS AND EGGS

ONE MORNING I stepped onto the elevator in the centre block of the House of Commons. In the elevator was the minister of agriculture with his unmistakable trademark. Eugene Whelan always wore a preposterous green Stetson. He served as minister of agriculture and the farmers loved him. Opposition leader Robert Stanfield was also on the elevator that morning. It was the day after the Russians beat Canada in the opening game of the 1974 Canada/Russia hockey series.

For weeks, Whelan had been under fire about CEMA, the Canadian Egg Marketing Agency. Based on the scandal, it was possibly one of the dumbest ideas the emanated from a town with plenty of dumb ideas. The scandal was that Canadians consumers were paying high prices for eggs while surplus eggs, converted to powder, clogged warehouses. Really, CEMA should have been called the Canadian Egg Purchasing Agency. Great at buying eggs but lousy at selling them. They had warehouses full of powdered eggs. They had enough eggs to make an omelet that could have fed the Chinese population for a couple of years. Whelan was getting clobbered in the House of Commons question period about mismanagement of CEMA. And he was largely being clobbered by Robert Stanfield.

Stanfield said to Whelan, "Gene, what do you think about the hockey series?"

Whelan looked out from under that large green hat and fiercely said, "Russians are going to win!" He had a defiant scowl on his face.

"Why do you think that?" inquired the puzzled Stanfield in his halting manner of speech. The elevator doors opened and Whelan made his exit. He turned around to face Stanfield and then just before the doors shut he replied.

"Canadians don't eat enough eggs!"

The elevator doors closed. Stanfield and I looked at each other. Nothing was said.

PARLIAMENTARY PRESS GALLEY DINNER

IN 1975, WHILE serving as executive assistant to Ed Broadbent I attended my first parliamentary press gallery dinner. In those days the dinner was off-the-record. Now they televise it. The prime minister, the leader of the opposition and the governor general delivered speeches to a room full of well-lubricated journalists and their equally inebriated guests. The third party leader, my boss Broadbent, was also given a shot. Musical skits performed by member of the press followed the speeches. Irreverent satirical lyrics set to the tune of popular songs were the standard fare— some clever, some just nasty. A rare few were both clever and nasty. The goal of the evening was humour usually self-inflicted and a bonding of the Fifth Estate, the press, with their subjects or victims—depending on your perspective.

As a first-time attendee of the august and ribald evening, I was told the story of a famous entrance at a previous dinner some ten years earlier. I believe columnist Allan Fotheringham recounted the story to me. At the time of the earlier dinner, the government of Prime Minister John

Diefenbaker was mired in a scandal. Gerda Munsinger, a German woman of great physical beauty and less robust morals, had already brought down Defence Minister Pierre Sévigny. She was also rumoured to have enjoyed a liaison with another cabinet minister, George Hees.

At that earlier press gallery dinner, the Honourable George Hees was escorted into the hall by Charlie Lynch, columnist and president of the press gallery. Painted for the occasion was a huge nude mural affixed to the wall depicting Gerda Munsinger—a thirty-foot nude of the woman in red that Hees had allegedly carried on an affair with, to the horror of the security folks and the embarrassment of the nation. The noise in the room died down. Loud conversation stopped. All eyes turned. Ears strained for Hees' reaction. Would he grow angry? Be shocked? Turn red in the face? Bolt from the room? Silence and anticipation greeted Hees as he surveyed the painting of his alleged former mistress. Hees gazed at Gerda, all of Gerda, took in every painted inch of her glorious body, and then turned slowly to Lynch and pronounced. "I don't think they got her eyes quite right."

Even Charlie Lynch had to roar at that one. Grace under fire. Hees, the old warrior. It would take more than a thirty-foot nude woman to throw George Hees off his stride.

The only way to attend the dinner was to be invited by a member who was in good standing in the parliamentary press gallery so named for their assignment of covering federal politics and in particular Parliament Hill. I was fortunate enough to be asked by a young woman who worked for Dow Jones. This was a night to let your hair down. Tell off your least favourite reporter or politician. Each gallery member was entitled to only one guest. Desperate politicians would sometimes feed leaks to media members to secure an invite. Not being at the dinner was a sign of unimportance bordering on insignificance.

The context of the April 12, 1975 dinner was that Trudeau had returned from two years of minority government to soundly defeat the Tories and regain a majority. Along the way the NDP lost their balance of power position and were cut in half from thirty-two seats. NDP leader David Lewis lost his seat and Ed Broadbent became the parliamentary leader.

Just as the 1974 election had been a mano-a-mano duel between the Ichabod Crane-like Stanfield and the charismatic Trudeau, so was the gallery dinner. With one big difference—unlike the election, this was the night that Stanfield won.

"Ladies and Gentleman," Stanfield paused, "and... Mr. Doug Ball." The crowd roared with laughter and applause. In four words "and Mr. Doug Ball," Stanfield had captured the hearts and laughter of the gallery. In the election campaign, Stanfield had been undone by a photograph of himself fumbling a football. The photo damaged Stanfield as a solid, capable statesman and former premier. It portrayed him as a fumbler, quite literally. The back story was that the first four takes Stanfield caught the football but the aforementioned Doug Ball kept insisting the camera had malfunctioned until they got the famous fumbled football shot.

After "Ladies and gentleman and Mr. Doug Ball" Stanfield owned his audience. He went on in his slow dry speaking manner that drew the audience to his every word. "I don't want to say the press was unfair to me." Stanfield continued. "Although," he paused, "although the morning I walked across Halifax harbour on the water—the headline read, 'Stanfield can't swim.'"

By contrast to Stanfield's self-deprecating approach, Trudeau offered a spirited speech bordering on savage. His first subject was a defence of his controversial swimming pool at 24 Sussex. Anonymous donors had financed the new pool to deflect criticism that taxpayers had bought a pool for their aquatic prime minister. The anonymous donors became the focus of sustained and nasty opposition questions in the House of Commons. The Conservative critic and determined questioner of the prime minister was Tom Cossett.

Trudeau began his remarks by suggesting that the Conservatives were guilty of hypocrisy in the pool matter.

"I was a little surprised," he began in his best nasal tone of absolute contempt. "I was a little surprised to receive a call from Progressive Conservative Party headquarters. They were inquiring about borrowing my new pool. Naturally I asked, 'What for?' 'We want it for a policy conference,' they replied."

Trudeau paused and smiled that barracuda smile. He knew what lay ahead. We did not.

Trudeau leaned into the microphone. "I replied to them, 'of course there is the shallow end.'" The audience laughed loud and long. Trudeau went on to suggest an event for the policy conference. "I told them they should stage a race in the pool. Tom Cossett and two sixteen-foot sharks."

The parliamentary press gallery dinner featured songs performed by members of the press corps in addition to speeches by notables. My faded copy of the evening's program reproduces the lyrics of the songs performed. In general the songs were familiar tunes with the lyrics rewritten to political satire.

Prior to his leadership of the federal Conservatives, Robert Stanfield served as the premier of Nova Scotia. To the tune of "Farewell to Nova Scotia," Bruce Phillips, Dennis Baxter, Peter Meerburg, and Iain Hunter sang for the first and likely only time the unique ballad, "Stanfield's Farewell":

My sun is setting, I'm over the hill.
But when will The Hill get over me.
In my garden I'll be digging, where that friggin' Gerry Riggin
Spends provincial tax to bribe the blacks, and acts like me.

Goin' back to Nova Scotia
The coast with the most
Had my fill of Upper Cana-dee
With my charismatic smile, I'll make merry all the while.
Will you ever find the time to pause … and … think … of … me?

I implored every Tory
To trust in me
While I bust my ass to keep the faith
But of this there is no doubt
Big Thunder has clapped out
Lost my clapper in the crapper on July the eighth

The chorus was then repeated.

If you ever need to reach me
You'll know where I am
You can ring me on the telephone
I'll be back in old Truro where the long johns ebb and flow,
Sipping scotch and heavy water by the old Clairtone!

Most of the rest of the dinner has faded with time but the image of the slow-talking but sharp-witted Stanfield and the arrogant and tough Trudeau remain. And much booze, far too much booze was consumed that night in the name of politics and journalism. I believe a good time was had by all.

CHAPTER FIVE

MANITOBA— THE SCHREYER GOVERNMENT

THE ELECTION OF the Schreyer government in 1969 changed everything for me. The event more than forty years ago marked the end of moral victories for me and for the New Democratic Party of Manitoba. I was sixteen years old on the night of June 25, 1969, when Edward Richard Schreyer was elected to be first NDP premier in the history of Manitoba. For me it meant being initiated gradually into the challenges and compromises of governing—the discipline of power as it is aptly named.

My government days began in the summer of 1972 when I was still an economics student at Harvard College. During my Easter vacation when I was home in Winnipeg, I went for an interview with the assistant planning secretary to cabinet in the Manitoba government. At that time, the planning secretary to cabinet was Jack

Weldon who commuted from his other life as head of the Department of Economics at McGill University in Montreal. His dynamic number two was a Ukrainian farm boy from Saskatchewan and then Transcona, Manitoba, who had rocketed through the University of Manitoba, off to Oxford on a Rhodes scholarship back through the federal public service, and home to Manitoba. Wilson Dwight Parasiuk, named after two American presidents, went formally by W.D. Parasiuk, but to all of us, he was just Willy.

The interview turned out to be easy. Summer student jobs were allocated largely on the basis of fit. Given Harvard and my knowledge of Manitoba, I was seen to be a good fit. My immediate supervisor, George Ford, was a dedicated, extraordinarily hard-working and somewhat overly serious young man. He had come out of the student Christian movement at the University of Toronto. Willy and George would play major roles in the rest of my career with the Manitoba government, as would Mr. Derek Bedson who I would not really get to know for another few years.

The letter arrived at my dormitory room in Harvard, offering me employment in the summer of 1972 for the princely sum of $417 per month. I was delighted. When I finally arrived in June to take up that job, I was not annoyed in the slightest to find that our offices were in the old Grace Hospital that was no longer in service. It was a good two kilometres from the Legislative Building, which meant that we had to commute there for important and for less important meetings. George Ford did this by pedaling his bicycle.

My first experience with the importance of symbols over substance, acronyms over programs within government came the second day on the job. The project on which I was working had to do with community-based economic development. We shared office space with a number of other projects and the one I remember most vividly had the title: Community Roles Analysis Project. Halfway through my second day, one of the people working on the Community Roles Analysis Project, discovered that the acronym was C.R.A.P. This created both great entertainment and amusement and ultimately alarm when word drifted back to our superiors in the Legislative Building. No premier wanted to be asked about the C.R.A.P. in question period.

It also became clear that analyzing the role of every community in Manitoba in over two or three months in the summer was an impossible task. Here, the skill of seasoned government officials became evident. The project was scaled down to cover not all communities in Manitoba but just those in the north. With the project renamed Northern Community

Roles Analysis Project, the acronym would now be N.O. C.R.A.P. This seemed to make everyone happy. The students on the project were happy because they had fifty or sixty communities instead of several thousand. Their superiors were also happy because they would not be ridiculed by ministers, or worse, the opposition, for the acronym.

I realized that in government as elsewhere what things were named was very important and that no crap is better than crap!

CHURCH HALL ORATORY

EARLY IN MY CAREER, I had occasion to drive the minister of labour who was also the deputy premier. Russ Paulley had led the Manitoba NDP before Ed Schreyer. He had an enormous capacity for telling a good story but did not enjoy robust health so occasionally one of us would serve as his driver for an out of town cabinet meeting.

On this particular occasion, I was driving Minister Paulley northwest of Winnipeg. We passed a hamlet near Gladstone. He pointed out a small church with a hall next to it.

"I spoke there once," he declared. "Not a great experience."

"What happened?" I inquired.

"When I became leader of the party I determined that I must go out to the country and speak every week." He coughed a rough smoker's cough. When the coughing finished, he continued his tale. "We would send out notices to a town or village and book a local hall. I would drive out by myself to speak."

"That hall," he gestured at the church hall now receding behind us as I drove north. "That hall was one we chose."

His coughing took over for a few more moments. "I arrived just on time for the speech. There was our notice posted right on the door of the hall. When I went in there was only one person present, an older man sitting right in the middle of the front row. I decided that I would show no disappointment. He had come for the speech and the speech was what he would get." The old warrior paused and then continued. "So I really laid into the speech. I used all the gestures. I pounded on the podium."

"What happened?" I asked.

"When I finished I asked. 'Are there any questions?' And I looked around as though the hall was filled with people. The man in the front row put up his hand.

'Yes sir, do you have a question?'

'Yes I do. I am the caretaker. I was wondering whether you are going to be using this hall for much longer?'"

We both laughed long and loud as the church hall receded in the rear view mirror.

RUSS DOERN

RUSS DOERN'S END was tragic. Who can ever know the pressures and internal demons that compel someone to commit suicide? Some of my fondest memories of Manitoba government days, however, revolved around Doern and his capacity to be entertaining; sometimes deliberately, more often inadvertently.

The most public and celebrated of his battles was with the shrewd mayor of Winnipeg, Steven Juba. Juba's own political career was a marvel. At one point, he was simultaneously a Member of the Legislative Assembly, sitting as an independent, which was a rare feat in Manitoba politics, and the mayor of Winnipeg. He sponsored such high profile political stunts as a contest on the colouring of margarine. City dwellers favoured colouring margarine so that it would look more like butter. Farmers and rural folk opposed colouring margarine as it would hurt butter sales. A free trip to Florida as a prize for the best entry on why margarine should be coloured like butter garnered enormous publicity for Juba and a populist following in the city.

Doern's clash with Juba came over Doern's decision, as public works minister, to build public washrooms in a park across the street from the Legislative Building. This was in the 1970s and Doern had become enraged by the long-haired hippie types trouping into the Manitoba Legislative Building to make use of the washrooms. This was a very practical thing for people to do since the Legislative Building washrooms were significantly overbuilt. Motivated by his desire to clean this rabble out of the Legislative Building, Doern had a large limestone washroom structure erected in the park. Juba, who was a good friend of the premier's, was nonetheless eager to seize any political advantage that he could. He accused Doern of slighting the veterans and the war dead by building a washroom in what was known as Memorial Park; a claim substantiated by the presence of the Cenotaph and War Memorial at the far end of the park. To drive home this point, Juba arranged for a portable washroom to be deposited on the front steps of the Legislative Building.

The press had a field day. Doern was slaughtered by the old political fox, Mayor Juba, in the public relations battle.

My own fondest memory of Doern was an incident which took place just before the 1977 election. Consistent with tradition, the Manitoba cabinet held meetings in various smaller centers across the province to have a greater visibility and to allow the premier's ministers to meet the local population. The overall political objective was to convince people that the government was not wholly Winnipeg-centric but interested in rural and northern Manitoba as well.

This particular meeting was held in the town of Killarney in the heart of Conservative southwestern Manitoba. The town hall had been borrowed for the occasion. Such was the dissension in the cabinet during the meeting and so loud were the shouts emanating from the hall that raised voices giving out election strategy could be heard on the Main Street of Killarney. It became necessary to provide some sort of camouflage. Two of the premier's aides were compelled to go out and try to make noise in the street to keep people from overhearing the raucous debate. Amidst this verbal jousting, Russ Doern provided what I always thought was the most outrageously simplistic view of the current political situation possible.

It is to be hoped that the premier's aides had succeeded in creating enough of a diversion on the street so that the good citizens of Killarney were not privy to the outbursts following Doern's suggestion. His comment was that he thought the NDP would have a great deal of difficulty recruiting Tories to vote for it. Therefore, and he unveiled this with a triumphant flourish, he felt that Schreyer should devote his efforts to courting the Liberal vote. Schreyer, normally a calm, polite and stolid chair of his cabinet, exploded in disbelief at Doern. "What in the hell do you think I've been doing for the last eight years?" was Schreyer's response to Doern's discovery of the obvious. Doern had no answer.

The NDP had been in power with the benefit of a social democratic, small "l" liberal coalition for eight years. Schreyer had expended much of his energies gathering the Liberals into his support base and holding the coalition together. He had personally recruited Larry Desjardins from the Liberals and had done everything in his power, short of joining the Liberals, to welcome them to the NDP. He had even suggested changing the name of the party to make it less painful for Liberals to belong.

By 1977, however, the NDP had lost popularity, as many governments do after two terms, and was facing a reinvigorated Conservative party led by a feisty and experienced leader, Sterling Lyon.

Another incident, which was told to me by a friend, a young political aide to Bud Boyce, involved Doern as minister of public works, Bud Boyce as minister of corrections, and Len Evans as minister of everything which affected his home town, Brandon. The occasion was the opening of a new correctional facility in Brandon or the sod-turning of the facility. I cannot remember which, but it was a three-minister affair. My friend related that as they prepared for the official photograph, he noted the most curious behaviour on Doern's part. He seemed to be making little shifting motions with his feet, hopping back and forth in the dirt from one foot to another. My friend was puzzled by these antics and was not quite sure what to make of them at the time. However, when it came time for the official photograph, all was revealed. At the very last moment, Doern, not very tall and quite vain about his appearance, hopped forward on a little mound of earth which he had been constructing by the shuffling of his feet. This served to make him several inches taller than his two colleague ministers and gave him a place of prominence in the photograph. My friend, while aghast at Doern's behaviour, proudly displayed the photograph in his office, proof that a little fancy footwork could gain you greater prominence in politics.

MR. BEDSON

WHEN I JOINED the government in 1972, Mr. Derek Bedson was clerk of the executive council and secretary of the cabinet. This was the most senior job in the government and one to which Mr. Bedson had been appointed in 1958 by the then newly-elected premier, Duff Roblin. Mr. Bedson (I never felt comfortable calling him anything else) had survived the transition from Walter Weir's ill-fated and short-lived Conservative government to the Schreyer government which was elected in 1969.

Mr. Bedson's survival in the Weir to Schreyer transition was a combination, I always thought, of at least three ingredients. Ed Schreyer was totally new to the process of governing and inclined, by his nature, to both generosity and tradition. This supplied two of the elements since Schreyer wanted, in the face of a nervous business community to give as much of an impression of stability and continuity as possible. For this reason, many senior officials were retained. Ed Schreyer considered Derek Bedson to be, first and foremost, an expert on protocol. I learned a decade later that Mr. Bedson considered himself to be anything but an expert on protocol and deemed the whole topic to be rather silly. But impressions are everything in politics and everyone had the impression that Mr. Bedson loved protocol.

The third ingredient was that Derek Bedson had served in the post for over a decade by the time Ed Schreyer arrived. He had earned respect from many diverse quarters of Manitoba society. It was evident that he was committed to integrity in government, to historic buildings, to culture, to the preservation of the French community in Manitoba, and to a number of other causes that were not overly popular and are still not in many segments of Manitoba society. Mr. Bedson defended noble but eccentric causes which won him a place in the hearts of many leading Manitobans.

What occurred through the Schreyer era was an erosion of the power of the clerk of executive council and the creation of a new planning secretary to cabinet. This created another senior official to cabinet who, at times, had far more influence on policy than had the clerk. Nevertheless, it was Mr. Bedson who attended cabinet as clerk and took the minutes from 1958 to December 1, 1981, when I was appointed by Premier-elect Pawley to replace him.

Mr. Bedson was a friend and a mentor to me in a different way than Wilson Parasiuk, George Ford and others had been. Mr. Bedson knew the history of the Roblin government and of the province and he was very graceful in sharing that knowledge with me.

In the early days, I was terrified of him. He was tall, well-dressed and articulate but stooped with a posture of one bearing the weight of his office He was a formidable figure, with a picture of, I think, King Charles I on his office wall. Mr. Bedson believed himself to be descended from Spanish kings and English nobility. Certainly, his distinguished bearing and dramatic eyebrows, when raised to signal horror, would have supported his claims.

By the mid-1970s, I was serving as a kind of unofficial number two to Willy Parasiuk who was running the planning secretariat. Willy was entitled, in fact, obligated, to attend cabinet meetings for what was called the planning part of the agenda and take minutes. It was my duty to stand in for him when he was away. The difficulty was that it was impossible for me, outside the room, to determine when cabinet had finished with the routine items of appointments, regulations and legislation and had moved on to the major policy items. In theory, I was not to be there during the routine items but to show up when they reached the policy matters. Mr. Bedson was not of a mind to call me when that time came since he considered the planning secretariat to be a wholly unnecessary creation of the Schreyer government. He seemed to be generous of spirit enough, however, to realize my dilemma and he let me know it was all right to phone occasionally to see where they were at.

One day I phoned and asked where on the agenda the cabinet might be. Mr. Bedson answered the phone. "They are on their favourite item," he said.

Not knowing what exactly this might be, I inquired, "What might that cabinet item be?"

Mr. Bedson replied, "The distribution of largesse in the boondocks."

As this description might apply to any number of items on a normal cabinet agenda, I was forced, for a second time, to test Mr. Bedson's patience by inquiring what exactly the distribution of largess in the boondocks might mean in the contest of this particular Cabinet meeting.

"The lottery, you young fool!" he thundered into the phone and hung up. That was more helpful. I was able to locate the distribution of the lottery proceeds on the agenda and turn up at the appointed hour.

Over the years, I spent many hours sitting in Mr. Bedson's office, often at high points in the minor drama of Manitoba politics, as he would recall what so-and-so had done, generally Premier Roblin, in a similar circumstance. His only real advice to me upon my appointment in 1981 was that I should go out to lunch every day and never eat in the cafeteria within the Legislative Building. He said, "If you let them (the cabinet), they will work you to death and make you eat here in that wretched cafeteria. After a time, all that will be left is a small grease spot on the carpet. That's all there will be of you, a grease spot."

At the time, I thought Mr. Bedson's view of the capacity of cabinet to wear down its senior officials to be exaggerated. Four and a half years later, it was my view that he understated the case. Going out to lunch proved a small salvation. Mr. Bedson's seemingly minor bit of advice masked its greater wisdom.

Derek Bedson had a remarkable collection of friends, many from his days in federal Department of External Affairs. He frequently spent his Christmases in Bermuda with William Stephenson, the famous spy, code-named Intrepid, from World War II. Mr. Bedson was also a life-long Conservative. He was Diefenbaker's appointment secretary when Diefenbaker was in opposition and later, prime minister. Mr. Bedson brought some order to the chaotic realms of the Chief's office. However, he was a staunch believer in a non-partisan civil service and I believe he gave advice that, while influenced by his years, never reflected a partisan bias. I endeavoured to follow his example.

LILY SCHREYER

I HAVE ALWAYS been taken by a story Lily Schreyer tells. It is about how, after she had been married to Ed for a number of years and he had been premier for several, they went back to her hometown of Grandview, Manitoba. The occasion was the official opening of a new senior citizens' residence. On a dusty August day on their way out of town, they stopped at one of the two or three gas stations in Grandview to fill the tank. In those days in Manitoba, the premier drove his own car.

When the premier emerged from the gas station, he noticed that Lily had been talking with some intensity to the gas station attendant. When they began driving, he inquired whether she knew the fellow.

Lily replied, "Oh, yes. Ed, that's a fellow I went out with in high school, long before we ever met."

Schreyer said to her, somewhat self-importantly, "And where do you suppose you would be today, Lily, if you had married him instead of me?"

Lily smiled her best smile and said, "Why, Ed, I'd be married to the premier of Manitoba."

FARLEY MOWAT

ABOUT THE LAST PERSON I expected to become friendly with while working for the Manitoba government was Canada's best-known environmental campaigner and bestselling author, Farley Mowat. A business loan, given by the Schreyer government in 1973 first attracted Mowat's attention. The loan was to an Inuit Co-operative in Churchill, Manitoba. The purpose of the loan was to allow the group to begin hunting the beluga whales that frequented Hudson Bay near Churchill. Mowat, who had just finished his book *A Whale for the Killing*, about the grizzly fate of a whale trapped in a bay off Newfoundland and used as target practice by the Newfoundland cowboy contingent, was enraged that any government would sponsor the further killing of the whales. He was particularly incensed because, as a long-time supporter of the NDP, he expected better from them. In his Mowat-like fashion, he laid siege on Premier Schreyer.

Schreyer, a good politician and an intuitive environmentalist, was also a fan of Mowat. He was amenable to Farley's suggestions. He told Mowat that if he could convince the Aboriginal co-op that there was more money to be made in building a tourist industry around showing people the whales rather than killing them, he would be just as happy to provide the money for the preservation and watching of the whales. Mowat, good as his word, flew to Churchill and persuaded the community and the Inuit that there was more money to be had bringing wealthy Canadians, Americans and Europeans to see these whales rather than killing and eating them as had been their traditional way. Surely Mowat has been vindicated by the popularity of whale-watching in Churchill. Some thirty years later, the Michelin Guide and other major tourist guides celebrate the whales of Churchill as a major tourist destination. In the process, he became friendly with Premier Schreyer and became, as we all were in those days and all remain in these days, completely enamoured by the wondrous Lily Schreyer.

Mowat was so charmed by the Schreyers that he decided to take up residence. He parked his small caravan in the backyard of their home. Ed signed him on as a dollar-a-year man for the government and Farley took to pounding out proposals on how to bring about some sensitivity to the natural environment. As a young functionary in the cabinet, I was assigned the task of being the go-between for Mowat with the departments. My role was to attempt to figure out who exactly should be responding to Mowat's proposals and to impress upon them the seriousness with which the premier took Mowat's ideas.

For many years, I still had a full file of what were, in those days, brilliant proposals, hand-typed by Farley on his trusty Underwood. They were somewhat ahead of their time and were regarded as coming from Mars by most of the timid officials with the Manitoba government. Needless to say, we did not get very far in actually implementing such imaginative proposals as a major log cabin building scheme, a writers' retreat, or a new publishing house. However, I believe Mowat did achieve some victories in terms of changing some of the attitudes of the staff in the Department Natural Resources when it came to the North and Aboriginal peoples. He also probably accelerated the political acceptance of the environment (although no one called it that in those days) as a central issue.

The task of managing Mowat, as it were, was an impossible one. He would show up when he felt like it and his passion for rum took a little getting used to. Not that I considered myself a timid drinker, but my first experience of a lunch meeting with Mowat went somewhat as follows:

The lunch was set for noon at the Old Swiss Inn and Mowat popped by my office at 11:15 and suggested we make haste for the restaurant, which was but a scant ten minutes from the Legislative Building. We had arranged for several officials from the Department of Natural Resources to join us at noon. We arrived at the restaurant at 11:30 and pounded on the closed door for admission. Once seated, Farley immediately ordered both of us a double rum and coke. It was a little early for me, but I thought that if the great man could order a rum and Coke at 11:30, so could I.

When the officials arrived from the department, Farley saw it as an opportunity to order another round of double rum and Cokes. In the first hour of lunch, I had consumed three double rum and Cokes, well above my capacity. Mowat was completely undiminished and seemingly unaffected by this large intake of grog. In a completely uncharacteristic move, I agreed to have a cigar at the end of lunch and went back to my office where I toiled usually unaffected by alcohol and as a lifelong non-smoker. This was the only occasion where Premier Schreyer stuck his head in my office and found me somewhat inebriated, with my feet on my desk, smoking what was left of the lunchtime cigar. I think to this day he still has the view that his staff did nothing but drink and smoke cigars when we were supposed to be doing policy work. It's with some irony that this was the only time I can remember either smoking a cigar or returning to work after a liquid lunch.

In those days I had returned from years in the concrete jungle of Boston and had decided that I must live in the country. To this end, I bought a very small house in the community of Starbuck, Manitoba. I painted the house barn red so that friends could find it and proceeded with some pretty amateurish renovations. Nevertheless, I extended an invitation to Mowat to visit, which he did with Lily Schreyer in tow. Ed was making a speech somewhere and that was about the only explanation offered. There was the compulsory bottle of rum which we proceeded to demolish.

Starbuck, I should note, is a small community and not one noted for radical tendencies of any sort. It was a warm summer evening and at about 10:30 p.m., Farley decided that he would see if the creek across the road from our house was suitable for swimming. He casually stripped nude, threw a towel over his shoulder and set off for the creek. However, as it turned out later, he stopped at a few neighbours' homes to seek directions for this creek as he was unfamiliar with the area.

Over the next number of months while I lived in Starbuck, I harboured the secret hope that Farley's celebrity was such that my cause had been helped and not hurt by his naked perambulations. The neighbours never said a word about Farley's appearance.

When I would run into Farley from time to time in the late 1970s, he would complain mischievously that Schreyer had never paid him the dollar the government of Manitoba owed him. With Sterling Lyon in power, there was no chance of him ever securing this dollar from the government of Manitoba for all his fine work.

FIRST FRENCH FARM

MY FIRST EXPERIENCE with the politics in Manitoba between the French and the English came on a summer's day when I was young policy analyst in the premier's office. We were approaching an election campaign and I had been dispatched, along with my boss, Willy Parasiuk, Premier Schreyer; and the premier's aide, René Chartier, to attend a cabinet meeting on the west side of the province. En route, we agreed to Chartier's suggestion that we visit his home town, the small French village of St. Lazare, Manitoba.

Chartier was driving the premier's car, a big Chevy, and Willy and I were in the back seat. We were rocketing along the smooth paved highway at more than a hundred kilometres an hour when suddenly and without warning the pavement ended. The car slammed into a large gravel hole in the road and (this was pre-seatbelt days) we were all catapulted upwards banging our heads on the roof of the car.

Premier Schreyer inquired angrily of Chartier what the hell had happened to the road. René Chartier replied calmly, "first French farm."

I learned later that the only piece of unpaved provincial trunk highway in Manitoba began at the first French farm on one side of St. Lazare and continued through the village to the last French farm on the other side, where the pavement resumed. Clearly the local branch of the Manitoba Highways Department had a large negative sentiment towards to the French inhabitants of St. Lazare.

Premier Schreyer was as enraged as Chartier had known he would be. On the premier's edict, the Department of Highways reported every morning on the progress of the paving of that road. The premier lost the 1977 election but carried the vote of St. Lazare by a large majority.

There was a postscript to this story. When I told it many years later at a two-day colloquium on Official Languages at Queen's University, Roger Turenne of the Manitoba government noted that there were now bilingual highways signs on that stretch of road as St. Lazare had been designated by the province as an area to receive services in French. My own view is that they probably much preferred having the road paved to having highway signs in their own language. Now the people of St. Lazare have both. So it goes.

BRITISH COLUMBIA POLITICS

THE WILDEST AND WACKIEST politics in Canada are indisputably those of British Columbia. Over the years, many visits to friends and business trips have taken me into the heart of that political culture. There is no concise way to describe it. It would seem that British Columbia tends to pick its politicians from people who would in other places make good hotline radio talk show hosts. In fact, there seems to be a great movement back and forth between the ranks of the elected and the ranks of the self-appointed. Politics everywhere is somewhat show business. In British Columbia, show business is politics and politics is show business; there are no real boundaries between the two.

For example, much maligned B.C. Premier Bill Vander Zalm had as his major qualification the development of an amusement park called Fantasy Gardens. A good description of the continuing situation of the government in B.C. would seem to be more like Fantasy Island.

In 1975, I narrowly avoided employment with the government of David Barrett which lasted a brief thirty months and which, upon careful analysis, greatly resembled the rest of the intervening several decades of Social Credit rule. Barrett at his most populist was little different from the Socreds. Although his rhetoric was of the left, his behaviour often seemed born of one-man rule and chaotic flailing about in the fishbowl of B.C. politics.

My first real inkling about the truly different nature of B.C. politics came when as a young official working with the Manitoba government

I was assigned to an obscure creation of the western premiers—the Task Force on Constitutional Trends which became known as the Intrusions Task Force. Led largely by strong provincial rights types in British Columbia and Alberta, the job of the task force was to ferret out every area in which the federal government could be argued to be intervening in an area of provincial jurisdiction. This was the sensitive ear of the early to mid-1970s. I believe that at one meeting, an Alberta representative suggested that the very existence of the Central Mortgage and Housing Corporation could be construed as an intrusion into an area of provincial jurisdiction. Through a series of meetings and working parties, we eventually catalogued a wide array of places where the federal toe was indeed across the provincial line.

The Honourable Rafe Mair chaired the Intrusions Task Force. He was a burly, broad-shouldered fellow with a beard. He looked like a well-dressed Mountain Man. He first introduced me to the significantly different career path of the politicians of British Columbia. He announced at the conclusion of one of our ministerial meetings that he had decided to resign from cabinet and as a minister of the Crown. He further announced that he would be appearing on a Vancouver radio station as host of a talk show. To those of us from outside B.C. this seemed to be indicative of some darker mystery. No one in Manitoba would resign from the cabinet to take up a radio hotline show, much as they might detest the existing legislature. However, to our amazement our B.C. colleagues treated this as though Mair had been the winner of a lottery or perhaps had been awarded knighthood by Her Majesty. Clearly, movement from the ranks of ministers to the ranks of live on-air hosts was a promotion. Later on, I was not a bit surprised when the out-of-work David Barrett, former NDP premier, went the same route.

YOUNG TURKS

THE PHRASE "YOUNG TURKS" has its origins in the Ottoman Empire rather than as an abbreviation of "Young Turkeys." Young Turks was a phrase used to describe a coalition favouring the overthrow of the Ottoman Sultan. It came to mean progressives seeking prominence and power.

The first time and only time I had the phrase hurled at me in anger was on the floor of an NDP convention. I had the enormously poor judgment that despite being an employee of the Manitoba government, I could still take part in active political debate. I found myself supporting a resolution on the convention floor that was critical of the premier's support of wage and price controls. Worse still the resolution passed. In his acceptance speech to the convention, Premier Schreyer declared fiercely, "I will not be dictated to by Young Turks from Ivy League universities." There were few present who would not have known he meant me.

My punishment was not long in arriving. A First Ministers' meeting was called for the day after the convention and I was included in the Manitoba delegation. I hid from the premier on the plane to Ottawa and at the hotel on Sunday night but could not avoid him on Monday morning. So early Monday morning we began our walk, the entire Manitoba delegation with the premier at the front and I as far back as I could manage without joining the Saskatchewan delegation behind us. We took the tunnel from the basement of the Château Laurier to the Conference Centre.

When we reached the end of the tunnel there was a phalanx of television cameras to broadcast our arrival back to the nation and Manitoba. As we exited the tunnel into the grand hall of the Ottawa Conference Centre, Premier Schreyer turned to me and uttered the words for which I remain grateful more than thirty years later. "At least they can't say I don't bring my Young Turks with me!" he intoned with an edge of kindness. I had learned an important lesson and I had been forgiven by a very gracious political leader.

I knew then that you had to make a choice. As a public servant you gave your advice to those you served with the door closed, not on the floor of a party convention.

CHAPTER SIX

MANITOBA— THE LYON GOVERNMENT

WHEN THE GOVERNMENT of Ed Schreyer was defeated in 1977, I was only twenty-five years old and serving at a fairly high level as acting planning secretary to the cabinet.

During the election campaign, Conservative leader Sterling Lyon had pledged to abolish the planning secretariat to cabinet. He labelled it as too political. He was not alone. Many civil servants in the line departments viewed the by now seventy-eight person planning secretariat as too closely aligned with the government of the day. This was the organization that I had been appointed to head on an acting basis when Willy Parasiuk stepped down to run in the election. Although the government was defeated, Willy Parasiuk captured the Transcona seat for the NDP making him a Member of the Legislative Assembly (MLA) and of the opposition caucus.

Before being sworn in as Manitoba's premier, Lyon set a tough tone for his administration by dismissing three deputy ministers whom he considered to have been too close politically to the Schreyer administration that preceded him. After taking office he met with all of the remaining deputy ministers and among the statements he made to them was that he favoured having "the managers manage." A few days later he appointed a Task Force on Government Organization and Economy and imposed tight spending controls. Lyon's proposed remedy for what he saw as the high spending ways of the Schreyer government was a period of "acute protracted restraint."

One of the restraint measures adopted was that any government grant over $500 had to come before the full cabinet for approval. Del Gallagher was deputy minister of tourism and culture at the time. He was a hard-drinking, tough-talking man from Atlantic Canada who brooked little foolishness in his world view. His department which made literally thousands of small grants to arts and tourism organizations was most affected by the new policy constraint.

At a subsequent meeting with the deputy ministers, Gallagher asked Premier Lyon, "How do you square your view that the managers should manage with your decision to have every grant of $500 or more reviewed by your full Cabinet?"

Premier Lyon replied carefully, "This is a temporary measure." He paused and then added, "We are just trying to slow things down so we can get a good look at them."

Gallagher exploded. "Who in the hell told you that anything in government moves fast enough that you had to slow it down to get a look at it?"

Del Gallagher's time as a deputy minister ended within days of this exchange. These events taught me that some things in government, particularly the end of a career, could move rather swiftly.

THE NEGOTIATION

I FELT AN enormous responsibility for the seventy-eight people who worked in the planning secretariat and whose fate seemed to be sealed. At my first meeting with Premier Lyon and Mr. Bedson, I put forward the view that since the premier had promised to abolish the planning secretariat, he should allow the staff and functions to transfer to line departments. He was not immediately receptive to this view.

"I want the planning secretariat dis-established" he pronounced firmly. I resisted the temptation to say that would make him a dis-establishmentarian knowing that would seem cavalier. Instead, I tried to engage him on the workforce itself.

I began again, "Many of the staff in the planning secretariat are civil servants from other departments who just happened to have been in the planning secretariat at this time."

"Many are not—they are political," he retorted.

"What about the secretarial and clerical staff?" I tried. "Surely they deserve a chance at a job that might be vacant elsewhere in the provincial government?"

The premier seemed unmoved.

I played my only trump card. "What about Sonia Smith?' I inquired.

"What about Sonia Smith?" the premier replied.

"Sonia Smith—do you think she is political and should lose her job?"

"The same Sonia Smith that worked as my secretary when I was attorney general?" demanded Lyon.

"Well," I replied, "Sonia is my secretary now."

"Of course not—she is a true public servant."

The newly-elected premier suddenly saw my point, through the lens of Sonia Smith. She was real to him. To Lyon, Sonia was a hard-working woman with no interest in politics.

I pressed my small advantage. "If the deputy ministers would request that staff from the planning secretariat be transferred to their departments would you let those transfers happen?" I asked.

"If the deputies request the transfers in writing, I would consider it," he replied evenly.

Mr. Bedson shot me a stern glance. I knew it was time to retreat.

"Thank you, Premier."

In this first round I held the advantage of knowledge. Despite the incoming premier's view of the NDP as profligate spenders, Premier Schreyer had been a very tough manager of civil service growth. Departmental expansion had been constrained not only by budgetary measures but also by headcount or staff-year controls. To hire new employees, departments not only needed the money to pay them but the staff-years or positions in which to put them. The planning secretariat had not only employees but also staff-years and budget to the end of the fiscal year, fully four months away.

Shortly after the meeting with Premier Lyon, I began my rounds of meetings with the deputy ministers. I knew all the deputies, some better than others. My proposal was straightforward: here are the personnel that are working in the policy area of your department, health, economic development etc. If you request these staff be transferred, you will have their staff-year (SY) as well as funding until the end of the fiscal year. What I asked in return was that they endeavour to retain the staff in their department in the next fiscal year. In essence the planning secretariat staff would have four months to prove themselves invaluable to the department. I had little doubt, given the calibre of the planning secretariat staff that they would do just that. My intention was to get as many of the staff placed as I could. I did not see an obvious continuing role for myself in the Manitoba government of Sterling Lyon.

Just as this process of meetings was getting underway, Mr. Bedson summoned me to his office.

"Would you be willing to meet with Sidney Spivak to discuss working for the task force?' was his question. I was willing.

I also met with Bill McCance, who served as the secretary to the task force. We were from opposite sides of the tracks in many ways but we hit it off. Bill's father, Ches McCance, had been Manitoba's athlete of the century. He had played for the Winnipeg Blue Bombers. My father as a young physician had been the team doctor. In Winnipeg this means you are related. It is a small town in things that matter.

I made great progress on the request for staff from deputies after joining the task force staff. Most of the government including the deputy ministers saw the task force as a "hit squad" and it seemed to them a good idea to have a sympathetic person on the staff. More important was that these senior civil servants had a belief in a second chance for their colleagues who had been in the wrong place at the wrong time. After two weeks, I had requests for virtually all of the planning secretariat staff from various deputy ministers on behalf of their departments.

I reported to Mr. Bedson and submitted all of the written requests. One morning I was summoned to a management board of cabinet meeting. The premier was there and extremely unhappy. I had done too well. I think he had expected that Sonia Smith and the other secretarial and clerical personnel would be requested but not the policy types. I had succeeded in obtaining transfer requests for nearly the entire seventy-eight employees. To be fair he had said at our initial meeting that they would consider the transfers not that they would automatically approve them. Now a further condition was added. In addition to the deputy ministers' requests, I now needed to obtain the agreement and support of each minister that would be receiving staff. Inwardly I despaired but tried not to show it in front of the premier.

"Fine," I replied. "I will seek the approval of each minister." The reason for my despair was simple. Unlike the deputies whom I knew, I had never met the incoming ministers other than the premier and Sidney Spivak.

I returned to the task force office and encountered Bill McCance. I explained my setback.

Bill smiled.

"What are you smiling about?" I demanded.

"I can help." He replied calmly.

"How can you help?" I retorted. "You have been in the government for two weeks."

Now Bill laughed out loud. "I worked with the premier on the campaign. I personally asked a third of the cabinet to run. They owe me and I intend to collect."

And so in the most improbable turn of events, Bill McCance, who had played a huge role in defeating the NDP government and who had been sent to watch over Sidney Spivak lest he stray from the Lyon line on acute protracted restraint, would help me save the careers of the planning secretariat staff.

We set off on our rounds to see each of the seven or eight ministers whose deputies had signed the transfer memo to have them countersigned. We were an odd couple touring around the Legislative Building. For most of the ministerial signatures, the mere presence of Bill and the written proof that their deputy ministers had signed was enough. We had only one really hard sell.

A minister who shall remain nameless declined. His department had requested nearly twenty of the seventy-eight. My heart sank.

"Don't want any of them," he began. "I hear they are radicals, political communists and the like."

I was ready to make a reasoned case but Bill stopped me.

He replied to the minster in the most unparliamentarily language imaginable. I remember this minister owned a car dealership.

"These are people. They are not goddamned cars. You don't get to slam their doors and kick their tires." There was then a very specific and unprintable threat about some misdeed of the minister's that obviously he and Bill knew about and I did not.

This moment was followed by Bill handing him a pen and the shaken minister signing the transfer request.

Lyon was not amused when I returned triumphant but trying not to show it.

"I don't know how you managed to hoodwink my entire cabinet," he began. "But a deal is a deal."

I suspected that he knew exactly the role Bill McCance had played and secretly respected that we had done everything in our power to save the employees their jobs. But this is mere speculation, to this day I don't actually know what he thought of it all.

He approved the transfers and seventy-eight employees found new homes in the departments. Some of them left over the first few months. Many stayed. A few went on to leadership roles over the next two decades in the government. At least one of them rose to the rank of deputy minister. Most served several governments with great commitment and ability.

And what was my reward for pulling off what I considered a major coup? The soccer team that I played for every weekend was comprised of political left-wingers. They met and unceremoniously kicked me off the team for what they took to be the treachery of collaborating with the Lyon government. While hurtful, my expulsion only strengthened my resolve to be a public servant. It also convinced me that in public service you had best keep your own scorecard and not be daunted by the reaction of others.

TASK FORCE ON GOVERNMENT ORGANIZATION AND ECONOMY

ONE OF LYON'S first steps in taking office was to appoint his chief rival, Sid Spivak, who he had ousted from the party leader's job, as a minister whose job it was to make the Manitoba government smaller and more efficient. He paired Spivak with a long-time, very successful Winnipeg businessman, Conrad S. Riley. You could not have found in Winnipeg two men with as many similarities—they were both successful businessmen, both wealthy, both conservative and yet there were so many differences. Riley was a pillar of the city's Protestant establishment. Spivak was a leader in the Jewish business community of Winnipeg.

In every aspect from the smallest detail to their broadest philosophy of life Riley and Spivak were opposites. Riley believed passionately in punctuality. He was never late for a meeting. Spivak took the proposed starting time of a meeting as a vague objective. He would appear half an hour late.

"My car didn't start."

Riley had a single automobile, a Jaguar if memory serves. It always started. He also had an airplane that he flew. It also started on command.

Spivak had several vehicles scattered about his long circular driveway. Sometime one of them started in the winter, sometimes none of them did.

Riley had a tidy moustache and a military precision to his speech. He believed in short sentences and a tone of command. Sidney Spivak never finished a single sentence in all the years I knew him. His mind raced on and his mouth struggled to keep up.

These were the two co-chairs of Lyon's task force.

The task force conducted its business through a series of working groups or committees established in policy areas such as education, health and Crown corporations. When it came time to select leaders to chair each of the working groups, each co-chair had his list. Riley went first:

"I propose Bob Jones the CEO of Investor's Group for the Crown corporations," he began.

The process moved on until they had a full list of proposed chairs and members for the various groups. They each agreed to phone those they had proposed to determine their willingness and ability to serve. We reconvened a few days later.

Riley went first. "Bob Jones—yes. Roger Murray yes…" In fact all of Riley's nominees confirmed except for Jack Ellis of Richardson's who had to ask his boss, George Richardson.

Then Spivak presented his list. These were not for the most part CEOs of large companies. Many were entrepreneurs. Several were out of the country and could not be reached. One man, Sidney noted, had agreed but had to ask his wife.

Riley drew himself up to an even more erect position than normal. Back stiff as a ramrod he said to Minister Spivak, "Sidney, none of mine had to ask their wives!"

Such were the differing world views of the two co-chairs.

I have often said and still believe three decades later that the task force gave the government of Manitoba some of the best and worst advice it could have received. Among the best advice was to separate the roles of chair and CEO at each of the Crown corporations. This policy when implemented recognized the inherent differences between these two jobs. It also meant that when the elected government of Manitoba changed the chair of a Crown Corporation, the CEO could provide managerial continuity.

The worst advice, not included in the final report, came from the working group examining education. The group chair demanded of the aging and well-respected deputy minister of education, "Dr. Lorimer why don't we just take the total education budget for the province and divide it by the number of students between Kindergarten and Grade 12 and send each student home with a bill for their parents to pay?"

Wes Lorimer, a staunch defender of public education, replied with barely contained fury, "If you do that, you and your kind will be voted out of office for the foreseeable future."

Both Sidney Spivak and Conrad Riley are gone now. It was my extraordinary experience to work with them in 1977 to 1978 in their capacity as the co-chairs of the Task Force on Government Organization and Economy.

MARVIN L. SALTZMAN—THE AUTHOR TOUR

AFTER THE CONCLUSION of the Task Force on Government Organization and Economy, I decided to try my hand at endeavours other than government. I worked several part-time jobs and I began writing and appearing on CBC Radio. One of those jobs was as a part-time role as publisher's representative, a fancy title for "book salesman" for the firm of Stanton and MacDougall. One of the duties of the publisher's representative was to arrange author tours for those visiting writers of books published by the many publishers we represented. I had successfully managed several author tours. Each consisted of a mix of media interviews and bookstore visits. They had all gone well. Author Marvin L. Saltzman was my Waterloo.

The day my best friend, Ron Bailey, saved my job began calmly enough. At dawn I felt organized. Although I did not allow smugness to embrace me, it was nearby. After all my plans for the author day were in place. Marvin L. Saltzman, author of the Eurail Guide to *How to Travel Europe and All the World by Train*, would be interviewed on CBC Morning Radio. Then he would visit the three key bookstores in Winnipeg and a second interview and then two smaller bookstores. It was the greatest number of events I had arranged in my several months as a publisher's representative for any visiting author. The missing feature of my planning—I had never met Marvin L. Saltzman.

Despite the luscious thickness of the corned beef, despite the delight of the tart kosher dill pickles, Marvin L. Saltzman remained impatient.

"What's next on the schedule?" he demanded.

I could not give a truthful answer. There existed no remaining schedule. Marvin L. had obliterated a full day schedule by covering it all in the morning. Every interview and every bookstore had already been done. My scheduler tank was empty.

"Just confirming a few appointments," I mumbled.

"Which ones?" Marvin L. demanded.

I turned my attention to my sandwich. My desperation mounted. Suddenly Ron Bailey appeared.

"Hi, Mike," my laid-back saviour began.

"Ron, great to see you—let me introduce, Mr. Marvin L. Saltzman,"

Marvin L. Saltzman, corned beef sandwich in his left hand extended his right hand to Ron. Fortunately, I thought, he lacked a free hand to whip the accursed book from its hiding place in his inner jacket pocket.

"Not THE Marvin L. Saltzman, author of the Eurail Guide." exclaimed Ron. With a broad smile, Marvin L. acknowledged the truth of his unmasking.

Ron continued, "Travelled Europe using your book. It helped us a great deal."

Ron took over. For nearly two hours, two glorious, lifesaving hours he kept Marvin L. occupied. Ron listened to his stories and prompted him with questions when he slowed his pace. I excused myself. From the back of Oscar's Delicatessen I called the remaining Winnipeg bookstores. I pleaded and when that failed I begged. Enough booksellers allowed that a visit, although unnecessary, would not be unwelcome.

At 5:00 p.m. I put Marvin L. on the train at Winnipeg's station to his next destination. I said a silent prayer for the person who would have him the next day. Then I went home to pour myself a large tumbler of scotch. I also decided that being a publisher's representative was not my dream job. I began considering a return to government.

STANLEY KNOWLES DINNER

I HAVE NEVER been a great fundraiser but that has not stopped various people from asking me to raise funds for worthy causes and it has not stopped me from agreeing. John Mallea was a very persuasive president of Brandon University and wanted to have an endowed Stanley Knowles Chair at the university. Stanley had served as chancellor for many years.

I said "yes" to raise one million dollars for this because I believed Knowles, as an honourable man, deserved the recognition. It was a fool's errand. The people who loved Stanley Knowles were not the "big donors." They were of modest means. It took an enormous effort and many years to raise the necessary endowment but it did get done with help from some unlikely places.

When I met with Jim Burns who was then running Power Financial Corporation, owner of two of Manitoba's largest corporations, his answer was blunt. "Stanley Knowles is a socialist and we are not honouring him with a donation." Then he paused and continued; "Now if you were to hold a big dinner in his honour, we could buy some tables. Then you could find some people, maybe senior citizens who really like Mr. Knowles, to fill those tables so we would not have to come."

That is exactly what we did. The talented Sharon Vance, an excellent organizer, pulled together a Stanley Knowles tribute dinner in Ottawa. The night arrived and we were overwhelmed by the positive response. The room was filled with the legends of Canadian politics and ordinary Canadians. Paul Martin Senior, Paul Hellyer, Ed Broadbent, Dick Martin and many others attended. All came to pay tribute to a man who had laboured so long and hard for justice and to build a decent retirement system for all Canadians.

A breathless young reporter for *Maclean's* asked me, "Why are there people who have led all three political parties here tonight?'

I replied, "Paul Hellyer is here. He ran for the leadership of three political parties all by himself."

The speakers and head table notables assembled in the green room before the dinner began. Stanley was tired and lay down on a long couch to gather his strength for the evening.

George Hees, aging Tory front bencher with his mane of grey hair and handsome face, arrived in the room. He spied Stanley and knelt down on the floor beside the couch where he lay resting.

Hees began, "Stanley, none of us are here because we have to be here. We are all here because we want to be here." He paused and then he added, "We all love you."

We all heard his words and there wasn't a dry eye in the room.

If I had not heard the words I would not have believed that they had been spoken. It was an act of love and generosity. It showed for an instant that beneath the indignation of question period that a brotherhood exists in Parliament that transcends party and politics. It was a magnificent moment.

Michael Decter, Clerk of Executive Council, right, with Farley Mowat and the Honourable Alvin H. (Al) Mackling, Minister of Natural Resources

Michael Decter in front of Taj Mahal Agra, India, 1984 with members of Manitoba delegation to India

Michael Decter receiving Order of Canada from Governor General Adrienne Clarkson in Ottawa, 2004

First Ministers Meeting, Ottawa, 1983
(front—left to right) Elijah Harper (M.L.A.), Honourable Howard Pawley
(behind—left to right) Honourable Jay Cowan (Minister of Northern Affairs),
Honourable Roland Penner (Attorney General), Michael Decter

Michael Decter on the Great Wall
of China, 1984

Michael Decter with President Bill Clinton,
Toronto, 2001

First Ministers Meeting, Ottawa, 1983
Honourable Jay Cowan, Michael Decter, Honourable Howard Pawley

Honourable Frances Lankin (Ontario Minister of Health) and Michael Decter
(Deputy Minister of Health)

Receiving Conference Board Governance Award, Toronto, 2003

Michael Decter, Chair Board of Directors Canadian Institute for Health Information (CIHI) and Richard Alavarez, CEO of CIHI

Ed Broadbent with all those who served as his Executive Assistant/Chief of Staff during his time as Leader of the Federal New Democratic Party

(left to right) Tony Pennikett, Bill Knight, George Nakitsas, Norm Simon, Ed Broadbent, Michael Decter, Murray Weppler, Jim Haynes and Dick Proctor

(left to right) Michael Decter, Jim Dinning (DM Integrated Government of Alberta), Norman Spector (DM Integrated Government of British Columbia)

(left to right) Michael Decter, her Majesty the Queen, Hon. Jake Epp, Premier Howard Pawley

MICHAEL DECTER:
Our token president can frequently be seen slushing down the slopes at Agassiz with a bevy of ski-bunnies in hot persuit. Our world traveller is reknown for his imported "Rossignol Strattos" skis and his Dad's 13 second Charger with which he holds the Kenora to Wpg. record. Next year it's on to Harvard and all those beautiful American women and watered down Yankee beer.

Kelvin High School yearbook, 1970

Skiing at Sunshine Village

(front—left to right) Premier Howard Pawley, Honourable Elijah Harper, Lieutenant-Governor of Manitoba Pearl McGonigal

(background—left to right) Honourable Judy Wasylycia-Leis, Honourable Leonard Harapiak, Honourable Gary Doer, Michael Decter (Clerk of Executive Council)

(standing—left to right) Algis Baronas (Secretary), David Henderson, Drew Cringan

(sitting—left to right) Peter Diamant (Alternate Member), J. Cliff MacKay (Chairman), Nick W. Diakiw, Michael Decter

CHAPTER SEVEN

MANITOBA– THE PAWLEY GOVERNMENT

I RETURNED TO the Manitoba government in December of 1981. My appointment as clerk of the executive council and secretary to the cabinet came at the tender age of twenty-nine. It was the same year Lucille and I married. I lost my father to heart disease a year later. Our son Riel was born the next year. It was a time of great emotion personally. Professionally, it was also a very heady time.

Lucille would later say of that period, "You jumped out of bed every morning at 6:00 a.m.. You were thrilled with your job—you just loved it."

And I did. I loved it despite the long hours, difficult challenges and the many setbacks.

MR. BEDSON II

THE PROCESS OF MY REPLACING Mr. Bedson was one over which I did not exercise a great deal of control. In 1981, Mr. Bedson was in his early sixties. He had survived transitions from Premiers Roblin to Weir, from Weir to Schreyer, and from Schreyer to Lyon. In both the Schreyer and Lyon eras, his power as clerk was considerably less than during the Roblin government. It was probably only the transition of power from the Conservatives to the NDP in 1969 which had seriously threatened him. However, in 1981, Howard Pawley was elected premier and he was determined to remove Mr. Bedson. Bedson was approached by Saul Cherniak, who was serving as one of the co-chairs of the transition committee and who had been a distinguished MLA, minister of finance and a major player in the Schreyer government. To Cherniak's surprise, Mr. Bedson would not hear the news from him; he wanted to hear it from me. It was also clear that he approved of my selection as his successor despite my relative youth. Mr. Bedson had faced the same hurdle as he was thirty-eight years old when he was appointed by Premier Roblin. In those days, he had been the youngest deputy and in my day, I was the youngest.

I telephoned and arranged to meet with Mr. Bedson who insisted that he would host me for lunch at the Squash Club, his club. I would be extremely surprised if Mr. Bedson had ever played a game of squash in his life. I felt awkward that I would present the news to Mr. Bedson that he was losing his job of twenty-three years at a lunch hosted by him. Nevertheless, that's the way he wanted it, and I would do my best to oblige.

The lunch might have gone off with some grace had not former Premier Lyon's press secretary wandered into the Squash Club just as we were sitting down. He stormed over to the table and proceeded, in a loud tirade, to denounce the Pawley government in very crude terms. His main complaint was the inevitable loss of his job as press secretary to a now defeated premier. Mr. Bedson was physically uncomfortable and unable to get a word in. Finally, he grabbed this fellow's arm, dragged him over to my side of the table and sort of thrust him at me, saying "I want you to meet Michael Decter. He will be taking my position in the government as clerk of the executive council." The unfortunate fellow mumbled a few words of regret and fled.

Our task then turned to what Mr. Bedson might do next. He expressed a strong desire to get back into the federal public service if only for a day. The federal public service has a far more generous pension than does the

Manitoba civil service. Mr. Bedson had served federally for thirteen years with external affairs and twenty-three years in Manitoba, entitling him to the maximum pension in either place. The federal pension had some better features. However, to receive the better federal pension, he needed to get back on the federal payroll, if only for an hour, so that he could retire on it. I undertook to see what could be done since it seemed to be a relatively modest request. Although new at the game, I had already done a small amount of business with Michael Kirby who was secretary to the federal cabinet for federal-provincial relations. I presumed, in the spirit of looking after old warriors, who one day Kirby and I might well be, that this kind of request was the sort of thing that could be accommodated.

I called Kirby after the lunch and he was very positive. He seemed to share my sentiments and he felt that if Mr. Bedson wanted to join the privy council office, perhaps even to undertake a bit of work for them prior to his retirement, then we should make it happen. At that time, neither Michael Kirby nor I knew that during the brief interregnum of the Joe Clark government, which had intruded so rudely, in the view of Liberals, into what they would call "the Trudeau Era," the Conservative Party had asked Mr. Bedson for advice on a number of things, but in particular, on Michael Pitfield who had been appointed clerk of the privy council federally by Pierre Elliot Trudeau in his first term as prime minister. Mr. Bedson replied in writing, which was probably a serious mistake. More ominously for our cause, that letter urging Joe Clark to get rid of that scoundrel, Pitfield, at the earliest opportunity had been placed, not on the PCO file where it would have been nicely sealed in the archives of the Clark government for twenty or thirty years, but in a file where the returning Trudeau and Pitfield were apt to find it. No doubt, someone wanted Michael Pitfield to find the letter and to know where he stood with this Mr. Bedson. I had a difficult call back from Kirby saying that what I had taken to be a minor piece of business was not likely to be easy to do. In fact, he reported Pitfield as saying that so long as he was clerk of the privy council, Mr. Bedson would not draw one penny of pay from the federal treasury. Since the object was not to have Mr. Bedson draw pay but rather pension, I wondered if we could skate it on those grounds. But this was not to be.

I lunched again with a somewhat subdued Mr. Bedson to report this setback. His suggestion was that Pawley and I take up the matter with Prime Minister Trudeau with whom he had worked in the late 1940s and early 1950s in Ottawa. This seemed to me to be an excellent idea. Surely

Trudeau could overrule Pitfield's vindictiveness on this issue. At least it was a chance worth taking. Pawley and I were scheduled to lunch with the prime minister so I phoned Kirby to say that if we could not reach some accommodation on this, I would ruin lunch by raising this subject, perhaps putting Kirby in the position of being caught between his political and his bureaucratic bosses. Kirby agreed to do whatever he could to avoid having me raise the subject and ruin what might otherwise be a productive intergovernmental lunch.

Mr. Bedson, meanwhile, had been hard at work with Bernard Ostry who was then deputy minister of industry in Ontario. Without revealing all of the details, the deal concocted by his co-conspirators eventually worked like this. Mr. Bedson would be hired by the privy council office with the authority of Michael Kirby. He would be transferred through the government's executive interchange program to the ministry of industry in Ontario by way of an agreement between Deputy Minister Ostry and Kirby. (This would fill Michael Pitfield's criteria since this transaction would happen so quickly, Mr. Bedson would not draw one cent of pay from the federal government.) Ostry would then second Mr. Bedson to the Ontario department of intergovernmental affairs which would post him to be the number two in their Brussels office. I considered this a masterpiece of negotiation, albeit that much of the negotiation had been undertaken by Mr. Bedson himself with Ostry and Kirby. Nevertheless, I was delighted.

At about that time, the provincial Conservatives lead by Grant Devine won a surprising election victory in Saskatchewan. Late one night the phone rang. Mr. Bedson, said Lucille, was in Toronto, changing planes for Regina not Brussels. I knew what that meant at once. All the clever negotiations had been for naught. Mr. Bedson was committing an act which I considered bureaucratic hari-kari. Mr. Bedson had deep roots in Manitoba and he knew the province in all its variety. Winnipeg was a city cosmopolitan enough that Mr. Bedson's strong views on many subjects were viewed as just that—Mr. Bedson's views on the subject. Saskatchewan, however, was a smaller place. He went anyway, becoming clerk of the executive council and deputy minister to the premier in Saskatchewan.

It never really worked out. Saskatchewan did not have the same traditions as Manitoba. Mr. Bedson's Manitoba history did not help him in Saskatchewan. He simply didn't know the territory. He was eventually done in over an incident in the legislature about which he thought only the premier and he could know the exact truth. The premier was in estimates when the opposition leader and former premier, Allan Blakeney, demanded to know if those working in the premier's office, including Mr. Bedson, had all received large raises recently. The premier bent over to Mr. Bedson and then straightened up and denied that such raises had been granted. At that moment, Blakeney tabled an Order in Council, the legal document approving the raises and signed by the premier. In the brouhaha that followed, Mr. Bedson went home and, in essence, took the rap for the premier's inadvertent or deliberate denial of events. As a consequence, Mr. Bedson made Europe after all, posted to Vienna as a representative of Saskatchewan Agricultural Development Corporation for two years.

This ended the saga of his Saskatchewan experience but not our friendship. When he returned to Winnipeg, we had dinner from time to time. He worked briefly for the Official Language Commissioner's Office before retiring. His untimely passing in 1989 was a time of great sadness for me.

I have a vivid memory of Mr. Bedson sitting in our living room at one end of a long knee-level coffee table. He was entertaining us with stories of Vienna when my son, Riel, then three years old, pushed a small tray of hors d'oeuvres very hard in Mr. Bedson's direction. Lucille and I watched in horror as the tray skidded along the table towards Mr. Bedson's lap. Neither of us was close enough or quick enough to stop this oyster and olive-laden missile from reaching its target. As the tray reached Mr. Bedson's lap, he simply parted his knees and caught the tray. Restoring the dish to the table with nary the loss of a single olive or oyster, Mr. Bedson continued his story without comment.

The antics of small children and of cabinet ministers, while different, led those having to deal with them to develop serenity amidst crisis. As Sir Humphrey Appleby remarked in the *Yes Minister* series on the BBC, "Ministers love to panic; it is their substitute for achievement." A little harsh, perhaps, but in Mr. Bedson's role (later my own) the olive and oyster trays were called cabinet submissions and they required careful handling.

I still have some correspondence from Mr. Bedson dating from when I was working on the Pictou Centre campaign in Nova Scotia. He wrote me and admonished me to remember him to Alexa McDonough, then the leader of the NDP, but not to her Grit brother, Robby Shaw. Throughout his life, it was the liberals more than the socialists who bothered Mr. Bedson.

Another reason for considering Mr. Bedson's death as unjustly premature was his deep affection for the career of Konrad Adenauer, particularly when the subject of retirement was raised.

"Michael," he would to say to me from time to time, "Konrad Adenauer sat in the library until he was seventy-two years old, when he became chancellor of Germany, and he was dragged kicking and screaming from office when he was eighty-nine years of age." Back in the day, I never checked Mr. Bedson's facts. I did know that Konrad Adenauer was chancellor of West Germany. Until Mr. Bedson's death, I always harboured a belief that Mr. Bedson would be back. That he had yet another career to go. Sadly, such was not to be. He did not live to enjoy a second career or any of the federal government pension which had required such collective ingenuity.

And Mr. Bedson was not far off the mark on the German chancellor. Adenauer began serving at age seventy-three and remarkably he left office as chancellor at age eighty-seven.

LUNCH WITH TRUDEAU

DURING MY TIME with the Manitoba government, Premier Pawley and I were invited to lunch at 24 Sussex Drive by Prime Minister Trudeau on two occasions. Both were fascinating experiences.

Our first lunch occurred immediately after Pawley was elected as premier of Manitoba in December of 1981. Pawley had asked me to give up my private consulting business and return to government as clerk of the executive council. In Manitoba, that title implied three or four jobs that in other larger jurisdictions were divided. As Manitoba clerk of executive council, I had responsibility as cabinet secretary. Also the premier was minister of what we plainly called "Manitoba Dominion-Provincial Relations" (which most other governments called intergovernmental affairs or federal-provincial relations). As the senior official for dominion-provincial relations, I accompanied the premier to lunch with the prime minister.

Premier Howard Pawley and I did not know each other very well. We had both worked in the Schreyer government but not as colleagues. His responsibilities were as minister of municipal affairs and minister responsible for the Auto Insurance Corporation while mine were as policy analyst and economist in the cabinet planning secretariat. Towards the end of the Schreyer government, in fact, right at its end, I was appointed as acting planning secretary to cabinet when my boss quit to be a candidate in the 1977 election. The Schreyer government was defeated and I was left to explain to Premier-elect Lyon, who did not believe in central planning, just who we all were. Somewhere along the line, Pawley must have been favourably influenced. I know that several on the transition committee were also keen to have me back.

The morning after Pawley's election victory, I happened to be at the Legislative Building retrieving some policy documents when a call came through from the prime minister's office. This was a delicate period in Canada's constitutional history. The government was about to introduce into the House of Commons the Constitutional Act of 1981 to formally repatriate the constitution. However, the outgoing government of Manitoba, in the person of Attorney General Gerry Mercier, had refused to agree to a provision pertaining to French-language minority education rights in Manitoba. As a consequence, as it was explained to me, the government of Canada might be compelled to bring two bills forward in the Commons, one pertaining to the country as a whole and one pertaining to Manitoba. What was being sought was the agreement of Manitoba that removed its reservation on this issue. Ottawa wanted Manitoba to support the minority French-language education provisions of the Constitution Act as proposed.

When I took the telephone call from Ted Johnson, Trudeau's executive assistant, I had no official position with the Manitoba government. I had not yet been asked to join the government as there was, in fact, no new government—it would be sworn in a week later. However, I was aware of the issue and the position of the Premier-elect Pawley and his colleagues. I had been involved in giving some policy advice during the campaign

As well, Lucille, as executive director of the Société Franco-Manitobaine, was keenly aware of the government's and opposition's positions on things which pertained to the rights of the French minority. During the election campaign, Pawley had put out a press release endorsing the constitutional protection of minority education rights. This press release, while it received little or no coverage, did represent the official position of the New Democratic Party.

I agreed to speak with someone involved in the constitutional process. A few minutes later, Michael Kirby, then secretary to the federal cabinet for federal-provincial relations called me back to discuss the situation. He explained the urgency. Kirby was very direct, candid and businesslike. My response was that the government of Canada was on good ground in presuming a change in provincial direction.

I also noted to Kirby that in return for this Manitoba would expect some significant consideration in the future. Kirby's reply was very much in the spirit of "let's make a deal." Little did I know how soon I would be involved in making that deal.

I learned later that as a result of our conversation, the government of Canada proceeded on the basis that the government of Manitoba would agree to constitutional change. This proved to be my first small effort in constitutional affairs. It was quite heady stuff when you consider that at that moment I was an official of no government and really had no formal authority to do anything. I explained the situation later that day to Premier-elect Pawley as we drove up to Hecla Island where the premier could plan his government. We did not dwell on the constitutional issue as the premier's mind was on other more pressing matters such as the selection of his new cabinet.

A few weeks later, with the government sworn in and a set of issues identified as provincial matters, Pawley and I got on a morning plane to fly to Ottawa where, at the prime minister's invitation, we would have lunch. It was to be a small group. Prime Minister Trudeau, Premier Pawley, Michael Kirby and me. The briefing book illuminated several broad issues on which the government of Manitoba was to make itself heard and also some specific financial issues. Pawley and I reviewed the issues which included assistance to modernize a Crown-owned forestry complex at The Pas; a return to fifty-fifty financing for Medicare; a specific transitional formula that the federal government had proposed and others. I realized that this would be a fairly difficult meeting.

Manitoba's new NDP government believed in practising modesty, so we took a cab to the prime minister's residence. No limousines for us. We were in the back of a ratty cab going to 24 Sussex. Premier Pawley turned to me and said "Michael, do you ever watch those detective shows on TV, those police shows?" I thought this was an odd question to ask en route to lunch with the prime minister but I said yes, I did occasionally watch television police shows. Pawley said "You know how they always have one good cop, one bad cop, you know, one nice cop, one tough cop." At this moment, a slow painful awakening was coming upon me. The premier concluded by saying "You know I'm really a very nice guy, so when we're having lunch, I'd like you to be the bad guy."

I thought Oh God, the premier who's just entrusted me with the top job in the public service wants me to tough cop none other than Pierre Elliot Trudeau, not only that, he wants me to do it, in his own house, at lunch.

My mission was to beat up on Pierre Elliot Trudeau, easily the most intellectually formidable prime minister in my lifetime and perhaps in the country's history. "Oh well," as Pawley said, "You wanted this job." Did I really want this job, I wondered.

I nodded grimly, and begin to think what an unpleasant lunch this historic occasion was going to turn out to be. While I was still lost in thought, the cab deposited us at the foot of the driveway of 24 Sussex.

The first inkling that this meeting might go awry was when the RCMP officer asked "Who are you and what are you doing here?" I said grandly, "He's the premier of Manitoba and we're here for lunch." thinking that this would have us promptly escorted up the driveway. The RCMP guy said "He's not the premier of Manitoba. I know the premier of Manitoba and he's a shorter guy, not tall like him." I explained that Premier Pawley in fact defeated the short guy and he was now the tall, thin premier of Manitoba. This alarmed Pawley, and did not placate the RCMP officer who presumably was just doing his job and didn't have the new pictures yet. The deal reached by me and the RCMP officer was that we would proceed up the driveway, ring the doorbell. One of two things would happen: We would be allowed in, proving that Pawley was in fact premier of Manitoba or we would not be allowed in, in which case, I would say to him grandly, you can shoot us right then and there.

The premier was a little alarmed by this thinking. Fortunately it was Michael Kirby who came to the door and ushered us in.

So there we were, swept into 24 Sussex, ushered into the living room by Kirby. We were admiring the magnificent room and view and pictures of Trudeau's kids on the table, when the prime minister bounced into the room. Pawley at this point was in his early fifties; I was twenty-nine. Trudeau was one of Canada's longest-serving prime ministers and was at the height of his power, having just succeeded in creating a Charter of Rights and bringing our constitution fully home from Britain. He was smaller than you would expect, well under six feet but filled with intensity and energy. He bounded into the room and asked with a mischievous grin "Which one of you is the premier of Manitoba?"

Now on the way to Ottawa, Premier Pawley had assured me that he and Trudeau knew each other from attending several meetings together when Trudeau was the federal minister of justice and he was Manitoba's attorney general. So he was completely taken aback at this non-recognition which really compounded the slight of the RCMP officer. He blurted out "I'm the premier!" to an amused Trudeau who replied "I knew that, Premier Pawley, I was just joking."

Pawley stepped forward and shook Trudeau's hand and they began, almost instantly, to discuss the fate of Sidney Green in the recent election. Green had been an extremely dynamic minister under Schreyer, a rival for the leadership, and eventually a renegade who left the NDP and set up a party of his own. Neither Trudeau nor Pawley liked Green. In fact, I think they were both somewhat afraid of the force of Green's personality and his extraordinary ability as a debater. Trudeau seemed relieved to learn that Green's attempt to win a seat under the banner of his new party had failed and that his party had been relegated to footnote status.

Michael Kirby was there and we chatted. Kirby indicated the similarity of the position I now found myself in and the role he had undertaken for Premier Gerry Regan a decade earlier in Nova Scotia. At a very young age, Kirby had had responsibilities on behalf of the newly- elected Regan government. I found Kirby sympathetic, direct and to the point, but I still dreaded what lay ahead.

Glasses of wine appeared and we were seated, the four of us, at a little table in the dining room. After a minimum of small talk, Trudeau pushed a little button on the table and a waiter appeared with soup. It was a perfectly dreadful soup and in the middle of it, Premier Pawley decided it was time for the first issue. He said, "You know, Prime Minister, I campaigned on the return to fifty-fifty funding for Medicare. I know your government chose to discontinue this in the 1970s but I believe it's an urgent national priority to return to fifty-fifty funding." I jumped in and made great mention of the premier's majority and the mandate he had from the people of Manitoba. He had a big Manitoba majority—i.e. three seats. Trudeau ate his soup, and when the two of us were finished, slammed his open hands on the table so hard that the entire cutlery jumped in the air. "Never!" he said. I glanced at Pawley and he lifted his eyebrows as if to say move on. I realized that this seemed to close the Medicare issue.

We dug in next on MANFOR for which the federal government had refused our request for $35 million of upgrading financing. The federal government had provided financing for the modernization of nearly every pulp and paper mill in Canada. The only difference with MANFOR was that it lost even more money than the rest of the industry and it was owned by the government of Manitoba. Public ownership seemed to be the major obstacle to funding. I raised the point that MANFOR was probably the largest employer of First Nations people in northern Manitoba, if not Canada. The point, I later learned, was probably a bit of an over-statement but it seemed to mollify the prime minister a little bit. However, it became quickly clear that the prime minister was not going to be sub-jected to an item by item interrogation or negotiation.

Trudeau sized the situation up and said to Premier Pawley, "Premier, surely we, as First Ministers, must discuss the important issues of jus-tice, the constitution and our nation." Pawley could do nothing but nod. Trudeau then turned back and said to Kirby and me, "Why don't the two Michaels go and eat their lunch on the porch and figure out all these mun-dane issues to do with money…" The way he said it made us sound like we were a couple of hardware merchants engaged in the selling of screws and bolts. It was not the first time I had seen sensible politicians were just as happy to let their officials, their Sherpas, find the common ground.

Kirby and I went out onto the balcony. Overlooking the Ottawa River in this magnificent setting, we negotiated some significant tradeoffs. It was decided that the government of Canada would look favourably on the transitional arrangement for equalization. The single provision, cooked up by our cunning lads in the Manitoba department of finance, Jim Eldridge and Pat Gannon, would yield Manitoba the better part of $500 million in additional federal assistance, although we did not know it or expect it at the time. We also received an assurance of assistance for MANFOR and I believe that in the end we got more than $25 million.

When Kirby and I returned from the balcony to report what we would recommend to the prime minister, we did not even get the chance. Trudeau turned to Pawley and said, "Well, if the two Michaels agree, I guess that's good enough for me." Premier Pawley was, I am sure, ap-palled at the notion that he would be bound by what had been discussed by two officials on the porch, but given the majesty of the prime ministe-rial imperative, he agreed.

So we finished lunch and left 24 Sussex in a waiting taxicab, with Premier Pawley fully unaware of the detail of what we had agreed to on behalf of the province. I thought this was not a problem as I would brief him in the cab and on the plane and by the time we had reached Winnipeg he would be as pleased as I with the progress made. What I hadn't counted on was that seated in the backseat of the waiting cab was a gentleman who turned out to be a reporter for the *Winnipeg Free Press* put there by the premier's office so he could interview him on the way to the airport.

I sat in the front seat with the premier in the back and the world's strangest interview began. An interview in which Premier Pawley was expected to tell the reporter what had been achieved at lunch with the small problem was that he had no idea what had been achieved at lunch. So we conducted an elaborate and ultimately successful interview which the premier would raise an item, and then I would jump in and say to the reporter, "The Premier was on him like a tiger. He fought for every nickel for that forestry complex. I believe we'll be getting our money." This proceeded all the way to the airport to the eventual high entertainment of the premier who found it sort of fun to put me in the line of fire with the reporter by saying "Well, how do you think we did on such and such, Michael?" I would then either have to skate for the boards or proclaim victory. By the time we reached the airport, the premier was vindicated as a champion of Manitoba and we went home feeling quite good about ourselves.

My assessment after that first meeting was that the prime minister was just as formidable as his reputation had promised and that Michael Kirby, although not a favourite with the other intergovernmental types over the constitutional issue, was someone who could be counted on in the "let's make a deal" sense to solve provincial issues. He had been very fair to Manitoba. In return, the prime minister had secured Premier Pawley's support on a range of constitutional issues including the Aboriginal constitutional process to unfold as a result of agreements on patriation and the Charter of Rights and Freedoms.

FIRST MINISTERS' MEETING

ABOUT SIX WEEKS LATER, we returned to Ottawa for the very unfriendly and discouraging First Ministers conference of 1982. The economy had taken a sharp negative turn, provinces were all eager for money from Ottawa and Trudeau was in a feisty, somewhat anti-provincial mood. Premier Pawley went off to 24 Sussex for an official dinner. It was a First Ministers-only dinner with no officials. Pawley expected to have a friendly time of it based on his successful earlier lunch with Trudeau. This was not to be the case. Trudeau was at odds with the premiers. He finally concluded the dinner by saying to them, "I have money. Why should I give it to you? You all hate me."

By his own account, Pawley stuck his hand up and said, "But I don't hate you." To which Trudeau replied, "You will soon." Pawley was skeptical that he would come to dislike the prime minister.

However, it was not long in coming. Later at that same dinner, Premier Pawley proposed a grand scheme for public housing that he felt would aid the nation. He was wounded and angered when Trudeau dismissed his proposal with the wave of his hand and said "Come, come now Premier Pawley, we're not here to build the socialist millennium."

In fact, Premier Pawley was there to build the socialist millennium and thought that Trudeau remained a socialist in liberal's clothing and was quite hurt by the exchange. There was a genuine prophecy in Trudeau's words that he would be driven to hate him, as most premiers did. Pawley, a gentle soul, chose not to hate Trudeau, only to strongly dislike him.

HOW WELL DO YOU COPE WITH FAILURE?

ONE OF THE EARLY CHALLENGES I faced as clerk was the aging leadership in the Manitoba civil service. Over the first few years of the Pawley government, a significant number of deputy ministers would reach retirement age.

The real issue was how to recruit new talent without falling in the trap of either politicizing the civil service or being wrongly accused of politicizing the civil service. After the polarized transition from Schreyer to Lyon, I sought another path.

Two steps proved invaluable. The most important of the steps was recruiting Ted Poyser to serve as chair of the Civil Service Commission. I had known Poyser when I began my career but had never worked directly for him. I respected him and knew that my respect was widely shared not only among civil servants but among politicians on all sides of the legislature. Ted was the quintessential public servant who cared deeply about advancing progress but hid it well. He had retired a few years earlier.

The next step was to advertise for deputy ministers as part of an open process. That had never been done before. It was a signal that we were not simply going to promote from within but we were eager to bring new talent to the Manitoba civil service at senior levels.

Paul Hart, who ran the Manitoba Civil Service Commission, Ted Poyser and I comprised the interview panel that recommended deputy minister appointments to the premier. In one of our very first interviews, we had a young and very energetic candidate before us. We took turns asking questions. Many were standard issues such as "How does your career and background equip you for this position?"

Then Ted asked, "How well do you cope with failure?"

I was taken aback. So was the applicant.

He declared, "I have never failed at anything in my life."

Later, nervous that he had not done well on his answer, the applicant asked Ted, "Did I get that right?"

Ted replied blandly, "There are no right answers, there are just answers."

After the applicant had left and Poyser and I were alone, I asked my own question of him. "Tell me why the question about coping with failure is important?"

"Public service is all about failure. The real question is how well do you cope with it." At the time, I was puzzled. It would be a decade later when I experienced my first major setback that Ted Poyser's words came back to me.

For interview purposes, it became our single most valuable question to separate the brash and ambitious from the calm and mature. What we were seeking were calm, mature individuals who could cope with failure and not be defeated by it.

FARLEY MOWAT II

FARLEY MOWAT CONTINUED to tour Canada making speeches saying he had been a dollar-a-year man to the Manitoba government and that the province was so cheap that it never paid him his dollar a year. Other than being mildly annoyed, there wasn't much I could do about this assault on our provincial honour until 1981, when I went back into government as cabinet secretary. Only then could I take action to silence the loquacious Mowat. Among the perks of my office, if one could describe it as that, was the chairmanship of an obscure cabinet committee, distinguished because it had in fact no actual cabinet ministers on it. It had the bland, innocent name, the Hospitality Committee of Cabinet.

This obscure committee had to approve all hospitality grants, grants for visiting conventions of elks, women of the moose and other fraternal orders. We had a modest budget and we also presided over Manitoba's prestigious Order of the Buffalo Hunt. This honour had been given randomly to curling teams and visiting dignitaries over the years. It struck me that in one fell swoop I could regain Manitoba's pride and do something nice. I conspired with the wonderful Rita Kurtz, the publisher's rep who toured Farley when he would be coming to Manitoba next.

I prevailed upon the premier, who heard me out on the story of Manitoba's honour being tarnished by Mowat's rather repetitive assertion that he was owed a dollar that he never saw. The premier of Manitoba invited Farley Mowat for a very special ceremony at which we presented him two items: a framed one dollar bill and recognition of his services to the province. And we created a new category of the Order of the Buffalo Hunt entitled Preserver of the Species in honour of Mowat's tireless work not only to save the whales of Churchill but also many other species. I think Farley was as delighted at the buck as by being named as the first Preserver of the Species, Manitoba Order of the Buffalo Hunt— an odd combination when you consider that we pretty much wiped out the buffalo on the Canadian Prairies. But I'm sure Mowat will have a book about that someday as well.

Farley and I remained friends although I don't see him as often as I would like. Many years later, I had the opportunity to find his old Manitoba manuscripts, wonderful ideas that he typed out on his Underwood typewriter. I felt the right course was to return them to him. He was reading at Harbourfront in Toronto some thirty years after he had typed these manuscripts. A mutual friend, his publisher Anna Porter, tried to introduce me to Farley back stage at the event. Farley turned— we hadn't seen each other in a decade—threw his arms around me and gave me a big kiss and said "Anna, you don't need to introduce me to my friend, Michael." This allowed me the perfect occasion to return the manuscripts to him and to tell a somewhat surprised Anna Porter that Farley was in fact the only living Preserver of the Species, Manitoba Order of the Buffalo Hunt.

PRINCESS ANNE

MY FIRST ACQUAINTANCE with British monarchy, a close encounter of the direct kind, came shortly after the election of the Pawley government in 1981. The clerk of executive council was expected to be the senior official of the government with regard to protocol matters. My predecessor, Derek Bedson, had been deeply involved in these matters but was little help to me when I sought his counsel. He stressed that everything must be done properly but gave no hint as to what "everything" was or what "properly" might mean. He seemed to think that I, being in his view, of sound mind, would figure it out for myself. The only other advice

Mr. Bedson offered was, "At the dinners make certain you seat them boy-girl-boy-girl."

My greatest coup was to capture Kathleen Brown as a member of my staff. Kathleen had served for many years in the office of the lieutenant governor. There had been a change in lieutenant governors and the new one wanted a bilingual person in the office. This made unilingual Kathleen available and it was she who, along with others, saved me from certain disaster on two royal visits and one visit by His Holiness the Pope.

Our first royal visitor was Princess Anne. Princess Anne has suffered for many years from a nasty reputation with the press; they had characterized her as a bit of a shrew. Later I was to learn first-hand that which the press objected to in Princess Anne: she was a thoughtful human being. She did not fit the royal stereotype; hence, she was an enemy to be dealt with.

Her visit was only a three-day affair. Nevertheless, it presented three harrowing moments. Prior to the Princess's arrival, serious negotiations had been going on for some months around the fate of Winnipeg's horse racing track, Assiniboia Downs. The Downs, which had operated under family ownership for many years, had been sold a few years earlier to a Winnipeg entrepreneur with an unsavoury reputation for defaulting on nearly everything he laid his hand to. This individual, whom I will not name, was the owner of the racetrack at the time. He was demanding financial support from the government and threatened to close the track if it was not forthcoming. Unfortunately, we had scheduled a visit to the racetrack in the misguided belief that Princess Anne, as someone who raised horses herself, would enjoy watching the races. I later learned from the Princess that she though flat track racing was cruel to horses. Her view was that it had nothing to do with jumping, which was the aspect of the sport she preferred. However, none of this was known to me at the time.

The owner of the racetrack called the premier after midnight one night to say that unless he had a commitment of one million dollars from the government by noon he would shut down the track, forcing the cancellation of the Princess's visit that evening. A number of the cabinet ministers were wholly opposed to giving in to what they perceived as blackmail. Others felt that although the tactics were crude the cause was worthy and that the money should be invested. The battle in cabinet was raging on when it came time for the premier to depart for the airport to fetch the Princess and welcome her to the province. All of us, including the cabinet, the speaker of the House and other worthies were then to adjourn to a lunch with the Princess.

The premier arrived at lunch escorting the Princess. He was as yet unaware of the final decision his cabinet had rendered on the racetrack financing. I was seated at the same table as the premier and Princess. It was my first experience with just how efficient the intelligence-gathering apparatus around the Princess was. In the middle of lunch she turned to the premier and said, "I believe I won't be going to the racetrack this evening?" The premier, whom I had not yet been able to brief on the cabinet decision, looked at me quizzically and then said, "Well, Princess, I had to leave for the airport before the discussion ended. Perhaps Michael can explain to us the state of Assiniboia Downs." This was my first time actually speaking in front of royalty and I was a little nervous. I was also reluctant to put the issue in blunt terms. For this reason, I began a somewhat long-winded, convoluted discussion about how the particular entrepreneur had run into certain financial difficulties. The Princess smiled, cut me off and said, "He's gone bust, has he?" At the moment I knew that I would probably get along very well with this Princess.

It turned out the she already knew he had gone bust, how, I can't guess. She went on to privately give me the advice that when an event was cancelled it was dangerous to try and reschedule another one. I had a dozen staff at the moment trying to secure Rainbow Stage for the evening so that we could take the Princess there. Heeding her wise advice, we simply cancelled her appearance at the track, forgot about Rainbow Stage and substituted a small dinner with our respective staffs. Later I learned that long-time, elderly season ticket holders at Rainbow Stage would have been forced out of their seats to accommodate the Princess. It would have been a public relations disaster.

The second incident during that visit was brought about by the persistent, ambitious mayor of Selkirk, the premier's home town north of Winnipeg. This mayor insisted upon hosting an event during the royal visit. At first we opposed the suggestion but eventually relented, knowing that the premier would favour a visit by the Princess to his own riding. The premier and the mayor being rivals, the premier was not eager for the mayor to gain the upper hand in entertaining the Princess. However, it was agreed that the mayor could sponsor a lunch. The mayor arranged for the cruise ship the Lord Selkirk, to be tied up at the dock and for its facilities to be available for the lunch.

We decided that it would be best to let the mayor run the event without our help but we did take the precaution of sending two food inspectors from the department of health to check out what was to be served. I thought that we should at least try and spare the Princess and her party food poisoning as a memory of Manitoba. The two health inspectors arrived at about 11:00 (lunch was scheduled for noon) and discovered that the chef had been completely overwhelmed by the enormity of his responsibilities. To steady his hand in the frying of the fish, he had nipped into a bottle of sherry. In fact, he had nipped into it so often that there was nothing left of the bottle of sherry and little left of the chef who promptly passed out. The two health inspectors realized that this was an occasion which called for service above and beyond checking the food. Most of the fish had already burned on the grill by the time they arrived. However, when they got there, they managed to get the unconscious chef off the ship and then went back to the ship's galley, rolled up their sleeves, and proceeded to do their best to save the lunch. They succeeded to the degree that they were able to salvage enough fish for the head table. So the mayor of Selkirk, his royal guest, and their immediate party sat and ate while several hundred invited guests sat with nothing to eat and merely watched. No doubt this did the mayor's political career no good in Selkirk.

The third incident came on the last night of the visit. The final event on the Princess's schedule was dinner at the lieutenant governor's residence. The wily lieutenant governor had endeavoured to stack the guest list with her Liberal cronies; the premier had retaliated with a list of his own, and so, in the nature of all things in Manitoba, there was a reasonably broad representation from across the political spectrum.

The premier was scheduled to present a gift to the Princess. The gift, a statue in porcelain by a Winnipeg artist of Hiawatha or some such not very Canadian scene, was to have been shipped over to Government House earlier in the week after having been on display at the Legislative Building.

I arrived at the dinner with my wife Lucille. We were seated at a table with three other couples none of whom worked in government. All was going well. The cameras were being set up to broadcast the presentation when I had the first inkling of disaster. Kathleen Brown came over, tugged on my sleeve, and said, "Do you know where the gift is?" I assured her that, to the best of my knowledge, it had been shipped over to Government House earlier in the week. Kathleen, who, due to her dismissal, was not all that fond of the lieutenant governor, took this as a mandate to ransack the house. A search of almost every nook and cranny of the large mansion was carried out under Kathleen's direction but yielded no gift. As we were approaching the time when the premier was to rise to present the gift, Kathleen became extremely agitated. I too began to be very nervous about the missing Hiawatha.

We caucused in the kitchen. Obviously, the spectacle of the premier empty-handed on province-wide TV would be an "incident." My solution was to direct that a large box be stuffed with newspapers and gift-wrapped. I felt that the premier could present this gift-wrapped box with the explanation that the gift was packaged for shipping and the Princess would not need to open the package. In order for this plan to succeed, I needed to ensure that the Princess would not in fact open the package, exposing the premier to ridicule and myself to ruin.

I crept up on to the head table platform, kneeled behind the premier's chair, and explained to him that the gift had gone astray and that we were gift-wrapping an empty box that he would present. I spoke loudly enough so that the Princess could overhear and thus spare the premier the task of explaining under the circumstances. The Princess turned with a mischievous grin, "May I shake and rattle the box?" I replied that she could do anything with the box except open it on live province-wide television. This seemed to be an awkward but successful resolution of the dilemma.

As I returned to my place at the table, a vivid picture of the gift sitting on the credenza behind the premier's desk sprang into my mind. Since the lieutenant governor's house was on the grounds of the Legislative Building, I decided that I might just as well run over to the premier's office to see if in fact Hiawatha was there posed on the credenza. I stormed out the back door of Government House, right into a torrential thunderstorm. My tuxedo and I were soon soaked as I ran up the long steps and into the front door of the Legislative Building. When I had left Government House, the television lights were on and the speeches were beginning so it was clear that I had little time. The security guard recognized me and I blurted at him, "Run for the premier's office!" He ran. It was a mistake as he must have weighed 275 pounds and was obviously in wretched physical condition. As we got up the stairs to the first landing, he was purple in the face and I was certain he was going to expire on me. Worse still, he had attached to his belt a ring which must have contained two or three hundred keys and I would have been there all night trying to figure out which key opened the premier's office door. So we rested on the first landing, waiting until he regained his breath, and then pressed forward. He identified the key, we opened the door, and there, in all its porcelain glory, was Hiawatha.

Tucking the statue under my arm, I sprinted out the door, completely forgetting the thunderstorm outside. As I came down the front steps and hit the rain slicked second step, I began to lose my balance. In contrast to not finding the statue, the prospect of falling and perhaps breaking my leg or neck and destroying the Princess's gift all in one foolish gesture, caused me a moment of great anguish. As I began to seriously lose my balance on the steps, I realized that if I manoeuvred correctly I could land butt first on the hood of the minister of government services' new car. This was a car that he had fought for in direct contravention with the premier's policy that all ministers should buy compact K-cars. This was a full-sized Chevy and with great delight I landed square on the hood, putting a sizeable dent in the car, but doing myself little damage other than a bruised butt and preserving Hiawatha in the process.

Delighted in my achievement, I walked slowly and carefully the rest of the way. I arrived in time to slide up on the platform to hand the gift to the premier. He presented it and all was well. The Princess later in the evening caught up to me.

"Michael," she demanded, "Do you have a box for Hiawatha?"

"Don't push your luck," was all I could reply after the harrowing events of the evening.

The Princess laughed long and hard. I did tell her that we had arranged special shipping for Hiawatha back to Buckingham Palace. I said she should be grateful to have Hiawatha at all and that she should not badger me for special packaging. We both laughed. Today, somewhere in the bowels of Buckingham Palace, along with treasures of thousands of royal visits to hundreds of countries, sits Manitoba's contribution—the triumphant Hiawatha.

ECUM SECUM

I DON'T REALLY remember when I first met Mike Kirby.

Everyone around politics has phrases they use to convey their point of view. Over the years I came to recognize one of his most intriguing sayings. When Mike was convinced that something wasn't selling he would say, "If it isn't selling in Ecum Secum, it just isn't selling."

As it happened during the federal election of 1984, I was in Nova Scotia visiting my mother. Brian Mulroney and the Conservatives were leading in the polls. Driving north of Halifax I spotted a road sign with an arrow indicating the direction to the village of Ecum Secum. I was mildly astonished, as I had believed Kirby had made up the name. After all, national columnist Allan Fotheringham referred often to the mythical town in the province of his birth, Saskatchewan. The town was named Upper Duck's Ass which even I knew to be an invention.

Twenty minutes later my rental car was cruising down the Main Street of Ecum Secum. It was entirely lined, each and every dwelling, with a blue Conservative election sign.

I decided to stop at the drug store and purchase a postcard. I addressed the post card to Mike Kirby.

All I wrote on the post card was, "It ain't selling in Ecum Secum."

I signed it and put my name on it.

A few weeks later, Brian Mulroney won his majority government. About a month later, I got a letter from Mike Kirby. It began, "It wasn't selling in Ecum Secum or anywhere else..." Kirby went on to pen a very coherent and lucid analysis of the campaign and where the Liberals had gone wrong—in short a full Mike Kirby!

MAIN STREET PETE

PETE ADAM WAS APPOINTED by Howard Pawley to the cabinet in the municipal affairs portfolio. One of the election commitments in 1981 had been to a Main Street Manitoba program. The responsibility for implementing the program had been turned over to the Department of Municipal Affairs, a department which would be well-suited to the *Yes Minister* approach of government. That department believed that every program should be delivered by way of a per-capita grant. They spent months seeking to convince the minister that Main Street Manitoba should be yet another per capita grant to municipalities. The reality was that not every municipality needed or wanted access to a program that would give them support to fix up their Main Streets; therefore, a per capita grant made little sense. Week after week in the legislature, Pete Adam would be assailed by the opposition for the lack of activity on the Main Street Manitoba program. They eventually dubbed him "Main Street Pete." Finally, one day, in response to an opposition member summoning righteous indignation to demand when the Main Street Manitoba program would appear, the Honourable Pete Adam rose, adjusted his jacket and said very slowly, "The program will be announced when I am good and ready to announce it." His slow, measured tone dissolved the house and the bubble burst.

A more memorable Pete Adam story was conveyed to me one morning by the gruff and entertaining federal Minister of Agriculture Eugene Whelan. I was attending an early morning breakfast meeting with the western committee of federal cabinet in my capacity as deputy minister for intergovernmental affairs, a part of my role as secretary to cabinet. A number of provincial ministers arrived at the Westin Hotel in Winnipeg for the same meeting. I bumped into Minister Whelan in the lobby. I commented on the early hour—it was about 7:15 a.m.—this drew a crack from Whelan about how that guy, Pete Adam, gets up pretty early. The story, as it emerged, was that the previous week, Whelan, Adam and a Saskatchewan minister concluded the long saga of the renegotiation of the Co-Op Implements refinancing. They had agreed that they would meet the next morning at 9:00 to announce the deal. Upon arriving, Minister Whelan discovered that Pete Adam had been there half an hour ahead of him and stolen the show. *The Globe and Mail* "Report on Business" gave Pete Adam sole credit for the saving Co-Op Implements. This was not Whelan's idea of co-operative federalism.

Stories about the Manitoba legislature, however, pale in comparison to the best story I ever heard about a parliamentary debate. It was in British Columbia—a livelier legislature. It involved a female MLA who represented the puritanical wing of the Social Credit Party. Apparently, she had introduced a bill in the house to change the word "sex" wherever it appeared in provincial legislation to the word "bolt." Her Puritanism was such that the mere use of the word sex, no matter its connotation, was obviously offensive to her. She was speaking on her private member's bill in the legislature to the hoots and catcalls of the opposition. Many members of her own party also considered the bill preposterous and an embarrassment. As the din grew, the MLA became flustered and demanded that the speaker bring the assembly to order. This provoked ever further catcalls. Finally, completely frustrated, she stammered, "Mr. Speaker, Mr. Speaker, please take that thing of yours and bang it on the table!" No doubt she meant the gavel but the house dissolved into hysterical and continuous laughter. Her private member's bill was no more. This is a story I told one night at a dinner at writer Allan Fotheringham's house. I was severely chastised by an angry Dr. Foth. It turns out he had written the story several years before in one of his terrific books.

HER ROYAL MAJESTY

TWO YEARS LATER we had a full royal visit to contend with, not a mere Princess but Her Majesty the Queen. The visit was postponed once due to the Canadian federal election but in the fall of 1984 it finally happened. I had been able to convince my old friend Jo-Anne McNevin to take up the task of organizing the visit. With Jo-Anne on the case I knew there would be no slip-ups. She did well coping with the extremely efficient Buckingham Palace staff and the rather more numerous and less impressive staff assigned by Ottawa to the visit. My own role was to be the final person who could fall on his sword if things went awry but I was confident, so confident in fact, that I declined the offer of a military driver and car to take me to the airport. I thought this ostentatious and unnecessary. If I could drive myself everywhere in the normal course of events, surely I could drive myself to the airport to be part of the greeting party for her Majesty's arrival.

I should explain that one of the banes of my existence with the government was the assignment of government cars. While purportedly free, the cars were more often in the garage requiring some sort of repair rather than actually working. However, my Ford LTD had been a loyal performer, although occasionally the cruise control would stick and one would rocket through rural Manitoba for ten or fifteen minutes trying to figure out how to slow the car down. In any event, I thought the car was in good shape and therefore did not make any special plans to leave early for the airport. I left right on time and was driving at a good pace along Portage Avenue when the car simply died. It did not sputter, it did not buck, it just stopped, went completely dead in the middle of Portage Avenue.

Panic began to creep in. Police officers were lining the route for the imminent royal motorcade and I realized that I could quite conceivably be late in arriving, that there could be an empty spot on the line-up. Thoughts of the press having a field day when the person allegedly in charge of organizing the event had not managed to organize himself to actually make it there goaded me into action. I got on a telephone and tried to raise somebody to pick me up and drive me the rest of the way, unsuccessfully as it turned out. A taxicab was the obvious solution but there seemed to be, as is usually the case when you need one, none in sight. Throwing myself upon the good graces of the constabulary seemed to be my last available option. I stopped the nearest police officer and explained my predicament. He wanted to be helpful but had no radio. We went to the nearest phone booth and he called police headquarters. They agreed to dispatch a car.

When it arrived, I was still five kilometres from the airport and about four minutes from being late. I jumped in the police car, a determined looking officer at the wheel. He was aware of how much time he had and he had obviously been told that this was important. I had never in my life gone down Portage Avenue at such a speed and I hoped never to do it again. It was, nevertheless, exhilarating. We ran every red light between my stalled vehicle and the airport. We also ran the gate at the air base, full sirens blazing, and I was there on the tarmac with thirty seconds to spare.

I was later interviewed and told my story on television. I sent the mayor a letter thanking this particular officer. I also wondered at the inadequacy of our security that someone in a police car could simply drive through, right on to the tarmac without being seriously challenged somewhere along the route. Nevertheless, I put these considerations aside for the royal visit had only begun.

When we reached the hotel, our Manitoba royal visit staff was assembled for a picture with Her Majesty as well as a brief audience. As the head of the visit I merited a slightly longer and more private meeting.

"Michael, here is a tie for the visit." Her Majesty passed me a very fine dark blue tie adorned with the Royal HR and three flowers. The flowers represented each of the three provinces Her Majesty was visiting on the trip—the trillium of Ontario, the crocus for Manitoba and New Brunswick's dogwood.

"I hope you wear it carefully," she added.

"Of course I will wear it with the utmost care, Your Majesty." I assured the Queen but she was not finished. In my haste I had interrupted her. Yikes, I thought, beheading to follow.

"Because if you spill something on that tie I shall be forced to visit another province."

I was taken aback. The Queen had a wicked sense of humour.

Later that evening, Jo-Anne McNevin told me a hair-raising story which could have had even more unpleasant consequences than my rather unimportant absence at the airport. We had decided upon the Summit Room atop the Westin Hotel to introduce Her Majesty to the royal visit party which is traditionally done immediately upon her arrival. The hotel had been advised that we would need the room between five and six o'clock in the evening and they had presumed that they could therefore rent it out for use during the day. However, the RCMP decided that security dictated that the room should be empty all day and they went up and confronted a group of oil company executives who were holding a formal planning meeting. The oil company executives objected that they had the room rented and it was the middle of their meeting. The RCMP threatened to turn their attack dogs loose on them. We placated the group of enraged and indignant oil company executives with a variety of small tokens of the royal visit and abject apologies from the staff. It was my first experience of where the RCMP was less than tactful in their dealings with the general public. Fortunately, the oil company executives had a sense of humour and a sense of loyalty to the monarchy so we were not confronted by an attack dog story in the next day's paper. And fortunately the royal visit occurred before the RCMP turned to frequent use of Tasers or we could have had electrified oil executives—a mixed energy metaphor.

There were many good moments on the royal visit. For me, the most moving was the visit to the Costume Museum in Dugald, a small agricultural community east of Winnipeg. The marvellous collection of costumes paled in comparison to the wonderful curator and driving force behind the museum, Winnifred Van Slyck. When she toured Her Majesty through the museum it was pure magic. Winnifred herself described it as one of the most moving days of her life.

As we planned and organized the visit, many stories emerged about earlier royal visits to Manitoba. I learned that on Her Majesty's previous visit in 1970 to celebrate Manitoba's centennial year, The Queen was scheduled to visit The Pas and The Pas Indian Reserve. Chief Lathlin, leader of The Pas Indian Band (later to be called the Opaskwayak Cree Nation) watched as graders and bulldozers descended on his reserve months before the visit to make certain the gravel road from the highway to the band office would be smooth for the royal ride. This was the only location Her Majesty was scheduled to visit. Observing the intense activity caused Chief Lathlin to fire off a telegram to Buckingham Palace. The telegram read:

"Her Majesty must tour the entire community by road or it will be an insult to our people."

The graders returned and fixed every road in the entire community. Such were the stories of royal visits past that were shared with us.

The final morning of the royal visit I met Her Majesty outside her suite at the Westin Hotel at Portage and Main. We descended together in the elevator. For once she seemed to not be briefed. The gala the evening before had run late and the schedule had been gruelling.

As the elevator descended Her Majesty turned to me and said, "I suppose I am doing something new and novel this morning before the plane home. Am I cutting a ribbon or unveiling a plaque?"

"One of each, Your Majesty," was my answer. We continued in silence as I considered how many thousands of ribbons cut and plaques unveiled marked Her Majesty's long reign as our Queen.

HIS HOLINESS

IN THE FALL OF 1984, immediately after the visit of her Royal Majesty Queen Elizabeth the Second, Manitoba was blessed with a visit by his Holiness, Pope John Paul the Second. This impending visit caused enormous excitement amongst the Catholic community in Winnipeg and I was appointed by the premier to oversee the visit. Luckily, I had an earnest young fellow who I put in charge of the details. He worked tirelessly and ably on the arrangements.

The oddity of Manitoba, of Winnipeg in particular, is it is the only place in the whole global Catholic dominion where there are three somewhat rival archbishops. There's an English archbishop, a French archbishop, and in those days, the Metropolitan Maxim Hermaniuk, who ran a largely eastern-European congregation in the North End of the city. The planning group for the visit was myself and the three archbishops aided by the premier's own emissary, a member of his caucus, Father Donald Malinowski. The premier, and myself to a lesser extent, had always presumed Malinowski to be a Catholic priest. Had I known about his wife and kids, I probably would have revised my view. Therefore it came as a bit of a shock, after our first meeting when I was taken aside by a very agitated archbishop who explained that in fact the Reverend Malinowski was not of the Catholic persuasion. This reality had been lost on the premier and me. We found other duties for Father Malinowski. The archbishops were for a time appeased.

The plan was for a very short visit, about eight hours in duration, during which his Holiness would be whisked from the airport to masses at the two English and French cathedrals and then out to a giant public open-air mass at Bird's Hill Park some 30 kilometres miles north of the city. The church forecast that over a million people would attend the open-air mass. Our own estimates were somewhat more modest given that the entire population of Manitoba at that point was only a little over a million and there were certainly some non-Catholics in that mix. However, the governor of Minnesota was coming and other prominent people from the region, so I felt it best that we make preparations for the full million even if our own polling suggested perhaps 125,000 would come. That is still a formidable crowd.

One of those most obvious and practical issues was how to provide toilet facilities for the assembled throng. Fortunately, or unfortunately, at that point in the premier's home constituency of Selkirk there was a plant that made nothing but park furniture—tables, benches and outhouses. The plant had a temporary lapse of work causing its largely Métis workforce to be laid off. This impending layoff was causing more than a little irritation for the town of Selkirk and premier's constituency. We rapidly solved this problem by placing a very large order for outdoor bathrooms which could be built at the plant, used for the papal visit and afterwards be shipped out for use at various provincial parks. It seemed an elegant solution.

We had not counted on the determination of the Metropolitan Hermaniuk, who was mightily offended that his North End place of worship was not on the tour. Clever man, the Metropolitan waited us out and then when the trip was nearly planned to the last second, fired off a telegram to the Vatican. In it he noted that having told his parishioners of the Pope's visit and having had them put up the better part of a million dollars to refurbish the North End cathedral, there was a great danger of loss of faith if the Pope did not visit. Hasty arrangements were made for a third whistle stop on route to the Birds Hill Park Mass.

The day of the visit began with my wife, Lucille Roch, standing at the Winnipeg Airport tarmac to meet his Holiness. Lucille's parents were Catholic. In particular, her father, Louis, was a devout and conservative Catholic. Given that it was a second marriage for Lucille, and given that I was not fully a Catholic with a Jewish father and one Catholic, although lapsed, mother, Louis was convinced that we would likely both be struck dead by lightning when we greeted his Holiness. I believe Louis Roch watched on television intent on seeing the exact moment at which the lightning hit me.

I had carefully briefed the Archbishop Antoine Hacault who was bringing his Holiness along, that my wife went by her maiden name, Lucille Roch, rather than by Lucille Decter. At the moment of our actual introduction, this proved too much for the archbishop who first looked at my nametag: Michael Decter, Lucille's nametag: Lucille Roch then looked at the list that read Michael Decter and Lucille Roch and introduced us to his Holiness as "Mr. and Mrs. Decter."

The rest of the greeting went well. I was made somewhat nervous by the report from the security forces noting that while I was greeting his Holiness on the tarmac I would be fully in the crosshairs of the rifles of two Swiss Guards in two helicopters who could, in the friendly words of the RCMP, drop me on the tarmac deader than a doornail. This caused me to resist any temptation to seek an autograph or scratch inappropriately.

His Holiness went off on his visits and I made my way to Birds Hill Park for the papal mass which went very smoothly with an attendance of just about exactly 125,000. Best of all—no one waited in line for a public toilet.

ABORIGINAL CONSTITUTIONAL AFFAIRS

ONE OF THE MOST POIGNANT experiences in nation-building that I participated in was a series of constitutional meetings of First Ministers on Aboriginal matters. These meetings were a compromise arrived at in the deal-making when Prime Minister Trudeau secured the support from a sufficient number of premiers to patriate our Constitution from England and to add a Charter of Rights and Freedoms. One of the areas of unfinished business was how to properly accommodate Aboriginal people and their rights within the now Canadian Constitution. Because of the complexities of the issues and much division among the provinces, the compromise was to mandate a series of First Ministers Constitutional Conferences on Aboriginal Matters.

Mike Kirby, secretary to the cabinet for federal-provincial relations, led preparations for the government of Canada. Delegations of officials had assembled in Winnipeg from every province, territory and Aboriginal organization as well as the federal government.

Kirby came to my home for breakfast before the meeting. As the Manitoba deputy, I was the co-chair. We had agreed on the timing of the First Ministers' conference. We had also agreed that it should be televised. My strong view was that the Canadian public would quickly discover that the Aboriginal leaders were articulate and had a powerful case to make. Television is a powerful medium to change views.

The meeting was supposed to last for a day, perhaps more. Mike Kirby secured, with my support, the agreements he needed and adjourned the meeting in less than two hours. Many officials were stunned and at loss to know what to do with the rest of their day. I was reminded of Nellie McClung's declaration that, "Never retreat, never explain, never apologize, just get the thing done and let them howl." The howling was not to be as the government officials were not a howling type of crowd.

I learned that day from Mike Kirby that any meeting should be just long enough to get the job done and no longer. It proved an important lesson in the meeting-intensive culture of the public sector.

THIS IS HOW WE PRAY—TRUDEAU AND THE FIRST NATIONS

THE SCENE: THE CONFERENCE CENTRE in the grand old Railway Station across from the Château Laurier in Ottawa on a Monday morning. In addition to the First Ministers, which included the prime minister, the premiers of the ten provinces and the government leaders from the two territories, there were also the elected leaders of the First Nations, Métis and Inuit groups from across Canada.

The Aboriginal leaders had met on the Sunday afternoon with Prime Minster Trudeau. By all accounts it was a sunny afternoon with a brilliant blue sky. Trudeau and the Aboriginal leaders stood at the large window in the prime minister's office looking out on the autumn splendour of the Ottawa River framed by red maple trees.

"Great day," declared Trudeau.

"Great day," echoed the leaders.

"Great day to be a Canadian," replied Trudeau.

"Great day to be a Canadian," agreed the Aboriginal leaders.

"Well, now that we have settled the issue of sovereignty," declared Trudeau, "we can move to other matters."

By the time I met the leaders later on Sunday evening, they were still angry at Trudeau's cavalier treatment of their aspirations for Aboriginal sovereignty which they largely acknowledged to be within the nation of Canada. It was typical of Trudeau's combative style to land the first blow before the fight even officially began.

On the first morning of the constitutional conference, loud rhythmic drums pounded and the First Nations elders were introduced to intone prayers to the Great Creator. The ceremonies went on for a very long period of time. It was easy to feel that we non-Aboriginals were the ones without spirituality or ceremony. It was also numbing and exhausting to hear the drums go on and on. It was easy to believe that this was in some measure payback for Trudeau's comments of the previous day. Finally the ceremony ended and everyone sat down. Everyone sat down that is except Prime Minster Trudeau who remained standing at the head of the vast conference table.

"Now let me show you how my people pray," said Trudeau firmly to all present. This surprised even Trudeau's own advisors who scrambled quickly back to their feet.

He bowed his head and he began the Lord's Prayer.

All of the delegates who had sat down after the drumming stopped clambered back to their feet. Trudeau carried on with his head bowed and recited the entire Lord's Prayer in English. When he finished everyone sat down in their seats again. Trudeau remained standing.

He paused only briefly and then began the Lord's Prayer in French. We all rose a second time.

Trudeau started the meeting having demonstrated that the Inuit, First Nation and Métis representatives were not the only ones present with a claim to having God on their side. And everyone in the room knew that Trudeau, alone, had established a measure of both combativeness and staked the high ground for the negotiation to follow.

JOHN AMAGOALIK

THE SETTING WAS A WELL-APPOINTED meeting room in the luxurious King Edward Hotel in Toronto. The players were each of Canada's justice ministers as well as Aboriginal leadership of the First Nations, Métis and Inuit.

Federal Justice Minister John Crosbie, a brilliant Newfoundlander, chaired the meeting. Crosbie's inability with the French language probably kept him out of his party's leadership and the prime ministership of the country.

One of the Inuit leaders was John Amagoalik. When it came his turn to speak John Crosbie tried to introduce him but stumbled badly over his name.

"Mr. Amm am a ama

Mr. Amaggwa gaw

Mr. Aga a molik"

After three halting tries by Minister Crosbie, John Amagoalik himself entered the discourse.

"Minister Crosbie," he interjected calmly and in a clear voice, "I am here to build the nation so it would be fine if you simply referred to me as John A."

The meeting erupted in deep laughter. John A. was the moniker given to Sir John A. Macdonald, Canada's first prime minister. In one sentence John Amagoalik had saved the justice minister embarrassment, declared that the Inuit were Canadians and more than anything else established that he fully belonged at this table where quick wit counted for as much as any other quality. And Minister Crosbie was very relieved to refer to Mr. Amagoalik as John A.

THINK OF THE ENTERTAINMENT VALUE

I WILL BE FOREVER GRATEFUL to Eugene Szach for a most wonderful moment in my governmental career. Let me set the stage. The year was 1983. I was cabinet secretary and clerk of the executive council in the Manitoba government. The government had lost an important constitutional court case. A speeding ticket received by George Forest was appealed by him on the grounds that it was not bilingual. The eventual judgment of the Supreme Court of Canada compelled the government to translate into French every law passed by the Manitoba legislature for over a hundred years. The cost would be enormous. The attorney general, the Honourable Roland Penner, set out to negotiate some other, more practical alternative with the Société Franco-Manitobaine, the group that represented Francophones in the province.

An important but little known historical point is that when Manitoba joined Canadian Confederation in 1870 it was an officially bilingual province. In fact, the majority of non-First Nations residents at that time were French-speaking. Shortly thereafter, Manitoba was overwhelmed with English or at least non-French speaking immigrants. Agreement was reached that Manitoba would provide certain services in French to its French-speaking population. In return for this, the province would be spared the expense of translating one hundred years of laws, including the dead, repealed laws. The deal would require a constitutional amendment to make it legal and permanent. Practical as this deal seemed at the time, its announcement inflamed passions. Angry shouts rang out in the legislature and in the province, English against French and opposition against government.

An illustration of the divergent views of Manitobans was evident in polling data at the time. Polls indicated that the question, "Are French-speaking Manitobans entitled to government services in their own language?" enjoyed eighty percent support. If on the other hand, the question was posed as: "Should Manitoba become officially bilingual?" one faced ninety percent opposition. Understand that Manitoba's ethnic, cultural and linguistic mosaic includes not only the French and the English, but very large numbers of Ukrainians, Germans, Mennonites, Icelanders and southern Europeans. In reality, people from all over the world had settled Manitoba. The government's efforts to pass this legislation met fierce resistance not only from the official opposition led by the formidable former premier, Sterling Lyon, but from large segments of the public. In fact, there were some acts of violence, including the burning of the offices of the Société Franco-Manitobaine and the smashing of windows of the home of its president. These acts underscored the depth of passion stirred by the language issue. Amidst this public controversy, hearings were held in the Legislative Building. Hundreds of angry Manitobans packed in the committee rooms, to shout their opposition to the legislation.

Enter the mild-mannered and soft-spoken Eugene Szach. Prior to being lured to government service by Attorney General Roland Penner, who he had known at law school, Eugene occupied the rather quiet and civilized post of librarian at the University of Manitoba law school library. I stood next to him watching the angry mob of protestors waiting to appear before the legislative committee considering the constitutional amendment.

Eugene gestured at the volatile gathering and said, "No regrets. Think of the entertainment value."

This was an uplifting thought at a particularly dark political moment. It became a touchstone, almost a creed for the beleaguered staffers around the premier. When the days were darkest, special assistant Ginny Devine would smile and say sweetly, "Think of the entertainment value!" We would all laugh in defiance.

THE ART OF THE POLITICAL APOLOGY

THERE IS A TIME in politics for the apology. That time is immediately. My observation would be that the longer it takes a politician to apologize, the longer it takes them to be forgiven. In many cases stubbornness proves to prolong the period of controversy far beyond the magnitude of the original incident.

Two contrasting examples presented themselves during the years of the Pawley government. In the first instance, two cabinet ministers, Muriel Smith and Al Mackling, attended a protest at the American Consulate in Winnipeg. Unbeknownst to them a violent act occurred. Someone at the back of the crowd burned an American flag. In my experience, nothing upsets Americans as much as the burning of their flag. It was bad enough when the burning is by their own disgruntled youth as it was during the Vietnam War protest of my young college days. But for foreigners, even Canadians, to burn the American Stars and Stripes is equated to a near act of war.

Not only did the incident rank front-page coverage but the presence of the two provincial ministers provided it with it a certain stature. These were not just the usual suspects but official members of government, albeit present in private capacities.

As I explained to the premier, there is no private time when you are a minister of the Crown. Her Majesty doesn't let her ministers off the duty hook at five o'clock or even at midnight—once a minster always a minister.

The premier defended his two ministers valiantly in the daily question period. After several days, it became apparent that the issue wasn't going away. A strong opposition can sense opportunity and they went to town. Each day came a renewed demand for an apology and each day featured the two ministers speaking at length to explain that they had not burned the flag. They went further to explain that they were not even aware that the flag had been burned.

It did nothing to end the issue. As day followed day, question period remained dominated by the "flag burning scandal or Flag-gate" as it became known. It is clear that in the post-Watergate era, all scandals have a mandatory "gate" tacked on to lend them some distant reflected notoriety.

Meeting with the premier and ministers only replicated question period, except with the door closed the premier was pushing hard for an apology. The ministers, both politicians of deep conviction, were not budging.

One of the unintended consequences of the combined stubborn ministerial refusal to apologize became clear to me at midnight a few days later. My phone rang very late. A formal military voice informed me that there was an urgent and secret communication for the premier.

"Where do I pick it up?" I asked. I wondered whether we were at war. If so CNN would have it.

"You can present yourself with proper identification at the Air Force base on the west side of the Winnipeg airport."

"National security," I mumbled to my sleepy wife before dressing and driving to the airport.

There, after my identification was carefully examined and I signed several forms, I was given a smallish envelope. I was directed not to open it. I cheated and opened it. It was a formal note of protest from the American Ambassador to Canada. The diplomatic note was extremely critical of Manitoba cabinet ministers participating in a violent protest at the American Consulate in Winnipeg. My resolve to obtain an apology from the two ministers strengthened as I drove home in the dark. For all I knew they could send these protest notes every few days. Embarrassing the government out of some stubbornness was one thing. Depriving me of sleep was quite another.

A far tougher meeting was held. A "frank exchange of views" is how diplomats describe such sessions. The premier who, after all is said and done, unilaterally appoints ministers, prevailed. Both ministers stood in their place in the legislature and apologized.

There was never a further question or newspaper story. After three long, long weeks, the issue was finally over.

In the second case, the cabinet minister in hot water was Elijah Harper.

The facts were alarming. The minister was reported to have driven his ministerial car into the back of a Winnipeg police department tow truck on a Sunday night. Alcohol was likely a complicating factor.

Harper was saved by two quick actions. First, his very able deputy minister drove him through the long night to the Betty Ford clinic in Minneapolis so by the time the news hit the papers Monday morning he was already in treatment for his problem. Second, the premier rose in his place in the Manitoba legislature that very afternoon and read a letter of resignation written by an apologetic Harper. He resigned from the cabinet and he took full responsibility for his actions. The premier accepted his resignation. There were no questions in the daily question period.

Three months later, Elijah Harper returned to the legislature and to the cabinet. He received a standing ovation from all members of the assembly.

I am certain that most of them felt a mix of personal affection for one of their own who had made a full comeback from the politically dead. They also felt a small measure of "there but for the grace of God go I."

The lesson for those in political or public life is clear. When you make a mistake—be it a big or small error—apologize immediately and fully. If you need help in the form of counselling or treatment, get it. You will be forgiven for being human but you will never prevail in denial.

LUNCH WITH TRUDEAU—AGAIN

THE SECOND LUNCH with Trudeau in 1983 was under far less happy circumstances than the first one. The subject was Manitoba's proposed constitutional amendment that would guarantee basic services in French instead of "full bilingualism" and the translation of thousands of outdated laws.

This ignited a flame of anti-French sentiment in the province. Some of this sentiment was the legitimate belief of Germanic and Slavic settlers of the Prairies that they were no less entitled than the French to some recognition for their language. More difficult for the government was the opposition leader and former premier, Sterling Lyon, who chose to exact revenge for his defeat at Pawley's hands by fanning these flames.

The New Democratic government itself was in disarray. Little unity prevailed on this issue within the party caucus and cabinet. The NDP, at its core, was a coalition government. The coalition was rooted in the shared economic view that the economy should not be left to big business to run, but rather that the government should take an interventionist stand. The New Democratic Party represented a coming together of the old Cooperative Commonwealth Federation, the voice of the farmer, and the unions. But in the coalition of voters that supported the NDP, just as there was little cohesive view on social issues, so too, there was little cohesive view on linguistic issues.

At the time of the prime minister's invitation to lunch, mass rallies were being organized in Manitoba against the government. There was beginning to be an aura of siege to the issue although it would be some months before the government in complete disarray, was forced to abandon the amendment. Speaker Jim Walding had the bells ring to summon all members of the Legislative Assembly to vote on the issue. The opposition refused to return. By refusing to silence the bells and take a vote, Walding allowed the opposition to defeat the majority government's will. He exacted his revenge for being left out of the cabinet by the premier. Walding is a classic case of the dangers of leaving those with expectations out of cabinet. Walding exacted an additional pound of flesh several years later when he voted against his own government's budget thus defeating it.

The cast of characters for this second lunch was somewhat altered. Michael Kirby had been replaced by a long-time official of the government, Gérard Veilleux. He proved to be both an intelligent and thoughtful official.

Veilleux began his career in the Quebec government and he also spent time in Manitoba. Gérard tells a wonderful story about being a young Quebecois working through the summer at the Manitoba Bureau of Vital Statistics. The bureau was where births, deaths and marriages were registered. Although enormous in terms of his personality and intellect, Gérard was a slight man physically and must have been even slighter in his youth. Apparently, a large, powerful Métis woman showed up quite regularly and pounded on the counter at the Bureau of Vital Statistics because she wanted to speak French. Because Veilleux was the only French speaking person there, he would be sent nervously to the counter. This woman had the view that she should change the names of her numerous children whenever she changed her boyfriends. So Gerard spent his summer filling out complicated reams of paper to satisfy the whim of one very determined citizen.

Over the three years that he and I had worked together, I had come to respect his ability to find a reasonable course of action when others were given to emotion or ego, but he would be hard-pressed in this climate to find an easy course of action.

Gérard was not the only new addition to lunch with the prime minister. Also in attendance was the Liberal boss of Manitoba, Transport Minister Lloyd Axworthy. Axworthy had become somewhat notorious for his pork-barrelling on behalf of the province. What was taken as normal behaviour for ministers from Ontario and Quebec was seen by many to be outrageous when it came from Axworthy when he tried to shake some goodies loose from the federal grab bag for Manitoba. I guess there is safety in numbers.

Before lunch, the conversation centered on Premier Pawley who described the situation in Manitoba and the difficulties posed. As we headed towards the lunch table, he was particularly emphatic with the prime minister that it must be a battle fought out in Manitoba. The premier was worried about the intervention of militant Quebecois ministers such as Serge Joyal, the secretary of state, in a way which could exacerbate the backlash in Manitoba. Just as we were about to sit down, it occurred to the premier that maybe his wording had been careless. In his statement that federal ministers should stay out, it might be taken to reflect poorly on Axworthy. In endeavouring to correct the impression, the premier went out of his way to praise Axworthy for his speech to the Chamber of Commerce the previous Friday, calling it courageous. In a chilling reminder of his dark side, the prime minister commented: "Well, Premier, that wasn't courage on Minister Axworthy's part. He merely wished to remain in my cabinet."

The remark had a jarring impact and, as the custodian of Manitoba's economic agenda where we were seeking funding for a number of important initiatives, I became immediately concerned that there would be no business done at lunch. Without meaning to, I intervened and said to the prime minister, who at that point was riding low in the polls:

"Well, just remaining in your cabinet these days takes a certain amount of courage."

As the words escaped my mouth, I thought that I would provoke a bout of the familiar Trudeau icy wrath and totally ruin the lunch. However, Trudeau, upon reflection, seemed to find the remark highly entertaining and amusing.

"Yes, I guess it does take a certain amount of courage to stay in my cabinet these days." He actually chuckled.

Lunch reinforced my overall impression that Prime Minister Trudeau was alive and intellectually stimulating when discussing things constitutional. The minute anything fundamentally economic came up, his eyes seemed to glaze over and he began to play with the food on his plate. As he was someone well-rehearsed in economics, I do not know if by the mid-1980s the prime minister had become so disenchanted with the advice he was receiving that he no longer had any interest, or if he had come to the conclusion that the economy was beyond management by government. In any event, it was far livelier to discuss the nuances of the Constitution with him than to attempt to sell him on the merits of further federal investment in Manitoba.

Our goal at lunch had been to secure support for the Manitoba economy while keeping the federal government at a distance on the constitutional amendment since their presence hurt our cause.

Premier Pawley and I rode to the airport in relative silence in the taxi. At one point Pawley looked at me and said, "I hope they don't send Serge Joyal."

I replied, "My sense is that they will do whatever they decide."

We looked at each other and laughed.

AROUND THE WORLD IN THIRTY DAYS

BY THE EARLY 1980s, it was beginning to become very clear to nearly everyone in government that international trade had become a dominant issue. In particular, the trading nature of the Canadian economy became more transparent and the need for government leaders to show an interest in trade became more evident. Premier Pawley was the first Manitoba premier to officially visit Washington. His reasons for going were to seek relief from a tariff on Manitoba hogs which some of the neighbouring states to the south of Manitoba, particularly South Dakota, had successfully achieved. It had become clear to Pawley, particularly through his friendship and discussions with Minnesota Governor Rudy Perpich, that succeeding as a leader in the 1980s required less of a stay-at-home attitude than in other eras.

Perpich was a particularly interesting case in point. He had served as the Democratic governor of Minnesota and had then been defeated. He had been born in the iron range of northern Minnesota and he had come to understand the Minnesota economy in terms of its resources, its agriculture, and, more importantly, the major multi-nationals based in Minnesota that carried that state's economy through periods of recession—Control Data, Honeywell, Pillsbury and others. After his defeat as governor, Rudy Perpich was hired by Control Data Corporation as a European vice-president based in Vienna. This tour of duty furthered his commitment to the view that to succeed in the global marketplace, Minnesota would have to become much more oriented to trade and its governor would have to become much more aggressive about pursuing opportunities.

Rudy Perpich returned to Minnesota and was re-elected governor. He undertook a massive amount of travel to points all over the world to promote Minnesota and its exports. To offset any criticism about the cost of such travel, the governor raised private-sector dollars to pay for his marketing trips.

In 1982 and 1983, Pawley had occasion to meet Governor Perpich. The governor's enthusiasm for world travel was great. His passion included the political magic of being seen as an ambassador of one's territory in the larger world. As a consequence of this, Premier Pawley agreed to a trade mission to Japan, China, India and then back through London. While involved in the organizing, it had not been clear that I would be invited on the trip. However, one fateful day, Pawley indicated it would be his preference if I could go.

What an adventure! Because we had some banking business in London, it was decided that we would go all the way around, spend a week in Japan, a week in China, a week in India and a final week in London. The departments assembled massive amounts of information and External Affairs provided thoughtful briefings on the countries we were to visit. The Japanese Consul in Winnipeg even had us over for dinner so that we could be schooled in some of the niceties of dining in Japan.

JAPAN—1984

THERE WERE MANY interesting adventures in Japan but what I found particularly fascinating was a glimpse inside Japanese politics. Two incidents were especially impressive. The first was when we visited the office of the Japanese minister of finance. It goes without saying that all ministers of finance are concerned with the state of their nation's currency but the Japanese minister carried this concern to a level of an obsession. On his office wall was a digital readout which changed every second. It showed the number of Japanese yen to U.S. dollar on a continuing and real-time basis. It was very difficult to maintain a conversation without being distracted and glancing away towards this large digital readout on the wall. There could be no doubt which policy variable had the most influence on the Japanese finance minister.

The second memorable incident of a political sort was a side visit to Oita, Japan. This is a prefecture, or province, in the very southern part of Japan. It has almost a tropical climate, allowing it to grow such things as kiwi fruit.

At that time, its governor was an individual named Morihiko Hiramatsu. Prior to his return to his native prefecture of Oita and his entry into politics, Hiramatsu has served as deputy minister of the legendary Japanese Ministry of Industry and Technology, MITI. The power of MITI rested upon the collaboration of Japanese banks, industry and government in post-war Japan. As former deputy minister of MITI, Hiramatsu had plenty of I.O.U's to call to aid the economy of his native Oita. He also had the most interesting approach to economic development of any leader I can remember.

When we arrived, our little Manitoba delegation consisting of the premier of Manitoba and several ministers and officials, was greeted by the governor and no fewer than five television camera crews. Someone could have mistaken us for a party of greater significance but it seemed, in talking to Hiromatsu's staff, that all visitors to Oita were a cause a for media show. Media reporting was aided greatly by the governor's showmanship. He unveiled a large map of the prefecture of Oita. Then he gave a brief lecture to all of us on the one village/one product philosophy which he was pursuing in Oita. It was a very successful strategy for diversifying and specializing the basically agricultural district. Hiramatsu prompted each village to identify one product in which it would become a world leader. One village had entered into the production of kiwi fruit and within five years it had displaced New Zealand kiwi fruit from the Japanese market. Another village specialized in exotic mushrooms. Dotted in amongst the agricultural one village/one product movement in the prefecture of Oita were some of the most high-technology factories on the globe.

We visited two factories, one of which was owned by Canon Camera and which produced vast quantities of 35mm Canon Sure Shot cameras. There were two assembly lines. One—the old line—still had some number of human beings working on it. The other, the newest assembly line, was made up almost entirely of machines. It was my first look at post-industrial society or, at least, post-human-involved industrial society.

The second factory that we visited was making machines, called sputterers, which spit out silicon chips for use in the electronics industry. The governor explained to us later that he had suspended visits to a third factory because North Americans found it too alarming and he did not want to spoil the delicious dinner that was awaiting us. Under questioning he conceded that the third factory was one where you could view robots manufacturing other robots using factory automation. This I would have found a little unnerving, although in 1984, it illustrated vividly how far the Japanese had been able to move in technology and robotics.

NO INFLATION IN CHINA

OUR VISIT TO BEIJING was extremely interesting. This was not the open Chinese society we know today from 2008 Olympics period. It was a closed communist society that provided handlers to most visitors.

The Chinese government had supplied us with a well-educated, knowledgeable guide from the Chinese Ministry of Foreign Affairs, called CPIFA for short. Miss Zhu had been at Harvard roughly the same time I had, although we had never met. To be sent from Beijing to attend Harvard University was a very great honour. Miss Zhu demonstrated the extraordinary intelligence that had earned her the experience.

We were transported from place to place on most outings in a small minibus and we were able to obtain large amounts of historical information. This ran the gamut from information of a purely tourist nature to all sorts of information on the process of the reform movement in China. However, there was one issue which presented a bit of a problem and that was inflation.

We had heard repeatedly from personnel of the Canadian embassy that rents and prices had gone up significantly in Beijing. They attributed this to the reforms which had allowed the rural population of peasant farmers to increase the prices of goods sold to city dwellers. However, when asked about inflation in China, Miss Zhu insisted that there was no inflation in China. We were baffled.

For a day and a half we mused over this contradiction. We knew that Miss Zhu was an intelligent, highly-educated young woman. We knew that there was inflation in China. Therefore, Miss Zhu must also know that there was inflation in China. That the government did not admit there was inflation in China was now evident. The issue became one of contention and we decided to take our case directly to Miss Zhu.

We confronted Miss Zhu that evening on the bus. We began by explaining that we were aware, from conversations with the embassy personnel and others, of the rising prices in China. We then acknowledged her statement that there was no inflation in China. Finally, we presented her with a polite request for a resolution of these seemingly irreconcilable differences. Miss Zhu responded that there was no inflation in China since inflation only existed in capitalist economies with markets. She then explained that prices had gone up in Beijing and in China, generally. Bingo! We thought—inflation.

Not at all, she said, what China had was not inflation but reform of prices.

When we asked the rate of "reform of prices," Miss Zhu acknowledged the reform of prices stood at six-and-a-half percent per year!

THE GREAT WALL

ONE OF OUR OBJECTIVES on the China mission involved the potential development of a potash mine in western Manitoba. Potash deposits had been developed and mined in the adjacent province of Saskatchewan. These deposits were originally the bed of a large ancient lake. Put simply the beach of this lake is in Manitoba.

The development of potash requires large amounts of capital to sink a deep shaft through water-bearing strata that lay between the surface and the potash deposits. The reason for approaching the Chinese government was its projected need to import vast quantities of potash to fertilize their crops and feed their nation.

One of our advisors was David Dombowsky, a previous CEO of the Potash Corporation of Saskatchewan. He was extremely knowledgeable about potash mining and about China. Our hosts from the potash sector in China were delighted to see David. One of them took me aside to tell me a story, through a translator.

"When you come to China, you go to see the Great Wall of China."

"Yes," I replied. "We are going on Saturday to see the Great Wall of China."

"When we go to Saskatoon, Saskatchewan, we visit the home of David Dombowsky," the Chinese potash sector storyteller said.

Unbeknownst to me, Dombowsky shared a passion with Winston Churchill—no, not for cigars, but for the building of stone walls. Around his property in Saskatoon he had constructed a long low stone wall.

"So when we go to Saskatoon," my storyteller continued, "we see Great Wall of Dombowsky."

I laughed almost as long and loud as did Dombowsky and the Chinese potash delegation.

Our meeting with the Chinese minister of agriculture proved more serious. Our hope had been to convince the minister to support the development of a potash mine in Manitoba by entering into a long-term purchase agreement with the province. The very small mining company that had the rights to develop the Manitoba potash mine could then use the long-term contract as a basis for financing the expensive mine development.

Manitoba Mines Minister Willy Parasiuk forcefully presented our case. Numerous scientific studies established that Chinese farmers needed to use more potash fertilizer to increase crop yields. Manitoba had undeveloped potash that would benefit China and Chinese agriculture.

"We need to use more potash fertilizer," began the minister of agriculture for the People's Republic of China after Willy finished. Our spirits soared. Dreams of returning triumphant from China to announce a new mine filled our minds.

But then the Chinese minister of agriculture continued, "We need more than raw potash fertilizer. We need ports to receive the ships. We need railways to carry the potash to the agricultural districts. We need bagging plants to bag the potash for delivery to 330 million farmers. We need trucks to deliver the potash. But most important of all we need twenty or thirty years of investment in agricultural extension to teach our farmers that they need to use more fertilizer, potash fertilizer."

By the time the minister finished, our hopes of an early mine had deflated. Thirty-five years later potash is soaring in price. All of the Chinese agriculture minister's prophecies have come true. But it was Saskatchewan that supported the agricultural extension. Manitoba has not yet built a potash mine.

Zhou En-Lai, the Chinese premier, is quoted as replying to a question about the significance of the French Revolution on the occasion of the 200th anniversary of the storming of the Bastille, "It's too early to tell." Perhaps Manitobans should remain patient and take the very long view as the Chinese do. Perhaps someday their potash mine will also arrive.

THE PREMIER AND THE ELEPHANT

SOON WE WERE ON the Indian leg of our journey. The Canadian high commission in India had arranged for cars and drivers so that we could visit Agra and see the Taj Mahal. While the journey was not long, the crowded nature of the road and the busy day in Agra meant that we would stay overnight, the Saturday night, and return to New Delhi in the morning.

The Indian government, for reasons which escaped both the premier and me, had assigned a bodyguard. This fellow accompanied the premier everywhere and carried quite a large pistol on his hip. I later learned that Indian politicians at all levels had bodyguards assigned to them, partly as a status symbol and partly as recognition of just how violent Indian politics could be. Slayings of politicians were relatively commonplace in the stormy politics of this country.

The drive from New Delhi to Agra was about one hundred kilometres. It was also a drive of a thousand years. Along that road one could see life and death. Funeral pyres and vultures with necks as thick as a man's thigh. Mercedes and elephants. Life and death, the past and the present, were all on display on that road to Agra.

None of the trucks seemed to have brake lights and passing was always into oncoming traffic. It was a hair-raising ride, even with a very skillful chauffeur.

We survived the journey and toured the magnificent Taj Mahal. Upon our return to the Hotel Sheraton Agra we were confronted by an intriguing Indian phenomenon. In the parking lot was an elephant with a sedan chair fixed to it. The elephant's owner was insistent that we pay him several rupees for a ride on the elephant. The premier was curious and decided to take him up on it.

I still have the picture. As the premier climbed up on the elephant for the ride, his bodyguard decided that His Excellency, as he had taken to calling the premier, was in grave danger so he hopped up behind him. The premier's experience was marred somewhat by the bodyguard who was wrapped around him. I am not sure whether it was out of a desire to protect him or whether he had a fear of heights, but the bodyguard held on very tightly. This was quite entertaining and the rest of the party watched with some amusement.

When the elephant knelt and the premier and the bodyguard had disembarked, the owner of the elephant demanded payment for two rides, one for the premier and one for the bodyguard. This enraged the sensibilities of our bodyguard who protested that he was merely doing his job and that His Excellency had no need to pay for the second rider. A violent Indian argument ensued. At one point in the dispute, the bodyguard drew his pistol and I was convinced I was soon be reading headlines in the *Winnipeg Free Press*: "Premier Involved in Elephant Shooting" or "Elephant Murder in Agra" or worse still "Premier Wounded in Parking Lot Shoot-Out!" Calmer heads eventually prevailed and the bodyguard declined to shoot either the elephant or the elephant's owner. His Excellency paid, I think, in enough rupees to take the whole community of Agra for an elephant ride and we escaped without peril, or, worse still, negative publicity.

VISITING BUCKINGHAM PALACE

WHEN THE BRITISH ROYAL VISIT staff led by Sir William Heseltine said goodbye to us in 1984 at the Winnipeg airport there was an invitation extended.

"Michael, if you are ever in London please come and visit with us for lunch at Buckingham Palace."

"Sir William, I thank you but I will understand if this is just your way of being polite. As a matter of fact the premier and I are leaving with a group of Manitoba officials on a trip to Japan, China and India shortly. We are coming back through London."

"Then you must do us a very large favour, Michael. Now that you know how a visit works, we need your help. Her Majesty has been invited to China. Can you do a preliminary advance and then brief us when you come through London?"

"I would be delighted to do that."

I thought to myself nice recovery.

Several weeks later I travelled most of the way around the world and endured a thirteen-hour flight from New Delhi to Heathrow Airport in London that was made even more miserable by the terrible news that Prime Minister Indira Ghandi had been assassinated. After an exhausting flight I staggered into the quaint Ryder Street Chambers where I always stayed in London.

As I entered the room the telephone rang. I was surprised. Few people knew I would be in this tiny hotel. It was the middle off the night in Canada and I had already called home. I picked up the phone.

"Michael, welcome to London. Bill Heseltine here, hoping you got our invitation and are able to join us for lunch on Friday."

"I just arrived from New Delhi, Sir William, I haven't even put my suitcase down. I have not received an invitation." As I was saying these words I noticed an envelope protruding from beneath the telephone.

The envelope had a red wax seal that seemed immediately regal. "Actually I have the invitation right here and I am delighted to accept."

"Look forward to seeing you Friday, Michael. Just present yourself to the guards."

I looked forward to Friday. Unlike China, Japan and India, the premier's schedule was much lighter in London. After the adventures of the Far East, I anticipated my quiet time in London, lunch at the palace and then finally home to my Lucille and Riel.

However, it was anything but an uneventful time for me in London. Although exhausted and with the premier facing a speech and a number of banking meetings, our hosts from Wood Gundy had proposed to take us to the theatre on Tuesday evening. The premier selected the long-running play, *The Mousetrap*. We were to assemble at the theatre at 7:00 p.m. for a pre-theatre drink.

At 6:30, I was dressed and trying to shake off the jet lag. I leaned across a glass-top table to retrieve my room key. I guess that too much of my weight went on the hand on the table. The table cracked and the lethally sharp and jagged edge of glass cut my right index finger. A long flap of skin peeled back exposing the bone in my finger. Blood gushed from the wound and I felt faint.

I wrapped my finger in a towel and held it aloft to reduce the bleeding. With my other hand I dialled 911 on the telephone. It already seemed absurd to call an ambulance for a cut finger so I inquired as to the nearest hospital with an Emergency Department. With this information in hand or rather in head, I took the elevator down and made my way to Piccadilly Circus where I flagged a London taxi. By now the entire towel was blood-soaked. I struggled clumsily using my left hand to do things normally performed by my right hand.

"Middlesex Hospital. Hurry," I said before slumping back in the seat. My finger now hurt like hell.

"Right, mate." The cabbie needed no urging on speed. We took off faster than I believed those large black cabs could accelerate. Within minutes, after some hair-raising turns in traffic, we were at the hospital.

I was seen immediately by a resident who expertly froze my wounded finger. A dozen stitches closed the gash. By 7:00 p.m., I was bandaged and free to go.

"No charge for our Canadian guest. Careful not to break anymore of those glass tables—they are all antiques you know," the doctor said in farewell.

I considered going back to the Ryder Street Chambers but did not feel like facing the ragged glass table top. So I directed the taxi to the theatre where I caught up with my party.

I told the story, making the wound seem small and the bandage overly and unnecessarily large. We went in to see the first act. During that act, the freezing began to come out. The pain was excruciating. I thought I was putting up a brave face but our host Trevor Spurgeon of Wood Gundy saw right through my own theatrical performance.

At intermission he said, "What do you drink?"

"Scotch," I replied in genuine agony.

"This should settle you," Trevor intoned handing me a very tall glass that had not a drop of water added to dilute what might have been a third of a bottle of extremely good scotch. I drank it all before the bell summoned us back to our seats.

The scotch worked its miracle. By the time I left the theatre for the Ryder Street Chambers I was feeling no pain at all. I may be the only person in the history of *The Mousetrap*'s thirty-eight-year run that cannot tell you anything about the second act.

By Friday morning I was able to replace the large bandage with a more modest one. I had no intention of turning up a Buckingham Palace looking like my finger had been fed to a meat grinder. Re-bandaged, my injured finger and I headed off on foot to the appointed hour at the palace.

I said as formally as I could to the Royal Palace Guard, "I am expected for lunch."

He marched across the gravel and I marched behind him. Eyes of several hundred American tourists drilled into my back as I crossed the gravel.

Lunch featured the Queen's staff. We began with a sizeable gin and tonic and then as the curator of the Royal Collections put it, "the other half," another large tumbler of gin.

We discussed the extreme challenges posed by "de-accession," the disposal of items in the vast royal collections.

Somewhere in one of those royal warehouses, Hiawatha and the Popsicle stick lamp from Dauphin, a surprise gift to HRM, had been carefully stored for posterity. I briefly thought what future archeologists would make of the lamp before deciding that the gin had fully taken hold of me.

After lunch, the staff took me on a private tour of Buckingham Palace. This is a palace that Harry Potter would love, complete with secret doors and hidden chambers where the royals could escape their Court.

We entered a large room. To my eye it seemed extremely garish. Red wallpaper with every inch covered with paintings. My hosts looked at me expectantly. I didn't know what to say.

Her Majesty's private secretary broke the awkward silence, "Hold your answer, Michael, we view this as only the second most hideous room in Buckingham Place. Let us show you the one we believe to be the most hideous before you decide."

They all chuckled. The other room was, in truth, even more garish.

NO MOU, NO SHOO

AS A CHILD, I JOINED my family in front of the black and white television to watch Ed Sullivan introduce his Sunday night show. Famously, Sullivan proclaimed each Sunday. "We have a really great show for you tonight." Except he pronounced show as "shoo" as though no "w" was involved.

Probably the most interesting and successful negotiation in which I was ever involved was the negotiation of the Economic and Regional Development umbrella agreement and related subsidiary agreements between the government of Manitoba and the government of Canada. These agreements (ERDA for short) were profoundly bureaucratic and uninteresting; however, the negotiation process was fascinating and the events leading up to the signing were dramatic—at least for those of us involved.

A bit of background is worthwhile. In the 1960s, the new prime minister of Canada, Pierre Elliot Trudeau, in proclaiming his vision of a just society also picked up some of the spirit of the U.S. war on poverty started by the Kennedys and continued by President Lyndon Johnson.

In Canada, part of Trudeau's vision was greater equality among the regions of Canada. To this end, he launched the Department of Regional Economic Expansion (DREE) and named his dynamic colleague, Jean Marchand, as minister of DREE. Marchand was one of the 'three wise men' of Quebec who had come to Ottawa as a group in the late 1960s; Trudeau and Gérard Pelletier were the other two. DREE in its early days was an amazing and talented array of some of the best and brightest young minds, determined to make significant progress against the regional inequalities and dire poverty of some regions of Canada. Much of the energy and dynamic, however, was lost over time as the department became bureaucratized. Limited to a small percentage of funding, less than two percent of the federal budget, it became apparent that DREE was not working.

One of the reasons that it was not working was that its preferred instrument for dealing with the provinces was something called general development agreements. These agreements allowed cost sharing. In most provinces what this meant was that programs would be launched by the provincial government after negotiation and agreement with Ottawa, and federal money would flow quietly to the provincial treasury to pay for anywhere from twenty-five percent to, in some of the Atlantic provinces, almost ninety percent of the program costs. This was eventually unacceptable to federal politicians who felt that provincial premiers and ministers got all the credit for the programming while the federal contribution was essentially invisible. The emergence of the separatist movement in Quebec exaggerated these tensions and fears. Further tension resulted from the efforts of Ottawa hard-line bureaucrats whose careers were made not by finding ways to co-operate with the provinces but by finding ways to reclaim federal areas of activity and jurisdiction from the provinces.

More important to the telling of this tale was that in late 1981, Prime Minister Trudeau announced the reorganization of DREE and its amalgamation with parts of the Department of Industry, Trade and Commerce to form a new department, DRIE Canada. This reorganization was undertaken to ensure that the federal government would get some recognition for its assistance with provincial economic development programs. The department would work with a series of federal economic development coordinators, one in each province who would have authority for organizing all federal economic development activity. To ensure their clout, they would be very senior officials of government and they would have access directly to a cabinet committee on economic and regional development. The idea was sound but as with all sound ideas in government, the eventual outcome is very much in doubt until someone gets around to inventing machinery to implement it.

By virtue of my position in the Manitoba government, the provincial responsibilities fell to me and to my colleague, Jim Eldridge. Much to my delight, the federal government appointed Jean Edmonds as the federal economic development coordinator for Manitoba. Jean had served in a number of positions in the federal government, including regional director of employment and immigration and of DREE, but she had retired and over a period of time had become very much a respected colleague and mentor. In fact, I was hopeful that she would be assisting us on a number of provincial issues related to the amalgamation when her appointment was made.

Also important to this account is Lloyd Axworthy, the only Manitoba member of the cabinet and a forceful voice for the spending of money in Manitoba. At that point, Axworthy was federal transport minister, which came to play a part in the negotiations. Transport was a large federal department with lots of ability to reallocate expenditures to Manitoba. When Jean and I met, it was clear that none of the machinery had been put into place to implement this brave new world of regional development. Jean's matter-of-fact approach was that we would simply have to invent it as we went along. Going first implied taking some risks since we would have no other province to follow. Leadership was risky but it also had the potential of reward. It allowed us to chart our own path.

After months of negotiation, we had achieved Canada's first Economic and Regional Development Agreement. As well, agreement on a number of subsidiary agreements, and for those subsidiary agreements the proposal was to exchange letters of clarification called memorandums of understanding or "MOUs." The major controversy centered on whether these MOUs would contain reference to the specific amounts of money which would be committed by the government of Canada. Officials of the federal government had been adamant that this was not possible. While officials of the province had been equally adamant that without a commitment of specific dollars there be no signing ceremony. Nevertheless, everyone assumed that someone else would blink.

So there we were in the cabinet room, the premier and provincial ministers lined up on one side of the table; the federal coordinating minister for the ERDAS, the Honourable Don Johnston, chairman of the Treasury Board, Lloyd Axworthy, Jean Edmonds and a phalanx of senior officials on the other. First the premier and then Don Johnson gave their warm, friendly, congratulatory remarks.

Soon the mood turned. From a mutual admiration society, the gathering began to resemble a war zone. With the press assembled outside waiting for a major announcement and all the press releases drafted, it seemed to me extraordinarily unlikely that there could not be some movement. The federal government after all was craving the photo op, recognition and a public show of support. However, Axworthy was clearly counting on Johnston to give some ground at the last minute and allow him to commit dollars in the MOU.

We decided to let the politicians cool in separate rooms while senior officials tried to find common ground. The ministers left and the senior officials sat in unaccustomed places across from each other at the Cabinet table. I turned to Jim Eldridge, then head of intergovernmental affairs and one of the finest public servants to ever serve the people of Manitoba, to get the ball rolling. Eldridge, summoning his best Ed Sullivan voice, intoned, "No MOU, no shoo."

That summed it up. We got the MOU, with the money, and the federal government got the Shoo. It was a triumph of what all provincial officials yearn for—the ability to capture the moment in a phrase, as well as the ability to deliver large chunks of federal dollars to their province.

THREE ENVELOPES

ONE DAY AT a federal-provincial meeting, an official from one of the Atlantic provinces remarked to me after a particularly lame performance by one of the premiers that it was "time for the three envelopes."

"The three envelopes?" I asked. "What three envelopes?"

The official took me aside and told me a story that so captures the essence of federal-provincial relations and the political cycle that it has stayed with me as a favourite for decades.

"The story," he began, "is not specific as to a province or premier but it is generally attributed to a smaller maritime province."

He continued. "The story begins the night after the swearing in of a new premier." He paused. "The newly-minted premier is in his office after the end of the business day. He is settling in. He is arranging his desk. There is a knock at the door."

My storyteller paused to cough a long rasping smoker's cough. Then he continued. "There was a knock, a hard knock on the great oak door leading to the corridor. The premier went over and opened the door. He was startled to see his predecessor, a man he had relentlessly criticized. He invited him in. The former premier demurred. Thrusting three envelopes into the new premier's hands he said, 'This is all the advice I have for you. When you get in trouble you should open the first envelope. When that advice does not work anymore, open the second envelope. And when that advice fails you, open the third envelope.'"

My new friend paused for a breath. "The new premier was puzzled and a little taken aback at the dishevelled appearance of his predecessor. They told me he was losing his marbles. Maybe they were right, he thought.

He did not take the envelopes seriously. He opened the bottom drawer on his desk. He tossed them in a drawer and in the warm glow of his first day in office he forgot all about them.

Three months passed. The premier had survived a tough day. The media were hounding him over a new deficit figure showing a large increase. He went looking in the drawer of his desk for a bottle of scotch and he came upon the three envelopes. He muttered to himself. 'It can't hurt.' He opened the first envelope. Inside was a small card that had neatly printed on it in block letters BLAME ME. The premier thought about it and chuckled.

The next morning, he called a full press conference and in lurid terms he described the huge financial mess he had inherited from the previous government. He blamed his predecessors for every penny of the deficit.

'If not for their reckless spending ways, our province would be in a surplus position,' he declared.

The headlines followed. "Previous Government Left Mess." Independent auditors were called in to chronicle the exact size of the mess. At every occasion the premier blamed his predecessor.

This worked extremely well for nearly eighteen months. Then one day a young reporter asked him after he had blamed a major environmental problem on the previous premier, 'We know the previous government was not very interested in the environment but could they have been responsible for this situation when the problem was not discovered until after your election?'

That night the premier took time to search through the now crowded drawers of his desk to find the two remaining envelopes. He found them and opened the one marked "2". Inside he found a simple card with block letters. It read BLAME THE FEDERAL GOVERNMENT.

The premier called a big press conference the next day. He blamed all of his problems, financial, environmental and others, on chronic underfunding of the province by the federal government. The press featured headlines that read: "Federal government blamed." This worked even better than blaming his predecessor. For nearly two years, the premier blamed everything that happened that was bad on the federal government.

One day the now slightly older, young reporter asked. 'Premier, we know that the federal government is nearly the Antichrist and they spend every waking moment thinking of ways of trying to make our province worse off but on this one issue isn't it possible that responsibility actually rests with your government?'

The premier knew the reporter was right. He was facing an election within the year. That night he put his scotch aside and searched the desk drawers until he found the third and last envelope. He opened it with enthusiasm and fond memories about how the advice in the first two envelopes had helped him.

Inside was the familiar card and block letters. The message read: PREPARE THREE ENVELOPES.

WASHINGTON

ALLAN GOTLIEB SERVED CANADA with great distinction as ambassador to the United States. He proved to be an extremely effective Canadian ambassador. He understood that for Canada to succeed in Washington he needed to have access. "Access is influence," he intoned to Premier Pawley when we arrived to Washington in 1985.

He also hired effective lobbyists to put Canada's case issue by issue to the powerful leaders in the House of Representatives and the Senate. In the American system of government, far less power resides with the president than resides with the prime minister in the Canadian parliamentary system. Gotlieb understood these realities and shaped a successful strategy to cope with Canada's need to influence its much larger southern neighbour.

Ambassador Gotlieb arranged a dinner for Premier Pawley. Two very knowledgeable Americans were invited. Gotlieb himself was unable to attend. Rudy Penner, who headed the Congressional Budget Office in the mid-1980s, arrived first to the Georgetown restaurant. He was soon followed by a former undersecretary of state for economic affairs, Myer Rashish. Both proved fascinating and insightful about how Washington worked, although we began on a sour note.

Rudy Penner explained that he grew up in Duluth. He complained to Premier Pawley that his family was frequently delayed at the border because of the Communist Penners of Winnipeg. Pawley replied that the son of the Communist Penners, Roland Penner, served as attorney general in Pawley's administration.

Myer Rashish began with a story about how he had been charged with organizing the Cancun Summit with President Reagan and Prime Minister Trudeau. He made an early trip to Ottawa to meet Canadian officials and to meet the prime minister.

"Trudeau and I were at the London School of Economics together in the 1950s," he began. "I wasn't certain that he would remember me."

Upon meeting Myer, Trudeau instantly remembered him and they had a warm chat. Myer explained that through hard work and diligence he had risen to his very senior position as Undersecretary of State.

He asked Trudeau how his career had progressed.

Trudeau replied, "Well, after LSE I bummed around and bummed around and well, they made me prime minister!"

Later in the dinner, Myer told one of those rare stories that captured real history.

In the early 1960s, Myer was already working at the state department as a young aide to then Secretary of State Dean Rusk. President John Kennedy had appointed his good friend and mentor in matters economic John Kenneth Galbraith as ambassador to India.

This was in the days before the internet had been invented. Ambassadors sent telegrams to convey their advice. Although his job was ambassador to India, Ambassador Galbraith sent very long telegrams on all matters that he deemed worthy. One of the missives was nearly one hundred pages on the steel industry. The length of the telegrams and their frequency was one problem. The more difficult dilemma was the ambassador's insistence in classifying all his telegrams, "For the President's Eyes Only." This caused a serious problem for the state department who were reluctant to deliver hundreds of pages of additional reading material to the president.

After the briefing of the president, the secretary of state asked for a few minutes with him. He asked Myer to stay with the large briefcase of telegrams.

"Mr. President, Ambassador Galbraith has been sending a large number of long, very long telegrams on issues not pertaining to the Indian sub-continent. He marks them all for 'The President's Eyes Only.' We are at a loss as to know what to do with them."

President Kennedy chuckled, then he said: "I love Ken like a brother but if you gave that man an enema—you could bury him in a matchbox. You deal with the telegrams, Mr. Secretary. You let me know if I really need to see any of them."

MULRONEY

IN CONTRAST TO the two lunch meetings with Prime Minister Trudeau, my one and only official meeting with Prime Minister Mulroney could not have been more different. The occasion was a somewhat emotionally-charged one. The Manitoba government felt that it was being short-changed some $72 million per year by the government of Canada on the Equalization Program. When Finance Minister Michael Wilson visited Winnipeg to meet with his provincial counterparts, one of his clumsy aides had left his briefing book in the hotel lobby. The briefing book contained material damaging to the federal side. It included a memorandum from Wilson's deputy minister, Mickey Cohen, indicating that Manitoba's claim of $72 million was quite valid. This touched off a great firestorm in the Manitoba press. In the national press the issue received slightly less coverage. Premier Pawley demanded a meeting with the prime minister. The meeting was granted.

We arrived on Parliament Hill with Premier Pawley, Cliff Scotton (head of communications to the premier) and me representing the province. We were ushered into a meeting room near the prime minister's office and we were joined by the prime minister, Mickey Cohen and Gérard Veilleux. The first difference I noted was the presence of a photographer. Some weeks later, we all received photos of ourselves meeting with Prime Minister Mulroney and a friendly note. This, to me, was the first evidence of the presidential style over substance of the Mulroney era—a souvenir of the visit seemed as important as the actual content.

This was not entirely unwelcome. A photograph does provide an Andy Warhol-like "fifteen minutes of fame" claim to one's place in history. I have shown my children the photo of their father and Prime Minister Mulroney seated at the same table. I do not know if it means anything to them. I do know that I would have treasured a similar photo with Prime Minister Trudeau.

In contrast to Pierre Elliot Trudeau's icy Gallic intellect, Brian Mulroney exuded a back-slapping, Irish politician's charm. He is what my Irish mother would call a 'chancer,' a wonderful Irish expression which is much kinder than suggesting that someone might be dishonest, but, heaven forbid, not an outright liar. A chancer is someone who is willing to take a chance with the truth.

As the meeting began, Prime Minister Mulroney turned to me and said, "Well, Michael, what is the sales tax in Newfoundland?" This was a skill-testing question for which I was not entirely prepared. I hazarded a reply. "Twelve, no thirteen percent." I was surprised that he knew my name.

The next question, in his lawyerly way, was, "What is the sales tax in Manitoba?" I believe that it was then six percent and told him so. He then thundered at us, "And here you are asking us for $72 million and you are collecting half the sales tax of those poor Newfs." I shuddered. We were clearly not in for an illuminating, intellectual discussion of the issue, but rather about as raw and ad hoc a political debate as you could imagine. Our issue was with the complexities of federal-provincial transfers, not with relative rates of sales tax in various parts of the country.

Mulroney went on to catalogue and praise each and every one of the great economic developments taking place in Manitoba, including the Limestone Generating Station, a major hydro-electric scheme. Premier Pawley properly objected on the basis that without appropriate federal financing, Manitoba would begin to lose its credit rating and be unable to develop the substantial resources of the province. The meeting was not a long one and I left somewhat shaken at the shallowness of the approach taken. As someone has remarked, the country may not want its brightest individual as its prime minister, which is a reaction to Trudeau, but it may not want its most affable, back-slapping Irish politician as its leader either.

I should be careful about the Irish remark. My late mother's entire family is still in Ireland and politics has long been a part of family history. When they were not serving time for their role in the IRA back in the 1930s when the IRA was not the despicable terrorist organization that it later became, they sat in the Dail, the Irish parliament. In particular, there was my Uncle Toady, Patrick McGilligan, who was, at various times, a finance minister, credited with bringing Keynesian economics to Ireland, and minister for hydro-electric development. I never met Uncle Toady, so I do not know for certain whether he would have felt a kinship for Brian Mulroney.

JACQUES PARIZEAU

PARIZEAU WAS NOT ONLY a brilliant economist, lecturer and professor of economics, but he was also extremely photogenic. His stout form and large, magisterial belly and wonderful moustache gave him the appearance of an actor playing a French academic in a very droll film. The story in question took place behind closed doors at the 1982 meeting of First Ministers. This was at a time when interest rates were hitting record levels of more than twenty percent. Hundreds of thousands of workers were losing their jobs and hundreds of thousands of businesses were going bankrupt. In the United States, banks themselves were going under.

An enraged mob of premiers descended on Ottawa determined to exact some explanation, if not a change of policy from the governor of the Bank of Canada. Prime Minister Trudeau, whether out of some concern for his personal safety or a reasonable belief that the governor was a decision maker independent of the government and should be there to speak his piece, agreed to provide Governor Bouey and the premiers with a chance to chat, not on national television, but with the doors closed. It was not a good day for the governor of the Bank of Canada. It was not clear whether Bouey was simply incapable of explaining anything with great clarity or whether he was unaccustomed to the forcefulness and directness of the premiers' approach. Whatever the reasons, the afternoon was going very poorly for Governor Bouey. He was having difficulty explaining to the satisfaction of the premiers the why of the high interest rate policy let alone any of the nuances of it.

Clearly uncomfortable in this circumstance was Prime Minister Trudeau. Extremely articulate and probably more familiar with some of Bouey's arguments than even the governor himself, Trudeau seemed reluctant to intervene lest he shift the brunt of the premiers' attack in his direction. Finally Jacques Parizeau, then finance minister from Quebec, who had been occupying Quebec's second seat at the table next to the diminutive and chain-smoking René Lévesque, intervened. In a few marvellously clear and colourful minutes, he described not only the logic of the Bank of Canada's position but also the flaws in that logic in view of the realities of the international monetary situation. In less than two minutes, Parizeau had so captured the attention of the premiers that the entire gravity of the room had shifted. The premiers began to direct their questions not at Governor Bouey but at Quebec Finance Minister Parizeau.

As officials seated back from the table, we could only marvel at this amazing shift of authority within the gathering. Parizeau's eloquence coupled with his knowledge of macro-economics gave him a powerful, near dominant position in the discussion. I wrote a note on a piece of paper, intended to be humorous, and handed it to Premier Pawley. It said simply "Jacques Parizeau for next governor of the Bank of Canada." To my surprise and concern, Premier Pawley signed the note and passed it to the premier next to him at the table. I watched as premier after premier smiled and added their signatures. There were an enormous number of nods.

Somewhere there is a piece of paper with the majority of the then premiers consenting to what would have seemed an extraordinary appointment of an avowedly separatist Quebec finance minister to the key post of governor of the Bank of Canada. Nevertheless, I believe that in that room there was sufficient political will to put Jacques Parizeau in just that position. It would have been a brilliant job for him, probably a better job than being leader of a political party.

J. ALFRED DOUCET

THE ELECTION OF Prime Minister Brian Mulroney caused great excitement among officials, better known as Sherpas, who toiled on the mountains of federal-provincial relations. The Trudeau era had ended with the premiers all at odds with the prime minister. A joke that emanated from Ottawa at the time captured Prime Minister Trudeau's unfavourable view of the premiers.

"How do you know when the premiers have landed in Ottawa?"

"The whining continues after the jet engines shut down."

By contrast, the well-regarded speech on federal-provincial relations and their renewal given by Mulroney in Sept-Îles, Quebec, before he became prime minster set out a much more conciliatory tone for the federal government and promised to usher in a new era of federal-provincial co-operation. When Mulroney became prime minster, a meeting of First Ministers was announced almost immediately. It was to be held in Regina. This was a positive gesture as historically almost all First Ministers meetings took place in Ottawa on the federal government's turf. We, the Sherpas of confederation, were summoned to Ottawa to plan the agenda and content for the First Ministers meeting. We arrived with a mood of anticipation of the new era and with a genuine hope of a much more co-operative relationship.

The meetings began slowly. The new key player from the federal side was an advisor to the prime minister. Prior to his elevation in the prime ministerial court, we had known him as merely Fred Doucet but the alchemy of power had transformed him into J. Alfred Doucet. It didn't matter to us whether Fred or J. Alfred, we were eager to hear from him on the new era that was to unfold.

The meeting proceeded through the morning with very little substantive discussion and a great deal of logistics and other administrative matters relevant to the upcoming meeting. The provinces indicated a new openness on a range of issues. Even Senate reform, a nearly impossible issue on which to make substantive progress, was within our grasp. There were indications of willingness from the requisite seven provinces representing more than fifty percent of Canada's population.

By the middle of lunch, however, we felt a rising tide of frustration. Henry Phillips, the representative of the government of Prince Edward Island, spoke for all of us when he inquired, "Fred, where are the new ideas on federal-provincial relations? What can we work on together? Senate reform? Equalization? What do you want us to do?" Phillips paused, then added, "Fred, we all wish to make this new era work, even Michael who represents an NDP government is ready to help."

I nodded my agreement. The answer from J. Alfred Doucet stunned us all.

He began, "Henry that is not how it is going to work. We are not going to hand down the ideas and proposals from on high in Ottawa. The ideas will spring up in the gardens of the provinces."

There was a moment of complete silence as we all absorbed two realities. Mulroney's pre-election posture as set out in the Sept-Îles speech had been rhetorical, not substantive and the new Emperor had no clothes on the federal-provincial front.

No one spoke for a long minute. Then Henry Phillips in his best Island vernacular said to our new federal counterpart.

"That's rich Fred, you drive and I'll spread."

Our hoped for new era in federal-provincial relations seemed over before it had really begun.

LEAVING THE MANITOBA GOVERNMENT

WHEN PREMIER PAWLEY was re-elected in 1985 I decided it was time to take up new challenges. After five years in the Cabinet Secretary post I was ready for something different. My final act before leaving was to assist at the swearing-in ceremony for three new ministers. Those three new ministers were Judy Wasylycia-Leis, Leonard Harapiak and Gary Doer. There was a sense of the future unveiled. Gary Doer went on to serve as premier for a decade. Judy served as a federal Member of Parliament after her time a provincial minister.

My new career began with the founding of a consulting firm that later merged into the international accounting and consulting firm KPMG, where I became a partner. A move to Montreal in 1988 took me away from Manitoba. It was not until 1991 that the siren call of public service summoned me to the next adventure in public service in Ontario.

CHAPTER EIGHT

ONTARIO
RAE DAYS

THE PAWLEY GOVERNMENT was my chance at a young age to participate in the debates and policy-making at the heart of a government. The Rae administration presented a new and immense challenge. The NDP had never governed Ontario. The scale of Ontario was daunting to a Manitoba boy. The health ministry was four times the size of the entire Manitoba government. As well, the nation entered into a serious and sharp economic downturn just before I joined the newly-minted government as deputy minister of health.

Bob Rae was elected premier of Ontario in 1990. He defeated the Liberal administration of David Peterson.

At that time, I was living in Montreal and working as a consultant to hospitals and other health organizations on strategic planning and re-engineering. I had no plans to rejoin the public service. However, when duty calls it is hard to say no, at least it is hard for me to say no.

My first involvement in the Rae government came in December 1990 when I was asked to lead the team in negotiating a new agreement between the Ontario government and the Ontario Medical Association (O.M.A.). Peter Barnes, the then very able secretary to the Ontario cabinet, called me to ask me to take on the assignment. I undertook this task as a consultant and continued to live with my family in Montreal. It was a very difficult negotiation but one that eventually led to an innovative agreement. One of the aspects of the O.M.A. deal was the so-called cap on billing, which wasn't actually a cap but a discounting, designed to shift work from over-worked older doctors to young doctors trying to break in. Believe it or not, in Ontario in 1991, there was a modest surplus of doctors and we were worried that unless the young doctors got a chance to enter practice and get some volume of work, they might leave the province.

The achievement of a deal between the government and the O.M.A. was seen as an unexpected success. After my role concluded, I returned to Montreal and my consulting practice. Most of my work was in the hospital sector assisting hospitals with strategic planning and efficiencies.

One day I returned to my office from lunch to find an odd voicemail awaiting me:

"This is Bob Rae, Michael. You may remember me. I am the premier of Ontario. Dr. Barkin has resigned as deputy minister of health and I would very much like you to take on that role. Call me."

I played the voicemail a couple of times to be certain. I had never received a job offer by voicemail. I called Premier Rae. That night Lucille and I discussed moving our family to Toronto and the next morning I called the premier back to accept his offer.

I made one other call that morning, to Dr. Eugene Le Blanc. A man of formidable intellect and memory, Eugene was a long-time public servant at the Ontario Ministry of Health. His support had been remarkable during the O.M.A. negotiations and his hard work and skills contributed to the attainment of an agreement.

I asked Eugene if he had heard any rumours about who the next deputy might be.

He replied, "No names. Likely they will choose someone political."

I asked, "How would you tell whether someone was a public servant or a politico?'

"You are only a public servant if you get the pension," Eugene replied.

"I will be your new deputy, Eugene." I responded. "Do you regard me as a public servant or a politico?"

There was a silence, unusual for Eugene who was rarely at a loss for words.

I spoke before he found words. "Eugene, I take your hesitation as uncertainty and I take that as a promising sign that someday I might be regarded by you as a public servant. I look forward to working with you."

And so my Ontario service began.

MY FIRST WEEK

THE FIRST WEEK on the job was in August of 1991. It proved to be a genuine challenge.

My predecessor, Dr. Martin Barkin, had passed on his government car. I noticed each evening when I drove home that the gas gauge registered full. I thought to myself what a great government garage—they fill the deputy's cars while we are working. I'll never need to fill my car with gasoline again.

On Friday of the first week, I was driving in heavy traffic on Highway 401 going to a meeting. My car phone rang. It was Barkin, "Michael," he explained. "I forgot to tell you that the gas gauge doesn't work in your car. It always registers full."

At the nearest gas station, the attendant said, "Wow, you must have been running on fumes."

I was beginning to feel that running on fumes might well be an apt description of the experience of a new deputy of health. One of my closest friends, Willy Parasiuk, who had served as a minister of health in Manitoba after I left the government described it to me this way. "You come in every morning and it is like being hit by Niagara Falls. You pick yourself up go home at the end of the day. And the next day it is like being hit by Niagara Falls all over again."

Early in my time in the deputy post I was called upon to attend a very large Ontario Hospital Association dinner honouring their CEO on the occasion of his retirement. My initial role was as a guest. Minister Frances Lankin was to deliver the speech. She called at the very last moment to say she couldn't make it and could I speak on her behalf. Of course I agreed.

I was lined up for the coat check behind two elderly gentlemen who were hospital trustees. As I waited for the line to move forward I listened with interest to their conversation.

"What do you hear about the new guy?"

"Worse than Barkin!" came the reply.

"Really!"

"Yes, way worse."

When it was my turn to speak, I recounted the car story and the story of the two trustees assessing my potential. The whole audience roared with laughter. Making fun of yourself is lesson one in trying to communicate with people.

ABSOLUTE POWER

AFTER A FEW PUZZLING MONTHS as deputy minister of health I went to meet with Ross McClellan, a key political advisor to Premier Rae and a former Member of the Ontario legislature. I was puzzled because much of the Rae cabinet, although not the premier himself, seemed to have a hostile almost adversarial relationship with the officials who worked in the Ontario Public Service.

"Ross, why are the ministers so hostile to the people in the public service?" I asked.

"Michael, do you remember the saying that power corrupts and absolute power corrupts absolutely."

"Yes, of course," I replied.

"Well I believe the opposite is also true. Powerlessness corrupts and absolute powerlessness corrupts absolutely."

I pondered this insight for a moment before asking, "So the ministers had no power in their previous lives?"

"Most were in advocacy organizations or the labour movement. They were always against those who held the power. Now they hold it and they need to be in opposition to someone so they are adversarial towards the public service."

A LYNCHING IN SUDBURY

INCO, THE DOMINANT EMPLOYER of the nickel town of Sudbury, had begun to cut back several thousand jobs and mechanize its mining in the 1980s. As a result, employment at Inco dropped from some 10,000 to about 5,000 miners. To try and replace the economic activity and the income,

Sudbury set out to become the regional centre for specialty medicine. It recruited a number of very talented doctors, but also a few of the most difficult and obnoxious doctors it has ever been my misfortune to encounter. Even within the O.M.A., the Sudbury local was viewed as a difficult. So it was not a complete surprise that Sudbury objected to the Cap.

The Cap, as it became known by those who opposed it, was most vehemently countered by the specialist community in Sudbury. The idea of discounting or the Cap was that the fee for service payment by the government through the Ontario Health Insurance Program (OHIP) to a doctor represented both payment for his or her overhead, such as office rental and nursing staff, and also a fee for their professional skill. As a doctor's volume of patients and billings increased, their rent and other fixed costs did not. The idea of the discounting was to continue paying doctors for their professional skill but not to overpay them for their overheads. It also had the goal of shifting work to newly graduated doctors to retain them in Ontario. Because the Cap was portrayed as taking income out of Sudbury, the doctors gained some strange supportive bedfellows including the trade unions.

I was invited to the public meeting in Sudbury to talk about the Cap. One of the local hospital CEOs invited me to dinner before the meeting. While at dinner I took a chance and said to the waitress,

"Do you know about the meeting they're having tonight?"

"That's not a meeting they're having," she replied.

And I said, "Oh, but there is a meeting tonight," and she said "It's not a meeting, it's a lynching. They've got some guy coming up from Toronto and they're going to beat the hell out of him." I decided wisely to ignore her mixed metaphor lest she reappear later as part of the lynch mob.

I thought, Oh, great! I'm the beat-ee from Toronto. After dinner we went over to Sudbury city hall where the meeting was to be held. It was in the bear pit of city hall, a chamber with seats—one labelled "Premier," one labelled "Health Minister," and one labelled "Deputy Minister of Health." I was the only one invited who had turned up to represent the Ontario government. When there is good news, the minister or premier delivers it. When there is bad news or angry doctors they send the deputy minister. It goes with the territory.

I declined to sit in my marked chair and said I'd stay with the people in the audience seats. Outside the meeting, there were women carrying babies and the babies were carrying picket signs that said "I'm glad I was born before the Cap!" as though if they'd been born after the Cap they'd be stuck in some room waiting for some doctor that would refuse to deliver the baby because he would get a discounted fee.

The meeting was mostly indeed a lynching. There were about thirty speakers, all of whom were opposed to the Cap, most of whom were willing to blame everything including the cold weather on the department of health. It was a horrible, abusive four-hour meeting. They had all those people speak before they had me get up to offer any sort of explanation.

When I did rise, I had some very powerful slides showing how the Cap (i.e. discount) actually did work and how it didn't constrain physicians even at a significant level of billings. I even put up some good examples showing how physicians could still be making a million dollars a year without suffering any affects of the discounting or the so-called Cap. This took a little wind out of the sails of the opposition. Two things alarmed me. One was on my way to the podium; a man near the front row shouted at me "Fuck you!" When I returned to my seat, I asked everyone if they might know who the man might be. Someone suggested they thought he was the editor of the local newspaper. This did not seem to bode well for the newspaper coverage. The second thing that happened was that I was seated next to a very large man from the mine and mill workers union. When I sat back down he said "Good speech, brother." I thought, aha. But he then added, "but that's not what we're here for tonight." They then unleashed another barrage of speakers to beat me into submission.

I went back to the hotel feeling only marginally good about standing my ground in the face of this. I couldn't sleep. I'd had too much coffee. They were replaying the meeting on television. And since I couldn't sleep and there were no other stations, I got to watch myself being beaten to a pulp all over again. I got about an hour's sleep before the 7:00 a.m. flight back to Toronto.

Miraculously, this foul-mouthed individual turned out to be someone other than the editor of the local paper. The editor of the local paper had in fact liked my presentation and had run an editorial on the front page of *The Sudbury Star* entitled "Doctors Medicine May Not be Right Remedy" in which he said a number of nice things—so nice in fact that I have reproduced a few sections of the editorial below. The article in its entirety is framed on my bedroom wall. I look at it on bad days to remind me to stick to the facts and to pray for a thinking journalist.

December 7, 1991 *The Sudbury Star*

OUR OPINION

Doctor's medicine may not be the cure

There are a good many people who find it difficult to support Sudbury's medical specialists, a group that is seeking an open ended exemption from new government regulations designed to halt the rapid increase in health-care costs.

The Sudbury Star can be placed in that category.

Amid the hoopla and the kangaroo-court atmosphere that existed at a Thursday night Civic Square meeting that pitted doctors, labour leaders, business people and politicians against Michael Decter, Ontario's deputy minister of health, one thing became painfully clear: the Sudbury specialists are not prepared to be open, honest, reasonable or rational.

The fact is, the government should be applauded for efforts to keep cost increases in check. About 34 per cent of the provincial budget (17 billion a year) is spent on health care, and doctor billings have been rising at a rate of 12 per cent a year.

On Thursday night, the health ministry's Decter gave a superb presentation under extremely difficult circumstances.

He was relevant, logical, understandable, and dealt with the known facts.

One specific item stands out among all others. In one situation picked at random from government files, Decter reported that one specialist had billings of about $1.2 million a year. That kind of puts the whole issue in perspective, Decter appears to be a reasonable man. Even after being hassled and goaded for three long hours, he held out an olive branch to the medical specialists, offering to meet with them individually or as a group in an effort to sort out the problems.

He was shouted down

Decter was serious. Indeed, Sudbury East MPP and cabinet minister Shelley Martel reiterates that offer in today's column on page A6 of *The Star*. But people with cooler heads than those involved in Thursday night's crude shootout should become involved.

Simply put, the doctor's arguments are less than credible. And creating fear in the community and publicly raising ridiculous and unsubstantiated debating points in efforts to receive special financial consideration is wrong.

That's especially true if the medical specialists are unwilling to provide the public with facts and figures that they claim would support their position.

The doctors should accept the government's offer to sit down and intelligently discuss the relevant matters.

They deserve to be treated fairly. But they don't deserve the open-ended contracts they are seeking.

As we noted, we're extremely uncomfortable.

Eight years after my horrible meeting in Sudbury, I went back. This time I was no longer deputy minister of health; I was invited to give a series of speeches on health reform in Sudbury. I admit to being more than a little nervous about returning to the scene of the thrashing. I knew that one or two of the most difficult physicians had moved elsewhere.

I wasn't prepared for the enormous goodwill, nor was I prepared for the great friendship extended to me by Dr. Roberto Grosso, a prominent physician in the community, and chair of the board of governors of Laurentian University. I had met Grosso previously through his daughter, Francesca, who produced the annual Pulse Conference, a major national health gathering. Dr. Grosso escorted me to my several speeches, all day, drove me around, took me up to the university and generally treated me with extraordinary kindness. At the end of the day, when I thanked him he said, "We didn't treat you very well the last time you were here."

He also noted that the troublemakers had been dealt with. I was grateful to him and was greatly saddened to learn a couple of years later of his death from cancer. His daughter worked with me to launch the Health Council of Canada. Later we co-authored *Navigating Canada's Health Care* and dedicated that book to the memory of our physician fathers.

I LIED AND I CAN PROVE IT

THE SUDBURY AFFAIR did not end with the favourable newspaper story. As I was enduring the slings and arrows of the meeting in Sudbury, Shelley Martel, minister of the Crown and member of the provincial legislature for Nickel Belt, one of the Sudbury ridings, was lighting the fuse in Thunder Bay on another bomb. In conversation at a cocktail party, Minister Martel was challenged about the Cap and events in Sudbury. The minister told to her antagonist, "If you had seen the doctors' billings you would not be defending them."

An enormous controversy ensued. The opposition demanded an inquiry into whether Martel had seen confidential doctors' billings that she should not have seen. The premier granted a legislative inquiry.

One of the stranger acts of defence in political life had to be Shelley Martel's determination to prove she had lied in Thunder Bay. Her claim to have never seen any doctors' billings was publicly buttressed by her lawyer who had her take a lie detector test to prove that she had in fact not spoken the truth.

Politics is a learned trade, not an inherited one. Sadly, this may not have been apparent to Premier Bob Rae in his initial days as Ontario premier. He chose novice Shelley Martel as house leader to take the post ably held by her father MPP Eli Martel. He had served as an MPP for twenty years from 1967 until he retired in 1987. She became house leader at the tender age of twenty-four. However, after a few bruising incidents early in her career Shelley Martel went on to solid and productive political service to her community and her province.

NO PHONE SERVICE

THE FIRST RITUAL of the working day at the ministry of health turned on the press clippings. Like an advanced military operation, the clipping of all press stories with a reference to health consumed much energy. One morning, leafing carefully through the morning press clippings, my eyes landed on an unusual headline. It read: "No Phone Service—OHIP!" Intrigued, I read further. The employees of a small OHIP office (who worked for the ministry of health of which I was the administrative head) became annoyed at the volume of calls they were receiving from the public. Their solution was to have their office telephones removed.

An effective remedy to be certain but not one a minister of health funded by taxpayers would likely defend. When I entered her office for the morning briefing, Minister Lankin, thorough as always, already had the package open to the precise clipping I dreaded. She was not amused. One of my jobs as deputy minister of health was to explain the actions of the 12,000 public servants who toiled for the ministry. Humour is often a defence. But this particular morning with this particular minister, humour did not work.

"Well, I can't call them!" I began. It was a mistake. I blundered on, "They don't have a phone!" The minister explained in what would be termed "frank and full" words the extent of her outrage at my weak attempt at humour. I indicated that I already had a staff member driving to this OHIP office to explain that phone service would be restored at the earliest possible moment. There were days when explaining the actions of 12,000 employees of the ministry of health proved challenging. This had been one of those days.

HEALTH MINISTERS

HEALTH MINISTER FRANCES LANKIN proved reluctant when it came to her first meeting of health ministers from across the nation. Her view was one of suspicion. The health ministers were from other political parties. She presumed that there would be little common ground for an NDP health minister and the others, Liberals and Tories. She was wrong. Health ministers, regardless of party, share the enormous burden of the responsibility of the largest portfolio in every provincial government. They have much common ground.

Russell King had served for nearly a decade as health minister for New Brunswick. He sat next to Minister Lankin at the first dinner meeting of their ministerial conference.

During dinner he said somewhat wistfully, "I used to have the best job in Canadian health care."

Knowing that he was a physician and general practitioner, Minister Lankin replied, "You mean being a family doctor,"

"No," replied King. "I used to be the opposition health critic."

THEY TAKE AWAY YOUR NAME

WHEN YOU WORK in a place as busy as the deputy minister's office at Ontario Health you become the job. They strip away your name as they would with a new inmate. Instead of a number you are assigned the job title.

I spent a fruitless week or two saying to staff, "Just call me Michael."

To which they would reply, "Of course Deputy."

I began to note that my own behaviour conformed to this pattern. Frances Lankin spent a year or more trying unsuccessfully to get me to call her anything other than "Minister."

Premier, Minister, Deputy Minister—the job becomes your new name. But, caveat emptor, best to remember these titles are on loan, you don't own them.

You could call someone below you in the hierarchy by their name but calling the Premier "Bob" caused the room to go silent. It was an error that few committed more than once.

No one was more amused and also offended by my new name, "Deputy," than my long-time friend and colleague Lloyd Girman. Lloyd had himself served ably as a deputy minister of northern affairs in the Manitoba government of Howard Pawley but Manitoba was more informal and even deputy ministers kept their birth names.

The elevator rose up the ten floors of the Hepburn Block in Toronto where both the minister and I worked, stopping at each floor. Staff of the ministry would enter the elevator, spy me, and with a nearly imperceptible nod of their head they would intone, "Deputy."

One day after we had enjoyed lunch together, Lloyd who was visiting from Winnipeg came back to the Hepburn Block with me. We got in the elevator together. After two or three floors this small ritual proved too much for Lloyd.

Lloyd would mimic the behaviour of those entering the elevator bowing his head slightly and whispering loudly at me. However he did not mutter or whisper, "Deputy," but rather "Asshole."

No comment passed from the startled ministry officials at this improbable and rude behaviour. They each pretended that they had heard nothing. I learned much later that a few staff thought that Lloyd might be either a new and unbroken ministerial aide or a somewhat mentally disturbed person, possibly an escaped patient from one of Ontario's ten psychiatric hospitals. I never shared this speculation with Lloyd.

UNCHARTED TERRITORY

IN 1993, THE ONTARIO CABINET decided it desperately needed to reduce an impending deficit of nearly $20 billion. I played a role in this decision. Sent by the premier and cabinet to New York with Deputy Treasurer Eleanor Clitheroe, we tested the huge numbers with our bankers carefully.

Dinner with senior officials of Goldman Sachs proceeded in a very civilized manner. Eleanor and I had decided to ease them gradually into the size of Ontario's deficit and therefore its borrowing requirement.

We started at $10 billion.

"What if we needed to borrow $10 billion next year?" began Eleanor.

"That shouldn't be a problem," came the calm response from the Goldman side. We continued to eat. After about ten minutes Eleanor inquired, "What if we needed to borrow $12 billion next year?"

This time there was a much longer pause before the answer came back.

"Manageable, tough but manageable."

The subsequent conversation became somewhat muted. A mood of dark anticipation settled over the dinner table. More wine was poured and consumed. Clearly everyone was bracing for the next round.

"How would an Ontario borrowing requirement of $15 billion be received by markets?" I asked.

When I mentioned the $15 billion a long and uncomfortable silence descended over the table. No one spoke. Finally Bob Hormats of Goldman Sachs spoke, "That would be uncharted territory for a non-sovereign borrower."

In plain language, no entity smaller than a nation had ever contemplated borrowing that sum of money in a single year. It was uncharted territory because no province or state or corporation had borrowed that much. Our hosts were far too polite to say it couldn't be done. They just said it had never been done. And they did not give us any reason to believe that this was a course that they would advise embarking upon.

Eleanor and I silently agreed not to try the $20 billion number. There seemed little point. Even $15 billion was a risk beyond the Ontario's advisors at Goldman to contemplate. Clearly the Rae government needed a new budget plan. We returned home and delivered the news to the premier, finance minister and cabinet. We were not received as conquering heroes. The cabinet mood was just short of "shoot the messenger."

THE ONTARIO SOCIAL CONTRACT

BOB RAE BECAME premier of Ontario at the time of a major recession. In fact, the declining economy likely contributed to his victory over the government of Liberal David Peterson in the election of 1990.

Premier Rae had nearly five turbulent years as premier of Ontario. Probably no event during this tenure stirred as much controversy as the negotiations that came to be known as the Ontario Social Contract.

After three years, the Rae government found itself confronting a gargantuan deficit. A sharp recession had clobbered Ontario manufacturing and sent provincial finances into a tailspin.

There was no escaping a role in solving this problem. As deputy minister of health, I had responsibility for forty percent of the province's spending. Over the previous two years beginning with the O.M.A. agreement, I had worked hard with the team at the Ministry of Health to rein in spending. We had demonstrated that savings could be achieved in health through tough-minded management. We had also proved that efficiencies through shortened length of patient stays in hospitals were possible without a reduction in the quality of care. This success drew me into the premier's sights as a leader for the most ambitious and contentious assignment I have ever been given. The role of chief negotiator for the Ontario Social Contract tested me to the very core of my being.

Eugene Le Blanc was a long-time public servant in the Ministry of Health. He was also much of the institutional memory of the place. He had worked in support of me when I served as chief negotiator in the 1991 negotiations with the Ontario Medical Association. We had achieved agreement when there seemed little prospect of a deal. Eugene was a logical choice to assist on this new and much larger mission.

Peter Warrian was transferred from the Ministry of Finance to serve as deputy chief negotiator. This was terrific. Peter was not only a solid economist but he had worked in the labour movement as head of research for the United Steelworkers. He knew labour and I could rely on him for negotiating advice. We set up six separate negotiating tables and assembled teams for each table. This was the largest labour negotiation ever attempted in Ontario and the most difficult.

At our first meeting of the full team I spoke with some passion on the urgency and significance of the mission we were embarking upon.

When I finished, Eugene Le Blanc said, "So let me be clear, if we succeed in getting this deal done we will all make less money for the next three years."

"Yes," I admitted. "You will make five percent less money but you will also get ten days off without pay."

Eugene answered, "You really know how to motivate a group, boss."

He meant it ironically and my observation over the next two months was that I had never seen a group work harder in pursuit of a difficult goal.

Peter Warrian, deputy chief negotiator, began each morning's team meeting with a quote from his favourite western movie: "It's a good day to die."

I tried not to let his dark humour undermine our optimism.

Premier Rae's own sharp-edged wit and propensity for the clever quip proved itself troublesome on at least one occasion during the negotiations. The public sector unions were led by four individuals representing the four major bargaining agents: Sid Ryan of the Canadian Union of Public Employees, Fred Upshaw of the Ontario Public Sector Workers Union, Liz Barclay of the Ontario Teachers and Ted Roscoe of the Service Employees International Union. The four were noisily critical of the Rae government, the Social Contract and pretty much every other aspect of the situation. Their rhetoric was always extreme. Words like "betrayal" and "traitor" featured prominently in their public attacks on the premier, the Social Contract idea and pretty much everyone involved in trying to secure a new approach.

Rae was asked at a private dinner how the negotiations for the Ontario Social Contract were going. He quipped that it would be going better if I were not forced to negotiate with "the four windbags of the Apocalypse." It was far too juicy a salvo to remain private for long.

When I arrived the next morning for the negotiations, the four labour leaders were sitting behind their table with their arms crossed in a gesture of hostility. From their body language I guessed that, just as the premier's smart remark had reached me, it had also reached them.

"So you heard," I began. They had. It was not a good day for me as I had to bear their anger at Rae's wit.

The brilliant quip of which Bob Rae is a master may not always win friends amongst those who are the butt of the quip. Rae is not alone in this weakness. Remember Prime Minister Mulroney's infamous comment on former Liberal Minister Bryce Mackasey. "There is no whore like an old whore."

Rae also landed another witty quip during the Social Contract talks. I had called him to seek his advice on how to convince Ontario Hydro, wholly owned by the government, to even attend the negotiations which they were boycotting. Rae had appointed the remarkable Maurice Strong to lead Ontario Hydro. I asked Premier Rae if there was any way to get Maurice's attention.

"Go to the nearest hub airport and wait. He should be through sometime soon."

This story appeared in Thomas Walkom's book *Rae Days* without clear attribution. Maurice Strong summoned me to his office to demand who said this about him. It was a humorous question as I suspect Maurice has travelled more air miles than nearly anyone on the planet. Nevertheless he was worried that the premier might have suggested he was travelling too much. After due consideration, I told him that David Agnew, the cabinet secretary, not Rae, was the quipster. If Maurice Strong is reading these words all I can say is that it was a small lie to salvage a situation. I have said my Hail Marys and sought forgiveness.

Wit is a virtue in playwrights and novelists. In politicians, it usually provides short-term pleasure for long-term pain.

One day during the Social Contract negotiations, I had a brief conversation with Ted Roscoe. He was one tough, shrewd labour leader. He was not as given to rhetoric as Ryan or Barclay and in my view was more effective at protecting his members.

"Last year we went to arbitration in the health sector," he began. "We wanted a ten percent settlement over two years but the employers wouldn't give it to us."

I nodded. I was very familiar with the history. So I continued, "You went to arbitration and asked for twenty percent."

"Yes," replied Ted, "And we got seven and eight—fifteen percent over two years."

"And you only really wanted ten percent."

"Yep."

"Well, Ted, all I want is that five percent back. The five percent you never really wanted in the first place."

"It don't work that way, brother," said Ted.

For a few fleeting moments, the ten days without pay that all government employees were confronted with were referred to as Decter Days. Despite the alliteration, politics won out and the days became known as Rae Days.

My brother Richard turned up at my home one evening. He had a pocketful of buttons the Canadian Union of Public Employees members were distributing that read DECTER IS A FOUR LETTER WORD. I wore it on my lapel the next day for the negotiations.

My more practical brother collected as many of them as he could and made them disappear. When asked by his union colleagues at city hall whether he was my brother he answered, "No relation."

I forgave him for denying we were brothers given the anger in the union ranks and particularly given his effective gathering of the offensive buttons.

Our Social Contract team experienced a roller coaster of emotions through the weeks of negotiations. At times we became deeply pessimistic at the glacial progress at the bargaining tables. At other times, we were much more optimistic as we had reports of breakthroughs at other sector tables. In the end, the labour leadership was not able or willing to contemplate a deal. The surprising reality is how close we came to a deal. The labour negotiators could see it. Our own team could see it. But the public sector labour leadership could not stomach it. If they were to give up ground then the government would need to legislate it rather than bargaining it. Ultimately they got their wish.

When I learned that the labour leaders had withdrawn en masse from the negotiations and vowed never to return, I assembled my exhausted team. I began what would be my final speech to this brave band that had worked incredibly hard.

"They say of opera that it ain't over until the fat lady sings." I paused, "sadly a few minutes ago as I walked through the lobby of this hotel I heard Liz Barclay leading the assembled labour brethren in a rousing chorus of 'Solidarity Forever.' So I believe it is over. No one is ever likely to thank us but you should all know that I have never been prouder of anyone that I have worked with. Thank you."

Left-leaning academics and journalists have written many books on this period. Most denounce the Ontario Social Contract as a betrayal by the Rae government of his party's labour roots and commitment to egalitarian principles. On the contrary, my view was then and remains to this day that the Social Contract was Rae's finest hour. He chose to sacrifice his government to prevent the layoff of 50,000 low-wage public sector workers without the protection of labour agreements. To find the $2 billion in labour savings he imposed a modest five percent reduction on the nearly one million Ontario public sector workers. When the labour leadership rejected the Social Contract, Rae's government responded by legislating the outcome. I left government after the failed negotiation.

The failure of the Ontario Social Contract negotiations haunted me. It took me many years to recover my confidence—and I still bear much scar tissue. I fully remembered Ted Poyser's question. "How well do you cope with failure." The answer in my case was—slowly and not very well.

JOSEPH STALIN

IT IS A RULE that as a government official or politician you should always presume a reporter is in the room. It is also a rule that diplomatic language is safest. Colourful language is a certain route to trouble. One night in Hamilton, I violated both rules and paid the price. Let me set the stage for my verbal gaffe.

During the negotiations of the Ontario Social Contract I was invited to speak to the Hamilton Academy of Medicine. The doctors of that steel town 45 minutes west of Toronto had invited me to address a dinner audience. I was exhausted before I arrived in Hamilton. It had not been a good day, one of many not good days in the Social Contract negotiations. What I said in my speech is lost to history—probably deservedly so. After I finished my remarks the angry doctors lined up at the lone microphone to have their go at me.

I made a decision—not a wise one. If I couldn't persuade them with logic, truth and the perilous state of the province's finances, then at least I could show them endurance. I resolved to stand at my place and answer every single question as completely as I could even if it took a very long time.

It went on for what seemed like hours. The doctors ranged in mood from sarcastic and angry to angry and angry. I remained calm and tried to give fulsome answers to each question. Finally there was only a lone doctor at the microphone and I dropped my guard.

The essence of the last question was, "Isn't health care decision-making too centralized at the ministry of health?"

It was a good and honest question. I happened to agree with the doctor who asked it. It had been a long day and a very long evening.

Instead of the bland careful answers I had given to what seemed like the previous hundred questions, I tried to be colourful. Anyone around politics and government knows that this is a very dangerous time to be colourful. However, I felt we were alone—just the two hundred angry doctors and myself. I had been told that no reporters were present. Obviously both the organizers and I missed the reporter from *The Hamilton Spectator*, the local daily, in that count of reporters. When you are being colourful, the difference between no reporters and one reporter is enormous.

What I said was this: "Yes, doctor you are correct, far too many decisions are made or not made on the tenth floor of the Hepburn Block where the minister of health and I both work. Far more of those decisions should be made locally. You should be part of those decisions as they are clearer to you in Hamilton than they are to us in Toronto."

Had I stopped there, no consequence would have flowed from my evening other than fatigue. Instead, I plunged on in a rhetorical flourish. I added, "You know if Joseph Stalin were miraculously reborn, and I hope he is not, but if he were and he came back to life in Ontario the only two organizations he would feel at home in would be Ontario Hydro and the ministry of health."

Then I went home exhausted, slept and dragged myself into the office for the morning briefing meeting with the minister. As I flipped through the press clippings I came upon a front page article from that morning's *Hamilton Spectator*. The headline read "Deputy Minster Calls for Return of Stalin."

"Oh Christ," was my first thought, followed by a reflexive "I guess there was a reporter present last night." Not finished with the Lord in this matter I uttered a silent prayer that the minister had not worked her way to page sixty-eight of the clippings package. My prayer was, of course, in vain. Frances Lankin read everything we ever gave her. She was a master of her files and had an unrivalled ability to absorb detail. She always read every press clipping. When I entered her office she had the clipping package opened to the offensive piece that would undoubtedly dog her day in question period.

I told my story emphasizing that I had not, in fact called for the return of Stalin merely reflected on what he might find if he had been reborn in the present day in Ontario.

"Perhaps, Deputy," she called me Deputy when she was very angry. The rest of the time she called me Michael. "Perhaps Deputy," she continued with a real edge to her voice, "for the remainder of the time you are my deputy you could refrain from mentioning the late Joseph Stalin in your public speeches."

A decade later, I was invited to address the editorial board of the *National Post* newspaper at a dinner with a group that shared none of my views on the virtues of Canadian-style Medicare. Of note, Terrence Corcoran, with whom I had previously clashed, was in attendance. I gave a spirited but calm defence of the merits of Medicare including the considerable competitive advantage it conferred on Canadian manufacturers in contrast to their American rivals who bore a far higher share of their employees' health costs. Towards the end of my presentation I told the above tale of Joseph Stalin and my night in Hamilton. My point was that

Stalin was a genuine centralist and I was a strong believer in decentralization and devolution of health decision making to local health councils as a way to reform health services. I was crystal clear on this point.

The next day, Corcoran's column described me as a Stalinist. I was completely indignant since I had said exactly the opposite the night before. I called *National Post* editor-in-chief Ken Whyte to complain.

"Ken you were there last night. I said exactly the opposite of what Terry claims."

"Well," Ken replied calmly, "Terry likely wrote his piece before he came to dinner."

There was no coherent reply I could make to this honest but unhelpful response.

Since that day until penning these words I have resisted the temptation to make any references to the late Joseph Stalin. As well, I also assume the press is omnipresent.

RABBITS AND HATS

SEVERAL MONTHS AFTER returning from the Social Contract negotiations to my job as deputy minister of health, I realized that I was too exhausted and dispirited to continue. The Social Contract negotiations had simply taken too much out of me. Even after a vacation where, to the dismay of my young children, I slept twenty hours a day, I was still drained and exhausted. Deputy minister of health is a nearly impossible job when you are in top form. In my diminished state, I was genuinely worried about not doing a proper job.

I telephoned Premier Bob Rae.

"Premier, it's Michael Decter, I am wondering if you could see me for a few minutes this evening?"

"I know why you want to see me and I don't want to hear it," was his reply, "but come at 7:00 p.m. I will be home."

I arrived at the appointed hour to his home.

"Why are you leaving?" the premier asked, anticipating my decision.

"Premier, my success as a public servant has always been pulling rabbits out of hats. Well, the hat got bigger and the rabbits got smaller and I just can't find them anymore."

EXPENSE ACCOUNT

THE LAST DAY I SERVED as deputy minister of health, I took a taxi from one meeting to the next. That morning *The Toronto Star* had featured a rather nasty shot at my expense account—based on a trumped-up, largely false attack concocted by Liberal MPP Tim Murphy.

The taxi driver and I listened to a radio account of my expense account. "Bastard bureaucrats!" he swore.

I paused briefly to reflect. Then I took the coward's way out. "Bloody awful." I meant it but perhaps not the way the taxi driver interpreted my comment.

Several years later when I was managing the Canadian end of a health care consultancy, APM Inc., I heard a story that fell in the category of "I wish I had said that."

Connie Curran, a senior partner in APM, was a nurse leader in the United States. She was also a powerful and highly intelligent Irish American from Wisconsin. Connie could be charming but she also had toughness acquired from life in the nursing and health care trenches.

She was hired by the then Manitoba health minister, Don Orchard. The APM mandate was to achieve significant financial savings in the Winnipeg hospitals. Here APM broke an important rule. If you are seeking savings in a hospital you need to have the hospital as a client. When you have government as a client there is less legitimacy at the hospital and more room for public criticism. In the Winnipeg job there was plenty of political controversy.

One night Connie was taking a taxi to the Winnipeg airport to return to her home in Chicago. Making conversation she said to the cab driver, "So what's new in town?"

"Haven't you heard?" replied the driver. "There is some bitch in town from the United States and they are paying her $5 million dollars to wreck Medicare."

A silence descended on the cab.

Connie tapped the driver on the shoulder. He turned around and looked at her.

"I'm the bitch," was all she said.

Silence again descended.

Then the driver spoke, "I guess I am not getting a tip tonight."

AND NO PHONES RANG

THE SAME DAY my resignation was announced in the press, my very first call was from Rob Prichard, then president of the University of Toronto.

"Michael, Rob Prichard, I am very sorry that you are stepping down. You did an outstanding job."

I thanked Rob for his kind words but he was not simply calling out of kindness.

"Do you have plans, a new job lined up?" he inquired directly.

"No," I acknowledged. "I decided to leave and then look for the next challenge."

"I would like you to come to the university. We have a place for you at the Centre for Bioethics. I have spoken with Fred Lowy who heads the Centre and he would be delighted to have you join him."

"Thank you, that is very generous."

Rob laughed, "I didn't say we had any money but we can put a roof over your head. Think about it and let me know."

"I will," I replied. And I did accept his offer.

The Centre for Bioethics at the University of Toronto was housed in an old church precisely one block from the Hepburn Block where I served as deputy.

There was only one off-putting reality of my new monk-like life. The phone never rang. As I worked on my first book, *Healing Medicare*, I would pick up the phone two or three times a day just to make certain there was still a dial tone.

I realized that in life you have your family and your friends but much of the noise and business comes not from you but from the job you are doing at the time. It is easy to mistake the popularity of your position for something more personal. For all the months that the phone did not ring, I remembered how it had never stopped ringing at the ministry of health. I also realized that in public service and in public life you need to keep your own scorecard and savour your own small triumphs along the way.

CHAPTER NINE

SPECTATOR AND COMMENTATOR

IN THE LAST FEW YEARS, my role in government and politics has been as more a spectator than a player. Since 1994, I have worked briefly at the Centre for Bioethics, University of Toronto, led two health care consultancies and for the past twelve years have built and managed what is now my own investment firm on Bay Street, LDIC Inc. I have also written six books, three on health care and three on investing.

During this period, I have chaired the boards of several health organizations, including the Canadian Institute for Health Information (CIHI), Saint Elizabeth Health Care and the Health Council of Canada. While my direct connection to government has diminished, my advisory role has greatly expanded. Whether working inside the government or advising you never lose the perspective of considering the entertainment value. Over the past fifteen years, I have had an opportunity to play a role in the formulation of health policy that rivals what I had when I was deputy minister.

MORNINGSIDE WITH PETER GZOWSKI

THE PRODUCT OF my labours at the Centre for Bioethics was my first published book—*Healing Medicare: Managing Health System Change The Canadian Way*. Early in the book tour, the publisher, Jack Stoddart, imparted to me his lifetime of accumulated wisdom with regard to being a Canadian author.

"Hold up the book at every opportunity," he declared. "Someone might even buy it."

He went on to add that if I were a bestselling American author on a book tour I would need security.

"What about a bestselling Canadian author?" I inquired, "What will I need?"

"A name tag," was his succinct response. Through the six books I have written I have found that a name tag is indeed a genuine asset.

One result of the publication of *Healing Medicare* was an invitation to appear on my favourite radio show, the beloved *Morningside* on CBC, and be interviewed by its host Peter Gzowski.

Although I had been interviewed hundreds of times in previous positions, an unfamiliar nervousness set in. I realized that as a first-time author I was terrified that the formidable Gzowski would demand, "On page 178 you wrote," and I would have no recollection of that sentence.

To add to my anxiety, the interview was scheduled for Remembrance Day which meant my two children, then ten and twelve, would be listening.

The fateful day arrived. I presented myself at the studio, author-lamb to the interview slaughter.

The red light went on. Peter Gzowski transformed himself into a plausible reincarnation of my favourite uncle, Canada's favourite uncle really. He asked questions motivated by genuine and transparent curiosity. After what seemed to me only a very few minutes, the red light went out. To my astonishment, we had spoken for thirty minutes. It had been a pleasure.

Gzowski smiled at me and said, "We are done." Then after a pause he added, "You know Michael, this is radio."

I nodded, somewhat bewildered by his comment, "I knew it was radio."

"So holding your book up for the whole thirty minutes interview didn't do you much good."

I blushed red realizing that in my nervousness I had the book raised in a fearful grip. We both laughed.

LLOYD ROBERTSON

IN THE MID-1990s I was asked to become chair of CIHI. This position made me the spokesperson for a series of very important health information releases. I became a favourite interviewee for reporters looking for comment on the facts of Canadian health care.

I will be forever grateful to Lloyd Robertson for teaching me the basic truth of television and brevity. Over the years, I had been interviewed many times by newspaper reporters as well as radio interviewers. The shared characteristic of all of these interviews was that there was lots of time. With CIHI I began to be interviewed on the national TV news. The national news is a different art form.

One evening I found myself sitting on the set at CTV National with Lloyd Robertson.

"I have three questions for you, Michael," he began.

The camera rolled and I answered each of his questions.

"That was excellent," said Lloyd when we finished.

I smiled.

Lloyd, possibly the nicest person in television, then went on to add, "And if we had five minutes for you on tonight's news we would be done. However, we only have one minute, thirty seconds."

I absorbed the evident truth that I had been, at least for national news purposes, long-winded.

"Fine," I said.

"Same three questions—just shorter answers," replied Lloyd.

The thirty-second clip—times three, I thought. The complexity of the future of health care reduced to three thirty-second clips.

Lloyd Robertson then asked me the same three questions again. This time I answered while watching the large clock tick off exactly ninety seconds.

When we finished he said, "Michael, I have to go but the technician will stay and show you both versions. You will be surprised."

I took his advice and watched my original five-minute version and then the second take at ninety seconds. What I expected was that the first version would be loaded with content and the second a mere shallow shadow. What I saw to my astonishment was not that at all.

In the long version, I had a long wind-up before I actually answered the question. "Well Lloyd, on one hand some critics say ... and on the other hand..." before actually saying what I thought. In the ninety-second version all of my wasted prelude had vanished and there were just the answers, direct and clear.

I will always be grateful to Lloyd Robertson for teaching me the art of the television interview and the power of clarity and brevity by inviting me to simply watch the tape.

CANADA AM

ONE EVENING, I received a call from *Canada* AM, CTV's national morning show.

"Could you come to be interviewed about tobacco legislation tomorrow morning at 6:30 a.m.?"

"If you can send a car and if I can bring my two children you have a deal," was my response. They agreed. The CTV limo was an aging Buick Riviera but it saved me from driving and trying to manage two sleepy children at the same time.

My children, Genevieve and Riel, were ten and twelve. I had been separated and was as a consequence a single parent. If CTV wanted me at 6:00 in the morning I needed to bring my kids. The children were excited about a limo ride, television and about meeting Valerie Pringle who was for them a television star. They wore their pyjamas with coats over top to the TV studio.

I had devoted a great deal of my time while deputy minister of health to tightening control on tobacco sales. In my mind, the most preventable health risk is tobacco. Reducing the smoking rate, particularly among teenagers, ranked as a major priority. I did not hold the tobacco industry in anything but contempt for its historical actions to undermine efforts to restrict use of a lethal substance.

Rob Parker, representing the tobacco industry, was scheduled to share the interview. He would be beamed in from a studio in Ottawa and I would be on the Canada AM set in Toronto with Valerie Pringle. I intended to make the case for tighter regulation of tobacco advertising on health grounds. Rob, predictably as the industry spokesman, would argue against restrictions on where and how they could advertise.

I waited and let Rob Parker go on and on making his points. I became angry when he described cigarettes as having "some health issues."

When he finished, Valerie Pringle turned to me and asked, "Michael, what have you to say?" I went for the dramatic. "Valerie," I asked rhetorically, "Is it all right to say bullshit on national television?"

I went on to add that tobacco killed people and that I did not consider this a minor "health issue."

Rob Parker remained calm. I had never met the man.

After the interview, I said to Valerie Pringle, "I hope I didn't get you in trouble by saying bullshit on the air."

Valerie retorted, "Why didn't you just say 'Fuck you Rob Parker' on national TV?"

I pointed to my now giggling children on the edge of the set.

My son said. "Valerie Pringle said the F word!" They both laughed.

Valerie blushed bright red.

On the way home in the chauffer-driven Buick, I was feeling pretty good about taking on the tobacco industry in unusually blunt terms, for me. Then my cell phone rang. It was Pamela Wallin, my partner at the time.

"I guess I forgot to tell you two things," she began.

"What?" I asked

"Rob Parker is one of my best friends in the world. Tonight you and I are having dinner with Rob and his wife."

"Yikes," was all I could say. "Probably better if you had mentioned this before the interview."

That night I walked up to the door of Pamela's home with a certain amount of dread. I had after all come close to accusing Rob and his industry of murder.

I shook hands with Rob Parker and mumbled something like, "An unexpected pleasure."

Rob responded, "Michael, I started out as a journalist, then I served as a member of the Mulroney caucus as a MP. Now I represent the tobacco industry." He paused, "I believe that I have been climbing the ethical ladder."

HEALTH COUNCIL OF CANADA

THE HEALTH COUNCIL OF CANADA was a recommendation of both the Romanow Royal Commission on the Future of Health Care and the Kirby Senate Committee.

Long negotiations ensued among the fourteen governments—the government of Canada, the ten provincial governments and the three territorial governments—over its creation, size, mandate and leadership. When I was approached to be the founding chair it was made clear that a long process had yielded little agreement. If I turned down the chair appointment, the council would be delayed further. I agreed with Kirby and Romanow; Canada needed a national body to create greater accountability for delivering the reforms frequently promised but infrequently implemented by governments. I decided to take on the challenge of a twenty-six member council with year-to-year funding from the government of Canada and an unclear mandate.

I had communicated my concerns about the weak mandate of the council to then federal health minister, Anne McLellan. In a note I used a quote from Winston Churchill to convey my concern. Churchill had always opposed joint planning committees of the air force the army and the navy.

His view, "Why you may take the most gallant sailor, the most intrepid airman and the most audacious soldier, put them at a table together—and what do you get? The sum of their fears." This notion was later borrowed by Tom Clancy as the title of his book, *The Sum of Their Fears*.

The official announcement of the council and the appointment of its chair took place in Toronto at the Royal York Hotel. The federal health minister was joined by Ontario Health Minister George Smitherman. I brought my daughter Genevieve. In the green room before the press conference Genevieve was quite nervous. She was there purely to support her father. As we walked along the corridor her nervousness was heightened by news that a protest would overshadow the press conference. The advocates for greater access to marijuana for medical purposes were to rally.

Just as we neared the door to the press conference room, Minister Smitherman turned his bald head toward Genevieve and asked her, "Is my hair okay for the cameras?"

She laughed. We all laughed and entered the press conference with smiles on, looking very jolly.

At our first full working meeting of the council, I got us in hot water with the then British Columbia Minister of Health, Colin Hansen. The council was being supported by a small group of staff hired and seconded from CIHI. As a start-up, we were trying to pull together a first operating plan for the council. One of the considerations, the most important one, was the mandate that ministers had bestowed upon the council. However, there was lots of room for interpretation of the role. I had directed Francesca Grosso, who worked on preparing the document, to put in "everything and the kitchen sink" that members of the council or staff had come up with. My intention was to remove the ideas that were outside our mandate through a council discussion.

Minister Hansen was hopping mad and launched an unpleasant attack on the council over the draft operating plan's "Blue Sky" document that he or any other minister were never intended to see. It was an idea-filled working document so the members of the council could pare it down to what we really wanted to do. I fell on my sword. I explained how the document had come to be and took the full blame. Minister Hansen was only barely mollified by my contrition.

Although an unpleasant way to start our journey, the exchange proved entirely beneficial to the council. Every member was indignant about Hansen's unfair attack and completely galvanized as a group. Suddenly we were the Health Council of Canada.

When we issued our first annual report, we launched it at an event in Ottawa. Our key message was that reforms were moving in the right direction but far too slowly. We generated considerable press attention.

Prime Minister Paul Martin, scrummed by reporters in New Brunswick, commented that I should be more patient with the premiers. This annoyed me but there was little I could do at the time.

The important lesson from my experience with the health council is that responsibility without authority is a difficult circumstance for any individual or organization. For the Health Council of Canada, year-to-year funding and the very short length of the "arm" in "arm's length" dramatically limited the scope of the council to be effective. Unlike a credible arm's length body such as the Canadian Institute for Health Information, health ministers undercut the council from the very beginning.

A second lesson that turnover destroys cohesion and undermines mission was also evident. The revolving door of provincial and federal health ministers made it hard to establish any continuity and sense of accountability.

JOINING LAWRENCE AND COMPANY

IT WAS ELEANOR CLITHEROE who suggested that I meet Jack Lawrence. She had served as deputy minister of finance when I was the health deputy. We joked that the health department spent nearly half the money that finance raised each year. We became friendly colleagues.

Jack was a legend on Bay Street. He had sold Nesbitt Burns to the Bank of Montreal. At sixty-one years of age, he had started Lawrence and Company as a venture investment firm.

In 1998, my investment book, *Million Dollar Strategy*, was published. Eleanor called and a lunch with Jack Lawrence was arranged. We met at the prestigious Toronto Club. Grant McCutcheon, a young lawyer working with Jack, accompanied him. David Peterson, former Liberal Premier of Ontario was seated two tables over. He spotted us and saw immediately what was up.

"Go ahead Jack—make a capitalist out of him," he shouted, disrupting the quiet intensity of the Toronto Club dining room. "You can do it."

With occasional heckling from Peterson, our lunch proceeded. Jack Lawrence's interest was in my knowledge of health care. His company had made several venture investments in start-ups in the health sector. Among these investments were Footmaxx, a company making foot orthodics, and Medcan, a health clinic firm and a dental floss manufacturer located in Quebec. My interest was in starting an investment counsel firm to manage publicly traded investments for clients. We agreed that I would help with the health care investments and further agreed that we would start Lawrence Decter Investment Counsel. And so I joined Bay Street.

A dozen years later, I am proud to have built a successful investment counsel firm, renamed LDIC Inc., with a terrific staff, wonderful clients and a strong future. Jack and I parted company five years before his untimely and tragic death in an airplane crash in 2009. I bought out his shares in LDIC Inc. and have continued the firm. Someday I may write another book about the Bay Street years.

MULRONEY LATER

THE NEXT OCCASION I had to speak with then former Prime Minister Mulroney was at Heather Reisman's fiftieth birthday party. This bash was held at the Indigo store at Yonge and Eglinton in Toronto. This was appropriate because Heather is the CEO and substantial owner of the Indigo chain. The party consisted of a veritable who's who of Canada. From Paul Martin to Brian Mulroney to Ted Rogers to Conrad Black and from Holly Cole to Little Richard—they were all present and accounted for.

At one point during the evening, I had occasion to chat with Brian Mulroney. I reminded him that we had met when I worked for Premier Pawley. He at least pretended to remember. I noted that his speech at the Manitoba Progressive Conservative Party meeting at the height of the French language controversy was a speech I greatly admired. Mulroney had supported the Manitoba government's position on French language services. This placed him in direct opposition to then Manitoba Conservative leader Sterling Lyon. The crowd had been hostile to their own national leader and he had not blinked. Here was a Conservative leader standing up for the rights of the French Canadians within Canada and confronting the issue in an adversarial way on hostile turf.

Knowledgeable insiders tell me that Prime Minister Mulroney never really recovered from that experience in Manitoba and regards it as his least favourite province, which may be the root cause of some of the federal decisions from 1984 until 1992.

"Michael, that was the only time in my whole political career where the RCMP said they could not guarantee my safety." Mulroney paused, his deep baritone voice, readying for the punch line. "So I did the courageous thing." He paused and the broad smile that played across his face foreshadowed what was to come. Then with the gravitas of a former Prime Minister he spoke, "I sent Mila out first."

A GAME OF INCHES

IN THE MOVIE ANY GIVEN SUNDAY, playing the role of the coach of a fictional, professional football team, Al Pacino gives a wonderful inspirational speech to his team. He argues that football is a game of inches. To quote a key passage:

"You find out life is just a game of inches
So is football
Because in either game
Life or football

The margin for error is so small
I mean
One half step too late or too early
You don't quite make it
One half second too slow or too fast
And you don't quite catch it.
The inches we need are everywhere around us."

This became a standard reference in my approach to health care reform. In response to those who wanted bold sweeping change my answer became the game of inches—that health reform was indeed a game of inches.

In 2004, I was in Ottawa. Preparations were underway for the federal government led by Prime Minister Martin to meet the provincial premiers to negotiate a new health care agreement.

Will Falk and I had worked together at APM in health care consulting in the mid-1990s. He had been seconded from his post at Cap Gemini Consulting to help Prime Minister Martin with preparations for the Federal-Provincial-Territorial Health Summit. I was in Ottawa to give a speech on health policy. Falk and I met in a hotel room. Will had the proposed agreement that Ottawa was about to share with the provinces. I read it carefully and grew exceedingly angry.

"Will, this is so weak and so flawed I don't think it is worth fixing. It is unbelievably bad." I threw the document on the bed in disgust.

Then Will Falk surprised me. He said forcefully, "You were the person who told me health care reform was a game of inches. You said that we should fight for every inch. Have you given up?"

I was taken aback. Will Falk, my friend, colleague and, in some ways in matters of public policy, my protegé, had just called my bluff.

"Well Will, I guess we should roll up our sleeves and see what we can do to improve this draft agreement."

We did just that. Sitting in the hotel room over the next hour or so we scribbled out a series of changes to the federal proposal for consideration by the prime minister's office and Health Canada.

Will took the changes back for consideration by senior officials. Nearly all of our changes were included in the final document sent to the provinces. As it turned out, health care reform is a game of inches just like football and life.

ORDER OF CANADA

THE MOST HUMBLING EXPERIENCE of my life in public and community service occurred in 2004 when I was awarded the Order of Canada. It was completely unexpected and a deeply emotional experience.

I had received a notice in the mail that I had a parcel to pick up at the post office. This was not an infrequent experience. My daughter Genevieve had a tendency to order clothing and other items such as contact lenses over the internet. I would go to the post office and pick up her purchases. Usually there was duty and tax to be paid. I had tried without a great deal of success to get her to pick up her own parcels. It was mildly embarrassing when the packages were from Victoria's Secret. The man at the post office would try not to raise his eyebrows but I was always certain that he was amused at my packages from that source.

On this occasion, I ignored the first two notices, leaving them for Genevieve. But when on a Friday I got the final notice I decided to go and pick it up on Saturday morning. When I had the package in my hands I looked at the return address. It was not from Victoria's Secret but from Rideau Hall, home of our governor general. I was puzzled. I noted that it was addressed to me.

I stood at the counter where others were sticking stamps onto envelopes and opened the package. There was a letter asking if I was willing to accept the honour of joining the Order of Canada. Tears welled up. I was stunned. The letter also admonished me not to tell anyone until the list was announced. In that moment I forgave Genevieve for each and every one of her non-pickups.

Several months later, I attended the ceremony at Rideau Hall in Ottawa with my two children, Riel and Genevieve, their mother Lucille, and my best friend Ron Bailey. Powerful emotions swept over me as I sat waiting my turn to have the Order of Canada presented by Governor General Adrienne Clarkson. I walked those short but memorable steps to the front of the grand room with pride and anticipation.

"We really like your letter," were the first words the governor general spoke to me. Her husband John Ralston Saul came over and shook my hand. He added his gratitude about the letter.

For a moment I was puzzled. What letter? I thought. I counted myself as an admirer of Governor General Clarkson. There had been criticism of her spending on international travel by a handful of members of Parliament. In most cases I suspect that their own international travel expenditures would not bear scrutiny. I had written a forceful letter in support of the governor general's international work. In particular taking Canadian artists and other cultural leaders to connect with the leadership of other nations seemed to me a very sound investment.

As I returned proudly to my seat amidst the other honourees I thought to myself they probably didn't get too many supportive letters if they remembered mine so clearly.

DINING WITH JEAN CHRÉTIEN

THE OCCASION WAS A DINNER at the York Club sponsored by CTV in honour of Pamela Wallin's appointment as Canada's consul general to New York. The head table included Prime Minister Jean Chrétien and CTV national news anchor Lloyd Robertson.

Much of the banter as dinner proceeded was between the prime minister and Lloyd Robertson. The agreement eventually reached was that they would resolve the issue of who would retire first by both retiring at the same time. However, as it worked out, Chrétien went first by several years.

Introduced to the prime minister as someone expert in health care, my introduction provoked the following conversation:

"Are you working for me or working for Romanow?" demanded the prime minister.

"Trying to help both your government and Romanow," I replied.

"So are you working for me or for Romanow?" came the pointed response.

Clearly Jean Chrétien's world did not countenance divided loyalties.

MEETING AL GORE—HOW *THE GLOBE AND MAIL* MADE ME AN ENVIRONMENTALIST

IN JUNE 2006, at the conclusion of the Montebello meeting of the Health Council of Canada, I let my fellow council members know that it had been my last meeting. My decision to step down as chair had several motivations. First, I had undertaken to serve for three years—my three years were nearly done. Second, the council had come through a near death experience several months earlier. All of the funding for the health council flowed from Health Canada, the federal department. However, the provincial ministers dragged their feet on approving our budget and that brought the council to within weeks of issuing layoff notices to our entire staff.

The most powerful reason for my decision to exit was the complete turnover of health ministers. None of the ministers who had asked me to take on the position of chair were still in their jobs after three years. In fact, there had been three prime ministers, five federal health ministers and thirteen provincial and territorial ministers in my time on the council. I stopped counting after twenty new ones.

In short, none of the ministers even remembered why the council had been created. My belief was that by stepping down I would cause the health ministers to select a new chair. During that process they would need to understand the role of the council and reaffirm or change its mandate. As well, the vice-chair Jeanne Besner, a nursing leader from Alberta, was an excellent interim chair. I was right about Jeanne and wrong about the ministers. They never did decide to replace the chair and Jeanne settled in.

I guess the lesson, and I am still learning lessons after all these years about politics and politicians, is never try to force the political hand. It is capable of ignoring you!

As I drove through the narrow roads through the green mountains and mixed forest from Montebello to Mount Tremblant where I was to attend an environmental policy conference. I felt a wave of relief. Unlike the Canadian Institute for Health Information that I chaired for six years, the Health Council of Canada had proven very difficult. The council, although comprised of good people, was large and was extremely draining to chair. I missed CIHI with its fifteen-member board. It had been much more manageable.

The conference at Mount Tremblant had been organized by Canada 2020, a policy group of which I was an advisory board member. The featured Thursday night speaker was Al Gore.

Gore spoke powerfully, delivering his trademark slide show on global warming that became the basis for his film and Nobel Prize. The audience, me included, was moved by his eloquence and the power of his thinking. So moved were delegates that the next morning the scheduled program of speeches was altered to allow those attending the conference to share their views on the Gore presentation.

Former federal health minister and deputy prime minister Anne McClellan was chairing the discussion. As she had been the minister who asked me to chair the health council, I thought I should make some mention of my departure.

When I got to the microphone, I said, "Before commenting on the question of carbon sequestration I just wanted to let our Chair Anne

McClelland know that yesterday I stepped down as chair of the Health Council of Canada." I added, "Now perhaps I will have time to pursue my education on matters of the environment that are so closely linked to our future health and the health of our children and grandchildren."

A reporter was present from *The Globe and Mail*.

Later that day as I was driving back to Ottawa to take the train back to Toronto, my cell phone rang.

A very agitated Paul Cantin, a savvy communications person for the health council, demanded, "What did you say?"

"About what?" I asked.

"About resigning from the health council to follow Al Gore on an environmental crusade."

"You must be kidding," was my first response.

"No, that is the story *The Globe* is running with."

"Give me the reporter's number."

I spoke with the reporter and tried to explain the sequence of events— that I had resigned from the health council and that there was no connection to my newfound interest in the environment. Nevertheless, *The Globe* largely stuck to its story.

A number of events followed. The premier of Ontario invited me to a roundtable on the environment. Many invitations followed to attend environmental occasions. Many friends in health care phoned to lament my decisions to leave the policy area.

I tried to be flippant at first. "Don't believe everything you read in *The Globe*." After a time I realized that I had been converted from a health person to an environmental person by one article. I was repeatedly asked by friends and those in government what I was tackling in the environmental world. At first, I stayed close to home. I repaired the windows on the third floor that leaked heat into the atmosphere. I bought carbon offsets for my non-green vehicles. More recently, I became involved as chair of a start-up biomass company. So the inaccurate *Globe* story actually catapulted me into some new and interesting adventures.

SONS—MEETING JUSTIN TRUDEAU

AT THE AL GORE DINNER at the Canada 2020 Conference at Mount Tremblant I had the good fortune to be seated with Justin Trudeau and his vivacious wife and Quebec television celebrity, Sophie Grégoire.

Before we sat down there were introductions.

"I am very pleased to meet you," I said to Justin Trudeau when we shook hands. "Actually," I added, "we did meet once before many years ago when you were quite young."

"When was that?" inquired Justin.

"It would have been when your father was prime minster and I was working for Premier Pawley of Manitoba. It was late in 1981. I remember how proud your father was of you and your brothers. He introduced you to the premier and me with immense pride. He was also very affectionate with you." I paused, then added, "Your father was such a formidable prime minister and intellect that it surprised me how warm and close he was to you."

After a moment, I continued, "My own son was born a few weeks after our meeting and I was thinking about what kind of father I would be. Your father set an example of how I hoped to be—proud and affectionate with my children."

Justin asked me several questions about my children as we waited for dinner to begin. I spoke of the enormous pride and affection I have for my daughter Genevieve and son Riel. By then, they were in their 20s and moving on with their own lives.

Just as dinner began, Justin said to me, "I believe you have become that father you hoped to be."

It was a nice moment and I knew with his wife Sophie expecting their first child that his thoughts were much like my own twenty years earlier.

JET BLUE SOLITAIRE

A YEAR LATER I was returning from a weekend trip to New York with my daughter. I noticed a man bearing a striking resemblance to Al Gore sitting by himself at an airport gate waiting for a Jet Blue flight.

My daughter, Genevieve, had complained that although the trip to New York had been a great success, she had not seen any celebrities. I returned with coffee and said to her, "Want to meet Al Gore?"

"What are you talking about?" she replied looking around our gate.

"Come with me."

We approached a man hunched over his laptop.

"Mr. Gore, we met last month at Mount Tremblant. My name is Michael Decter."

Al Gore stood up. I was relieved that it really was Al Gore not some look-alike. He was very friendly. I introduced Genevieve and we chatted for a few minutes. He was skeptical of Prime Minister Harper's new-found commitment to the environment. I was a little more optimistic.

As we went to our Air Canada gate, I looked back. The man who would win the Nobel Prize and an Oscar in the next twelve months was alone pounding away on his laptop, one more road warrior—albeit one with a mission of saving our planet.

MONIQUE BÉGIN

ONE OF MY FAVOURITE PEOPLE in the whole world is Monique Bégin. A charming, elegant and determined advocate for health care, she served as federal health minister, introducing the Canada Health Act in 1984.

One evening, Monique and I, along with Roy Romanow had been invited to a dinner discussion of health policy. Our host was Prime Minister Paul Martin and the dinner was in the meeting room adjacent to his office in the centre block of the Parliament Buildings.

When we arrived, two uniformed RCMP officers barred our way. One of them asked us for identification. I fumbled for my wallet. Madame Bégin made no move to produce identification or to stop.

Instead, she declared with some force, "Je suis l'ancien ministre de la Santé, Monique Bégin (roughly translated—I am the former minister of health)." Her tone implied that they must be fools for not immediately knowing this truth. The two RCMP officers stepped back allowing her to pass.

I smiled and said, "I'm with her."

The RCMP let me pass as well. Later in the meeting, Monique had roughly the same impact on the prime minister as she had on the RCMP guards. She is, as they say, a formidable woman.

STEPHEN HARPER

I HAD ONLY two brief encounters with Stephen Harper. Both occurred before he was prime minister. The first time was on national television. It was a discussion of the Canada Health Act and health reform. It was many years before he became prime minister.

During that first encounter, Harper advanced the idea that the Canada Health Act was a straitjacket preventing provinces from undertaking reforms to Medicare. He went on at some length on this theme. Finally, the interviewer turned to me to ask my view. I replied somewhat harshly that, "Anyone who holds the view that the Canada Health Act is a straitjacket has never read the Canada Health Act."

I went on to add, "The closer someone gets to sitting in the prime minister's chair the fonder they become of the Canada Health Act."

It was not intended as a prophecy but several years later Stephen Harper was elected prime minister. One of his early actions proved to be signing a letter to Alberta strongly supporting the principles of the Canada Health Act. He signalled that a Harper-led government did not regard the Canada Health Act as a straitjacket needing to be removed from the provinces.

Several years ago, I attended a parliamentary press gallery dinner at which Stephen Harper, then leader of the opposition, spoke. Thirty years had changed some aspects of the dinner. Earlier it had been private with no reporting of speeches. Now it is televised. What has not changed is the spirited humour, the best of which is self-deprecating. Harper's memorable line of the evening took me back all those years to Robert Stanfield.

"If political parties had warning labels as food products do," began Harper, "then my party, the Conservative Party would have a label that read. 'Beware—May Contain Nuts!' "

MEETING PRESIDENT CLINTON

MY FIRST OPPORTUNITY to hear former President Bill Clinton deliver a speech in person came in 2001 in Toronto. The occasion was a dinner following a golf tournament at Magna International in Aurora just north of Toronto.

We arrived at the reception in the lobby of Magna's global headquarters. It was a champagne and hors d'oeuvre affair. I began chatting with Ontario Premier Mike Harris. Off to the side of the reception were Clinton and former Ontario Premier Bill Davis, who was the master of ceremonies for the subsequent dinner. Next to them were two burly secret service men with the requisite earpieces. There was a small roped-off area. A long line of guests waited outside the ropes to have their photograph taken with President Clinton.

I had two thoughts that collided. On one hand, I really wanted my picture taken with Clinton. On the other hand, the line was too much like a petting zoo for my taste. I resolved to wait for the last possible second, until the line was gone and then rush over swiftly and pose for the presidential photo. My timing was thrown off by an engaging conversation with Mike Harris. When I turned and rushed over, the secret service had closed the rope barrier and said, "Sorry, we are going to the dinner now."

I was momentarily disappointed that my reluctance had cost me the desired photo. We are all groupies, I thought. Some are just more successful than others. Silently I cursed my shyness and pride that had caused me to miss the photo op.

As I started to turn away I heard Bill Davis's voice saying firmly to the secret service, "Let Michael through."

The ropes parted and I strode rapidly forward towards the two men. Davis and Clinton were together on the other side of the rope. In my view, William Grenville Davis had been one of Ontario's greatest premiers and William Jefferson Clinton, one of the great American presidents. Both had continued as important elder statesmen after their time in office. I had never worked for the Davis government but I had met him and admired his stewardship of Ontario. I also had great respect for his generosity, a quality often lacking in those hardened by decades of political combat.

As I approached, Davis turned to Clinton and said, "Michael was one of our very fine public servants in Ontario."

Clinton replied with a broad grin, "That is a really fine thing for this guy to say about you."

The photograph of Clinton and me shaking hands captures our mutual smiles. That framed photograph of Clinton and me has a proud place in my home. Every time I look at it I think about the generosity of Bill Davis.

At the subsequent dinner, Clinton demonstrated his own generosity. As we assembled for dinner, a jazz band played. Two young women wailed away brilliantly on saxophones. The crowd completely ignored them. The diners continued to talk loudly fuelled by the abundant pre-dinner champagne. By the time Clinton had been introduced to speak, the two dispirited sax players were just inside the door of the room holding their cigarettes outside.

"I know you are feeling dejected," Clinton said at the microphone. "You played your hearts out on those saxophones and you think no one listened to you. But tomorrow the people in this room will be driving along humming a tune. They won't know where the tune came from but it will have come from you." The two young women beamed at Clinton's praise.

Politics is not in its nature a generous profession. It is adversarial and combative. The core value that Davis and Clinton share is their generosity. That is likely the reason they both remain so popular.

REFLECTIONS

MY MEMORIES OF CANADIAN POLITICS and politicians began when I delivered pamphlets in south Winnipeg. Those memories deepened as I listened to the oratory of Tommy Douglas and John Diefenbaker in the old Winnipeg Auditorium.

On re-reading this manuscript, I realize that all of the journeys of my life have been shaped by a combination of optimism and naiveté, tempered by scar tissue acquired along the way. I am reminded of Randy Newman's words in his satirical song Rednecks, "Good old boys from LSU, went in dumb, come out dumb too." I am still an optimist. My hopes are undiminished by the years and events that could reduce anyone to a cynic.

On good days, I like to believe that naiveté is more honourable than just remaining dumb. Perhaps a better epitaph for this life and my refusal to say "no" to public service is found in Paul Simon, "Still crazy after all these years." Whichever song is most apt, I have no regrets about the years I spent in government and around politics. I have my share of scar tissue but I also have many achievements of which I am proud. Scar tissue can fester as a wound or it can heal as humility and experience and even, over the years, wisdom.

I have many memories of small kindnesses. I am grateful for those who mentored me in the early years. And I feel profound respect for those in political life who exhibited generosity.

Most days, I still have the hope of my younger years. After it all, I remain devoted to the belief that public service is a noble cause, perhaps the highest calling. It helps if you have boundless optimism and the hide of a rhino! I am also convinced that a good sense of humour is essential for the journey.

ACKNOWLEDGEMENTS

I EXPRESS MY DEEP GRATITUDE to all those who have shared their political stories with me over the years. There are many fine storytellers around the corridors of power and politics. The two finest in my own experience were my late mother, Una Barry McGilligan Decter, and my friend, Bill Fox. Likely it is their shared Irish blood that loves and weaves a good tale. It is a shame they never met. I would have delighted to listen to the political story fest that would have surely ensued. Someday, I hope Bill will find time to write his stories so that many more people can enjoy their humour. Better still, he should tell them on the radio. His rich Timmins Irish voice would be well worth the listening.

There are many others to whom I am indebted. Among those with a fine ear for the nuances of a good political tale were Stanley Knowles, Tommy Douglas, Murray Weppler, Ron Bailey, Lucille Roch, Gene Long, Hugh Segal, Bill Knight, Pamela Wallin, Mike Kirby, Jon Johnson, Charles Kelly, Francesca Grosso, Mike McCarthy, Les Benjamin, Julian Porter, Anna Porter, Jim Eldridge, Graham Scott, Gary Doer, Ginny Devine, Lloyd Girman, Derek Bedson, Bill McCance, Jean Guy Carrier, John McNevin and Jo-Anne McNevin.

I am grateful to Francesca Grosso, my co-author on *Navigating Canada's Health Care*, for reading this manuscript with such care and making so many excellent suggestions for its improvement. I am equally thankful to Lucille Roch for reading the manuscript and catching so many errors that I had missed. I am also grateful to Caroline Grosso and Steve Paikin for their encouraging comments on the manuscript.

Ingeborg Boyens has been a fabulous and supportive editor for which I am in her debt.

In my years in public service, it was my privilege to work with a number of premiers and ministers. While there were too many to be certain that important people have not been missed, I unreservedly thank the following for whom I toiled or to whom I gave advice—Edward Schreyer, Howard Pawley, Sterling Lyon, Bob Rae, Edward Broadbent, the late Sidney Spivak, Frances Lankin, Ruth Grier, Willy Parasiuk, Eugene Kostrya, Vic Schroeder and Paul Martin. Thank you for your patience with me and the many lessons you each taught me. Sorry for any trouble I caused you in my naïveté and enthusiasm.

There are also a number of authors who have captured the telling of political tales in their work. Several authors stand out for me. Robert Caro began with his remarkable biography of Robert Moses, *The Power Broker*. And then he continued through his masterful chronicling of the rise to power of Lyndon Baines Johnson through the three volumes of *The Years of Lyndon Johnson*. I also loved T. Harry Williams' extraordinary biography of Louisiana Governor Huey Long. On the Canadian side of the border, Dalton Camp's memorable and insightful *Gentlemen, Players and Politicians* tops my all time list but Ron Graham's *One Eyed Kings* and Richard Gwyn's *The Northern Magus* rank close by.

A remarkable book that encouraged me to tell these stories was written by Herb Schulz, who served as an assistant to Premier Schreyer in Manitoba for the eight years of his premiership. *A View From The Ledge: An Insider's Look at the Schreyer Years* is a fascinating and well-written account of politics in that period. It has a special place because of my own formative years in the Schreyer government.

I had the enormous good fortune to grow up in a political home. My parents debated politics fiercely. My early days in electoral politics were spent as a deliverer of leaflets. Later, I graduated to canvasser and organizer. After university my career took me into public service. Most recently, in a decade of managing an investment firm, politics became for me largely a spectator sport. Throughout these decades and different times of life my love for a good political story has never diminished.

INDEX